AMERICAN ASPECTS

AMERICAN ASPECTS

by

D. W. BROGAN

Harper & Row, Publishers
New York and Evanston

AMERICAN ASPECTS. *Copyright © 1964 by D. W. Brogan. Printed in the United States of America. All rights reserved. No part of this book may be used or reproduced in any manner whatsoever without written permission except in the case of brief quotations embodied in critical articles and reviews. For information address Harper & Row, Publishers, Incorporated, 49 East 33rd Street, New York 16, N.Y.*

FIRST EDITION

LIBRARY OF CONGRESS CATALOG CARD NUMBER: 64-25109

To
LAURA RAUCH

CONTENTS

PREFACE

IN 1948 I published a collection of occasional papers called *American Themes*. Now, sixteen years later, I publish another collection of occasional papers on American topics. In the interval, I have written, I suppose, at least several hundred thousand words on American themes and from that mass of ephemeral writing I have chosen less than a hundred thousand words which may well prove to be just as ephemeral as those I have rejected.

Nevertheless, there has been method in my selections and rejections. I have discarded a great deal of straight or mere reporting; nothing dates more, nothing needs more irritating annotation. I have a fondness for some of what I wrote under the pressure of urgent news. What a pity I didn't keep a copy of that well-informed speculation about President-elect Dewey's cabinet! It was a highly 'educated guess' which was never published because by the time it reached *The Observer*, Governor Dewey was no longer President-elect. Other pieces of reportage turned out to be mistakes. Thus I was induced by a well-informed but, as it was revealed, partisan American friend of mine to put forward his views on the necessary and right evolution of jazz, provoking violent letters of protest in *The Guardian*. I learned that various sects of jazz fanatics could give cards to early church councils for the power of polemical bitterness and the readiness to invoke anathemas on heretics. Other admirable pieces that I wrote I forgot to file and I cannot now remember what they were about or where they appeared. That, no doubt, is why they seem admirable in vague retrospect.

I have in this collection systematically discarded pieces that had to be tailored to the space needs of the magazine sections of daily newspapers or the elegant middles of weeklies like *The Spectator*. I have discarded pieces written for continental markets in France,

Germany, Italy, as well as a number of solemn pieces destined for trade papers (I mean academic journals).

What I have kept have been pieces of a length that allowed some development of the theme and had for subjects themes of more than a mere news interest. Of the merits of what I have chosen, I am naturally no judge but I have read some of the pieces with an agreeable sense of learning anew, and to be candid, with approval. I have noticed that I have certain trade marks that may irritate readers but so, I have learned from the Reverend Dr. Morton of Glasgow University, have the epistles of St. Paul. Such as they are, I throw these pieces on the waves, proof, if of nothing else, of the fascination all aspects of American life have had for me since I first read *The Last of the Mohicans*, 'Buffalo Bill' (in paperback) and Mark Twain in the days of President Taft.

Lincoln's Birthday, 1964   D. W. BROGAN

ACKNOWLEDGMENTS

'The Presidency' first appeared in *Encounter;* 'The Illusion of American Omnipotence', 'A Fresh Appraisal of the Civil War' and 'Unnoticed Changes in America' in *Harper's Magazine;* 'The Remote Revolution—A British View' in the *Proceedings of the American Philosophical Society,* Vol. 106, No. 1; 'America Through British Eyes' in the *Saturday Review;* 'The First Roosevelt', 'Uncle Tom's Message: the Book of War and Freedom' and 'Another President' in the *Times Literary Supplement;* 'The End of Illusion?' and 'Anglo-American Relations: Retrospect and Prospect' in the *Yale Review,* copyright Yale University Press; 'Citizenship in the United States' in the *Virginia Quarterly Review;* 'The American Personality: a Critique of New World Culture' in Wayne State University's *Graduate Comment,* Vol. 5, No. 1; and 'The Catholic Politician' in *The Atlantic Monthly.* 'The Unimportance of Being Adams' originally appeared as the Introduction to the Sentry Edition, *The Education of Henry Adams,* Copyright 1946 by Charles F. Adams. Used by permission Houghton Mifflin Company. We are most grateful to all these for permission to publish.

1

THE PRESIDENCY

THE ASSASSINATION of President Kennedy has brought out, in an agonizing way, the realities of the American presidency and has again demonstrated its unique function as a political organism. The first truth to be asserted about this great office is that the President of the United States is a monarch. The Constitution, in deliberately ambiguous terms, entrusts to him the whole executive power of the Union and in addition confers on him the separate office of Commander-in-Chief with complete control of the armed forces. This, of course, does not mean the President is an absolute monarch. He has to share power with Congress (as President Kennedy painfully discovered in his three years in the White House); and both he and Congress share power with the Supreme Court.

Nevertheless, it is important again to insist on the monarchical character of the American presidency. It is monarchical in two ways: monarchical because of the concentration of power in the hands of one man, monarchical because he, more than any other institution (and every President is an institution), embodies *We the People of the United States*. In the President, in any President, the American people see their embodied power and see their own driving force personified.

In another sense, the President is a monarch. For he performs many of the ritual functions of an hereditary monarch. He is the universal patron of good causes, a role that the late President Kennedy took very seriously. His precedence is as automatic as that of the Queen. He lives in the most historical building in Washington, the only one that has an aura of majesty about it. American boys are continually told that they can, when they grow up, become President of the United States (girls are not yet told that they can). Under the

easy and democratic exterior, the protocol of the White House is as
severe as the protocol of Buckingham Palace. The presidential
inauguration is a kind of quadrennial coronation. And even the
President who has made an immense number of enemies remains
President and is entitled, except among the most pathologically
minded, to respect and indeed, for his office if not for himself, to
reverence.

The White House itself symbolizes the character of this great
office. On the one hand, it is a princely residence; on the other, it is
a power house. It is what Versailles or the Hofburg were in the days
of the great monarchies of Europe. Beside, behind Buckingham
Palace, there is 10 Downing Street; there is nothing beside, nothing
behind the White House. True, General de Gaulle in the *Elysée* at
the moment performs a double function as political leader and as
the mandatory of the Sovereign People. But General de Gaulle is a
phenomenon, he is not an institution. The *Elysée* has none of the
magical, none of the sacred character of the White House. Nor does
General de Gaulle, as President of the Republic or in person, impose
on his enemies a reverence that the presidential office imposes on the
enemies of any President of the United States.

*

Washington is a great pilgrimage city. To it come from all over the
United States hundreds of thousands of visitors, especially parents
bringing their young children to the sacred shrine of the Republic.
The White House is not unique in Washington. Many children are
brought by parents to see the Supreme Court in session and are
suitably touched by the usher's proclamation at the beginning of
each session of the Court, '*God Save the United States and this
Honourable Court.*' Some children are possibly impressed by the
Senate, some possibly even by the House of Representatives. But
neither of these bodies has any air of the sacred about itself, and it
can hardly be said that in recent years this refusal to give to Congress
the reverence given to the presidency has been an act of manifest
injustice. The Speaker of the House of Representatives, the leaders
of the Senate may be and in the past sometimes have been great
men, but they are not august; there is no charisma attached to their
office.

Children and their parents pour through the White House during
the visiting hours, entering a shrine far more august than that of the

Supreme Court, not to speak of the Capitol. For one thing, the building is much more a part of history. It has been altered inside and out, it has been tactfully extended, but it is fundamentally the building into which John Adams moved while it was still unfinished for the last month or two of his unhappy term in office. It has known the horrors of war. It was burned by a British army, and there is a legend not totally vindicated that it got the name White House because of the paint put over it to hide the scars of burning. It was called the White House by the American people long before Theodore Roosevelt made that the official name of the Executive Mansion.

An elegant piece of Dublin architecture transplanted to the United States, it is perhaps the only important official building in Washington of intrinsic architectural merit. But it is not to admire this copy of Leinster House in Dublin (which now houses the Dáil) that the pilgrims come. They come to what may not extravagantly be described as the Parthenon of the American Acropolis. It is a house soaked in history and soaked in blood. The great ghost that walks through the White House is that of the greatest of Presidents, Abraham Lincoln, and this gives the necessary tragic note to this national shrine. It was to the White House he returned after his visit to conquered Richmond; it was on the way to the White House upon the Potomac that he recited, '*Duncan is in his grave. After life's fitful fever, he sleeps well.*' It was here his body was brought, and the Lincoln Room is still the most sacred part of the White House.

But not all memories of the White House are as dark as those of the Good Friday of 1865 on which the first assassination of an American President took place. The first real tenant of the White House, and one who left his mark on it, was Thomas Jefferson, and it was characteristic of the late President Kennedy that when he gave his famous party for the American Nobel Prizemen in literature and science he should have said there was more talent and genius gathered in the White House that night than there had ever been except when Thomas Jefferson dined alone.

Other great makers of the American tradition haunt the White House. Across Lafayette Square is the absurd and endearing equestrian statue of General Andrew Jackson, one of the great makers of the presidential office. The first man to dare to tamper with the sacred structure was Theodore Roosevelt; and the President under whose direction the White House was totally reconstructed within is still alive, Harry S. Truman. To see American families going through the public rooms of the White House which are shown to them (and which are far more attractive now than they were a few years ago, thanks to the energy and good taste of Mrs. Kennedy) is to get a lesson in the intensity of American reverence for American history and the degree to which that artificial construction the United States of America has gained blood, flesh, and spirit since it was launched uncertainly in the dread year 1789. In that year there was a King of France, a King of England, a Holy Roman Emperor, a Tsarina of all the Russias, a very powerful and sagacious Emperor in Peking, a powerful Shogun and an impotent Emperor in Japan. Of all these strictly monarchical offices, only one now remains, that of the Queen of England. Yet the office that Queen Elizabeth II holds is very different indeed from the office held by George III, while the office that President Lyndon Johnson now holds is basically the office to which George Washington was unanimously elected.

We tend to think of America as having no history or having a short history, when in fact it has the longest effectively continuous political history in the world, marked by only one great breakdown, the Civil War—and that ended in the triumph of the Union, a triumph won at an immense expenditure of blood and an immense expenditure of national feeling—a loss from which the United States is still suffering, and of which it is indeed possible that President Kennedy's assassination is one of the long-term consequences.

*

The White House is open not only to tourists, it is also open to not very important visitors to parties and receptions, and I was myself struck and moved by seeing on television the East Room where the dead President's body had been brought and where I had seen and talked with him and his wife—one full of energy, the other dazzling —only a few months before.

But there is, of course, another side to the White House which gives it its double character. There are the private rooms where the President and his wife, and his children if he has them with him, can take some refuge from the intense pressures of the publicity that beats on any American President. President and Mrs. Kennedy were especially successful in preserving something of the air of a private house in the midst of this great national monument of publicity and power. But the real contrast is not between the public and the private quarters. It is between the White House as a residence, as the great official American home, and the White House as the centre of power of the most powerful state in the world. Its weight of power can be felt, it seems to me, oddly enough in the silence which at times pervades the administrative quarters, the two wings on each side of the White House which accommodate the closest members of the presidential staff. They of course have floods of visitors in the daytime, and the President, however hard he tries, cannot always protect himself against intrusive visitors, including some whose impudence startles a European. But I have been in the White House executive wing at night and felt its powerful silence. These corridors, half underground, are indeed 'corridors of power'. Kipling, in a famous passage describing how he received the Nobel prize in Stockholm during the period of Court mourning for the death of King Oscar, remarked that the only sound in the vast palace was the click of the decorations on the chests of the Court officials. There are no decorations worn by non-military officials in the White House, but there are Court officials all the same.

The White House is a court because the President is a monarch. I used to be asked frequently during the last war by British officials posted to Washington what was the best book to describe the strange new world they were entering on. I didn't recommend Tocqueville or Bryce or even Brogan. I recommended Saint-Simon. I used to say, 'You must remember you are going to a Court. You must abandon all your regular Whitehall ideas of official priorities and hierarchies. You cannot estimate the power of some people you will meet by their official title or by the quality of their carpet. You must watch out for those who have the ear of the President, the only ear that really counts.'

In F.D.R.'s day, it was advisable to notice who saw the President in his bedroom, before he put on the crippling apparatus which alone allowed him to make public appearances. Sometimes the *eminence grise* took public office, as Harry Hopkins did, and as Colonel House did at the time of the negotiation of the Treaty of Versailles. Sometimes some of the most powerful figures round the President have been officials of nominally secondary rank. Yet it is as certain as things can be that Mr. McGeorge Bundy was a good deal more important under President Kennedy than some members of the formal cabinet. Confidants rose and fell, grew in favour or became an intolerable political burden, as happened to the unfortunate Governor Sherman Adams under President Eisenhower. But all of their importance came from their access to the President, off the record, unofficial, or in some instances official but still off the record. The White House is very much smaller than Versailles, but the corridors round the President's private offices are like the Grande Galérie or the Oeil-de-Boeuf at Versailles. One could almost feel the hopes and fears, the desires as strong as sexual lust, in the breasts of some who had, and others who wished to have, access to the *arcana imperii*.

It is for this reason that the President of the United States must be 'a lonely man'. If he has too many friends, especially friends of the wrong kind, and if he too openly abandons to them the prerogatives that the nation has conferred on him, he goes the way of Warren Gamaliel Harding. The power must finally be in his hands. As Mr. Truman put it on the little brass ornament he kept on his desk, 'The buck stops here'.

It is because the buck stops there, the final decision—for example the dread decision to blockade Cuba in 1962, made by Mr. Kennedy after long and careful consultations, but made officially and alone by him—that the presidency has in the eyes of the American people this sacred character. The President is given a charge like that given to the Roman dictator of old, 'that no harm befall the Republic'. As the greatest of Presidents, Lincoln, asserted more than once, he alone took the special oath which the Constitution imposes on the President, 'that I will faithfully execute the office of President of the United States, and will to the best of my ability, preserve, protect, and defend the Constitution of the United States'. Most Presidents have done their best in trying to live up to that oath, and some have died by violence in trying to carry out their duties, as Abraham Lincoln and John Kennedy did. It is a savage thing to say, but I have no doubt that some of the sacredness of the presidency comes from the fact that it has had its martyrs.

The presidency was never a mere secular office after the murder of Lincoln. It is true that his mantle has been thrown over some rather curious successors. Harding, by universal agreement the worst President ever to hold the office, was lamented with great sincerity when he died suddenly—and not a moment too soon. William McKinley was generally regretted, with fairly good reason. But so far as most of the presidential deaths in office, by violence or by the work of nature, are concerned the change has not necessarily been great or more than merely political. But the most recent death recalls two previous deaths which were shocks to the American people because they brought into play this religious reverence for the presidential office and this sense of the immense importance of that office, never so great as today when the President of the United States could destroy the human race.

*

The three deaths which have given this kind of shock to the American people have been the deaths of Abraham Lincoln, Franklin Delano Roosevelt, and John Fitzgerald Kennedy. Contrasts are obvious enough. In age, in background, in length of service, they differ greatly. But each was, in a very visible sense, *the* leader in a time of troubles. Lincoln had a well-authenticated premonition of some great event about to occur, and may indeed have had some premonition of his death in the days before Good Friday, 1865. He was struck down in the moment of victory after uttering in the Second Inaugural the noblest speech of a victorious leader in history. His death provoked an outburst of horror and grief, especially among the Negroes, which has been equalled only in November 1963.

The death of F.D.R. was less unexpected, although it was not expected at that time; it had come suddenly and especially shocked millions of young Americans who had never known any other President. As there were 'myths after Lincoln', there were myths after the death of F.D.R. When his body was brought through New York on its way to his ancestral home in Hyde Park, a black cloud settled over Manhattan and moved the superstitious to reverie: it was an old story, '*When beggars die, there are no comets seen: the heavens themselves blaze forth the death of princes.*' What legends will grow up around the death of John Kennedy it is too early to say.

But this sudden death of the youngest man ever elected to the presidency brings out another side of the great office. '*The King is dead, long live the King.*' President Lyndon Johnson is the eighth American Vice-President to succeed to the presidency by the death of the incumbent. No Vice-President is chosen because he is openly regarded as the next President. President Lyndon Johnson had far more serious claim to be considered a presidential candidate than had most Vice-Presidents in American history; but he has come to office through violent death. The point to notice is that he is as fully President as if he had been elected by the American people to that office, as much as the legitimate heir—the Prince of Wales or a Dauphin—succeeding to an ancient throne.

Mr. Truman has told us of the horror and astonishment and shock with which he received the news that he had suddenly become President of the United States, an office for which he had very little preliminary training. We know with what courage and energy Mr. Truman rose to the height of his responsibilities. President Johnson has far more training for the presidential office than had Mr. Truman. It is not only that at once the new President is surrounded by the secret service and that all the vast machinery of Federal Government is under his hand, it is that the American people turn with sympathy and with trust to the new incumbent. Presidents succeeding in this way have sometimes disappointed the hopes of the American people; sometimes they have much more than fulfilled those hopes. There is a famous story which underlies this character of the presidency, the legitimacy of the succession. Chester Arthur, who succeeded the assassinated Garfield in 1881, had been a noted playboy, and the friend of some of the most dashing men about town in New York and Newport. Shortly after his accidental accession, he was in that great centre of the American rich, the Newport Yacht Club, when an old social companion walked up to him, clapped him on the back, and said, 'How are you, Chet?' The new President turned, said nothing, looked at his old companion who blushed and shambled out of the room. Chet Arthur was now President of the United States; his old companions were as welcome to the new President as Falstaff was to Henry V.

President Johnson has far better training for the job than President Arthur ever had, but he has a far more difficult job to fulfil. For now he is not only President of the United States, but the leader of one of the two great coalitions into which the world is divided. Like his predecessor President Kennedy, he is and must be our leader as well as the leader of the American people. But he is above all the leader of the American people, the embodiment of the power and majesty of the American state.

1964

2

THE ILLUSION OF AMERICAN OMNIPOTENCE

I

I AM WRITING this on the Pacific Coast, before the election, but in the conviction that the result of the election will very little affect the problem that I want to discuss. Even if the Republicans should make a clean sweep, even if the State Department is cleaned out, from the Secretary to the doorkeepers, even if the Pentagon is purged from the Joint Chiefs of Staff to the leaders of the rescue teams who find lost visitors, one problem of American policy will remain: the problem of the existence, in the American mind, of what I call the illusion of omnipotence. This is the illusion that any situation which distresses or endangers the United States can only exist because some Americans have been fools or knaves.

Such a situation may exist because of conditions about which the United States has, and will have, little to say. For America, powerful though she is, is not omnipotent. A great many things happen in the world regardless of whether the American people wish them to or not. I deeply regret this state of affairs; like Bertrand Russell, I would gladly settle for an American hegemony; but we are not representative characters, and American hegemony not only does not exist, but is not even universally expected or desired.

I should, perhaps, say that the illusion of omnipotence to which I refer is not shared by all Americans. Nothing could be sillier than to attribute to nearly 160,000,000 people one common attitude, or to assume, as many European intellectuals do, that there is such a thing as 'what the American people are thinking'. Nevertheless, the idea that I am trying to describe is expressed by Senators and columnists, by candidates, by preachers, by people overheard in taverns and club cars, in drugstores and restaurants—the idea that the whole world, the great globe itself, can be moving in directions annoying or dangerous to the American people only because some elected or non-elected Americans are fools or knaves. When something goes wrong, 'I wuz robbed' is the spontaneous comment—the American equivalent of that disastrous French cry, '*Nous sommes trahis*'.

It should also be said that I am not reproaching the American people, or even any important fraction of them, with the sort of mere arrogance that the British displayed in the nineteenth century, the arrogance that made the humiliation of the Boer War so refreshing to the rest of the world. There would be plenty of justification for reproach if the American people were as pleased with themselves today as the English were around the time of Queen Victoria's Diamond Jubilee. But except in the Tribune Tower and a few other strongholds of the spirit of Jefferson Brick, Americans are not overflowing with self-satisfaction.

*

It would not be surprising if they were self-satisfied. For twice, in a not very long lifetime, America has redressed the balance of history. But for American intervention in the first war, it would have ended in a draw. But for American intervention in the second (which began with Lend-Lease, not with Pearl Harbor), Hitler would have had, with his Axis partners, a free hand. One result of this would, in the long run, have been war with the United States; but that long-run consequence matters little in this context. What does matter is that what stopped the Second and the Third Reich was American power. By 1945—with the greatest fleet, the greatest air force, and one of the two greatest armies in the world—the United States had become a world power such as had never been seen before. Never had ploughshares been beaten into swords so fast and on so large a scale.

And never were swords beaten back into ploughshares as fast as in 1945. As a demonstration of power, and of pacific intention, the scenario was perfect. The crowd that formed a conga line round the White House on V-J Day represented the American temper of August 1945 to perfection. So did Mr. Leo Crowley cutting off Lend-Lease; so did the immediate pressure to end all the controls and get the boys home. True, there was the atomic bomb—but the thought that there would soon be a world in which the atomic bomb would be a very present hope would have shocked nine Americans out of ten. The war had been won; the fascist menace had been destroyed. True, there was no such mood of high hope as in 1919; but the lesson of 1919 was not lost. America would not again take mere victory for enough, would not again walk out on the job.

And America has not walked out on the job. American policy since 1945 has, on the whole, been wise, far-seeing, magnanimous. Compare it with the policy of the years after the first war, with the policy of the years of Harding and Coolidge, and the growth in wisdom and responsibility is remarkable. Had there not been such a growth, the Kremlin would have won without firing a shot.

It is partly because the American people feel—rightly—that they have used their great power generously, that in 1952 they are perplexed, distressed, angry, and to some extent deluded. Why is it that, given the power, given the generosity of its use, the United States should be involved in the Korean mess? Why should so great a part of the world have passed into hostile hands? Why should the United States still be in danger, know the irritation of the draft in 'peacetime', suffer, in Korea, one of the most humiliating of American military defeats, and nominate, for the Presidency, a soldier not merely or mainly as a reward, but because the times seem to call for a soldier in the White House?

It is my opinion that one reason for American distress is the American belief in American invulnerability and American omnipotence.

II

Belief in American invincibility is, on the whole, a good thing. A corresponding English belief in 1940, without nearly as much material justification for it, probably changed the history of the world. 'The English always win, don't they?' asked my intelligent four-year-old son. The English won, but at a cost that has taken away the taste for victory. The Russians won too, but in the recent past they had lost. Probably the only people in the world who now have the historical sense of inevitable victory are the Americans. This belief, in its most extravagant, or McCormick, form, assumes that America doesn't need friends. In the less romantic, or Taft, form, it assumes that America doesn't need friends much. But even in the case of people who laugh at the Colonel and swear at the Senator, there is a lingering suspicion that there must be something grossly wrong when American policy suffers rebuffs; when, in despite of American opinion and interests, things go awry.

That grave mistakes have been made need not be doubted. As Mr. Walter Lippmann keeps on reminding his fellow-countrymen, one of the most obvious was the decision to exploit the victory at Inchon, regardless of the natural interest of the Chinese Communist government, of *any* Chinese government, in the arrival of a victorious American army on the Yalu. For that decision, Mr. Truman, Mr. Acheson, and General MacArthur are responsible, in that order. (For the actual military dispositions, General MacArthur is responsible, unless we are, belatedly, to blame Lincoln for the errors of General John Pope before Second Manassas.) That a naïve view of the world was displayed at Yalta, and long before Yalta, by many powerful Americans, is true. Eyes were kept on the conniving British Empire, as they are still kept by Colonel McCormick, Mr. George Sokolsky, and others—eyes which had better have been directed elsewhere. But even had those eyes been more prudently fastened upon Russia, even had American policy been controlled by a Richelieu or a Bismarck, some of the present disillusionment would have occurred all the same. For America, the most powerful nation in the world, was not omnipotent and a great many things in the world were going on and going their own way regardless of the views of the American people.

For, great as is American power, it is not so great as to quell, by its mere existence, all opposition. In the good old days an English fleet could sail into the Bay of Naples and tell that able Bourbon, King Charles III, that he could be neutral or have his capital blown up around his ears. In the good old days before the 'good neighbour' policy, the United States (or the United Fruit Company, if they could be distinguished) could lay down the law in the Caribbean. As Cleveland's Secretary of State said, the fiat of the United States was law in America, if the United States chose to insist.

But those days are gone. The United States could insist if she wanted to, but at excessive political cost. Even that American by-blow, the Republic of Panama, can defy Washington, up to the point where the safety of the United States is directly and indisputably involved. These facts are accepted. Yet a great many Americans, when China gets out of hand, or into the wrong hands, think this can only be because of some gross error or even crime on the part of the official rulers of America. Even so simple an explanation as that Chiang made the mistake denounced in all the military textbooks, and exemplified in the careers of Jefferson Davis and of Hitler, of commanding at long range and through favourites, is ignored. People feel that Chiang's defeat (a disaster for America, I freely admit) *must* have been due to American folly or American treason. People refuse to believe that it might have had other, more important causes, above all the one admirably described by Senator Tom Connally: 'If he's a generalissimo, why doesn't he generalize?'

The Chinese situation is, at the moment, the most important of these American preoccupations and causes of bewilderment. But the sense of bewilderment is visible in some American attitudes towards Europe too. Why hasn't Marshall aid won over the French Communists—that is, ended a schism in French society going back to the Commune of 1871, if not to the Commune of 1793? Why hasn't it converted 'Red Emilia', the Italian district that was in a violent revolutionary uproar in Wilson's first term? Why is it not certain that the inhabitants of the 'People's Republic of Germany', after being fought over, and driven here and there, and after having had their social structure destroyed, following the disillusionments caused by the collapse of the Hohenzollerns, the Weimar Republic, and the Thousand-Year-Reich, will welcome slogans admirably designed for Cincinnati or Oakland? In such perplexities there is embedded, at the foundation perhaps, the illusion that the world must go the American way if the Americans want it strongly enough and give firm orders to their agents to see that it is done.

III

This illusion of omnipotence is best illustrated by a very common American attitude towards the Chinese Revolution. In this attitude— apparently the dominant one at the moment—there is a curious absence of historical awe and historical curiosity. The Chinese Revolution, an event of immense importance, is often discussed as if it were simply a problem in American foreign and domestic policy and politics. The Communist triumph in China is discussed as if it were simply the result of American action or inaction, the result of the mistakes, and worse than mistakes, of General Marshall,

Secretary Acheson, President Roosevelt, and the Institute of Pacific Relations; and as if the Communists or the Russians would not have 'captured' China had American policy been represented and controlled by Representative Judd—or even, perhaps, by Senators Cain and Jenner.

Is this not to display the belief in American omnipotence in a very striking form? What is going on in China affects the oldest civilization now in existence. It affects about a fifth of the human race. It must have roots, deep roots, in the Chinese problem as seen by the Chinese. This is no matter of a régime imposed by Russia on a helpless small nation like Rumania or Hungary. It is a historical phenomenon that may turn out to be more important than the Russian Revolution. It may well turn out, also, to be disastrous for us and for China. But the first thing to notice is the size of the phenomenon; to notice, for example, that there are five Chinese for every two Americans. What inherent necessity is there that the decision in China is, was, or ever will be in American hands?

It is not only a matter of scale. There is distance. China is six thousand miles from the Pacific Coast of America. How was and is American power to be effectively exercised at that distance? I anticipate one answer—that Russian power *is* being exercised, and that it was Russian power (in the absence of American power because of American folly and treason) that 'took over' China. This is not demonstrated and in this crude and popular form is not probable. But even if it were true, Russia is not six thousand miles from China. Russia has had a common frontier with China for three hundred years, and as Russia's centre of industrial gravity moves eastward, Russian power gets nearer China and can be more readily exercised there. In a straight contest for control of China between the United States and the U.S.S.R., with the Chinese regarded as vile bodies, the U.S.S.R. would hold the trumps. To ignore that is to show the attitude of mind of those who have complained that, at Yalta, F.D.R. 'permitted' Russia to become a Pacific power. Russia was a Pacific power before the United States existed. And she was and is an Asiatic power, which the United States is not. Lake Baikal and Lake Superior are on different continents. Vladivostok and Peiping are not.

But the real lack of historical reverence and realism is in the assumption that Russia 'took over' China as she took over Poland. Even if we assume that there is as united an opposition to Communist rule in China as I believe there is in Poland, the scale of the taking-over ought to impose reflection. By what miracle was it done? Could General Hurley or General Chennault have prevented it? Would a sounder understanding of what the Communists were have prevented the Communist triumph? If it would have, then China is a more torpid body, more open to mere manipulation, than it is pleasant to think. If so great an event as the Chinese Communist Revolution could have been prevented by a different American policy, China is 'a corpse on the dissecting table', as Charles Gavan Duffy said of Ireland after the Famine. In that case, Mao and Stalin may dissect it and make a monster of it like Dr. Moreau in H. G. Wells's prophetic story. If it was taken over as easily as all that, it will be kept taken over even more easily.

*

There is some reason to believe and to hope that it is not quite as simple as this. We are in danger of being obsessed with the important and indisputable fact that world Communism is a real and potent force and that it is controlled from Moscow. We tend, therefore, to see the hand of Moscow everywhere and attribute to it an initiating and dominant role that may not always be justified. The Chinese Revolution, we should remember, has been going on longer than the Russian Revolution. Sun Yat-sen was the successful leader of a revolution when Lenin was an obscure and not too hopeful exile in Switzerland. But, I shall be told, that was a *different* Chinese Revolution; that was the *good* Chinese Revolution, the one that deposed the Manchu dynasty and abolished the pigtail and the binding of feet; that was the revolution which was inspired and encouraged by American missionaries and American-trained students. But isn't it a truism of history that when you start a revolution, you can't be sure where it is going and how far?

It wasn't Lenin who overthrew the Tsardom or Robespierre who stormed the Bastille. In a long, bloody, and profound revolution, the extreme party has many advantages. It may not win; it may not stay victorious; the Jacobins learned that. But it may destroy the old order, the old ruling classes, the rival revolutionary parties, Social Revolutionists or Girondins. It doesn't need, in a genuine revolutionary situation, outside aid, outside doctrine, though it may get and benefit by both. The Chinese Communists got aid; they got doctrine. They probably benefited by both (though in 1927 they might have done better without either). But to deny that the Chinese Communists are a large, native Chinese party is to fly in the face of all the evidence. Their leaders may be docile tools of Moscow, but that doesn't alter the fact that the Chinese Communist party which survived the Kuomintang war against it, which survived the 'long march', is a formidable indigenous party. On the record, it seems to have been the most formidable indigenous party—the one that, had both the U.S.A. and the U.S.S.R. stayed out, might have won anyway.

Could it have been prevented from defeating the Kuomintang by the provision of 'massive and controlled' American aid? I have already suggested that the Russians could play that game too, and their aid could have been both more massive and controlled than the American. But even assuming that they did not so react to open American intervention in a civil war against their political allies, in a neighbouring country, how was the aid to be made massive and how was it to be controlled?

Does anyone think that a continuation of what arms aid had been given, or even a stepping-up of such aid, would have done the trick? The Washington wit who said that supplying arms to Chiang was simply a roundabout way of Lend-Lease to the Chinese Communists was a jester, possibly frivolous; but he was not altogether wrong. Lend-Lease to Britain, Lend-Lease to Russia was direct and massive aid to coherent, united, and combative governments. It was not aid to a divided party in a country torn and tired by a generation of foreign and domestic war. More aid to Chiang might have prolonged the war; it might have saved the situation south of the Yangtse; but would it have brought conquest of the Communists by Chiang's forces?

And how was American aid to be controlled—except by exercising a degree of American authority which would not only have inflamed the *amour propre* of the Generalissimo, but would have deprived the Kuomintang of its last political asset, its claim to be 'nationalist', to represent the independence of China? Could the aid have been effective without active American participation—without keeping the Marines in China, without sending in more troops, without, in fact, involving the United States in a greater Korean war? Does anyone who remembers the temper of the American people in 1945, from the White House and Capitol to churches and bars, believe that such a policy was politically practicable?

I have been in America every year since 1944 with the exception of 1949. I have sometimes been twice in America in one year. I have been in all regions. At no time before the Korean war did I find anything like the resolution to make great sacrifices to save China which alone could have saved China.

IV

At first sight, the growing American distress at the continuance of the Korean war seems to show something very different from a sense of omnipotence. It shows, indeed, a sense of frustration, dismay, bewilderment. To find hundreds of thousands of American troops fighting in a remote country, seven years after 'the end of the war', is baffling enough. To suffer over 120,000 casualties in such a situation is worse. The Korean war is already, in terms of losses, the third most serious war in American history. An American mother lamenting the fate of her son is a figure to inspire sympathy and understanding. It is natural that the American people should want, not on any terms but on some terms, an end to the Korean war.

But in addition to this common and natural sentiment, there is another American attitude that is less defensible and decidedly dangerous. It might be likened to the attitude of the prosperous and pompous citizen who, in a jam, firmly tells the cops, 'You can't do that to me.' Many, very many Americans, it seems to me, find it inconceivable that an American policy, announced and carried out by the American government, acting with the support of the American people, does not immediately succeed. If it does not, this, they feel, must be because of stupidity or treason. That the Chinese Communist government should defy—and successfully defy—the policy of the United States, seems to them to fly in the face of a truth which they hold to be self-evident.

Yet such situations exist and may well continue to exist. It is by no means certain that American forces will easily be withdrawn from Korea, or even that they may not have to take part in other wars of that kind. Mrs. Kathleen Norris can no more alter that fact than Senator Taft can really guarantee to keep the military budget to a fixed proportion of the total. In the great power vacuum created by the decline of Europe, the United States is forced, and will be forced, to do a great many disagreeable things—or to surrender. This is a new story for the United States, but it is an old one for Europe. What the American people are enduring now is what the French, the English, the Russian peoples, even the Spanish and Italian peoples, suffered in the process of extending or trying to retain their empires.

But, it will be objected, America is not trying to extend an empire; she is defending public order and morality in Korea. This is very different from the piratical adventures of the old world, from the French in Africa, the English in India, or the Russians in Samarkand or Armenia. Morally, this is true. But, just as the purity of the American cause does not win all American families to an acceptance of the Korean war as necessary and tolerable, so the moral turpitude of European enterprises added very little to the burden of empire. And that burden was heavy in terms of lives lost.

It has been calculated—and I do not think it is an improbable calculation—that the French conquest of Algeria cost the French 150,000 lives. (What it cost the Arabs, resisting civilization, no one has paused to compute.) I don't know what the British wars in India cost either in great battles, in minor battles, or in disease, but they cost plenty. Even the British peace, imposed on India, cost plenty to the 100,000 white troops permanently garrisoned in that remote, unhealthy land. Do you think it mattered to a French mother that her son, dead in Algeria, was an agent of imperialism? All she knew was that he had paid what Marshal Gouvion Saint-Cyr candidly called a blood tax. And the same story can be told of Indochina seventy years ago—and now. It is one of the minor themes of a once-famous novel, Loti's *Pêcheurs d'Islande*. 'It's a long way to Carcassonne,' said the soldier of the Grande Armée, dying in the snow on the retreat from Moscow; and it is a long time since Virgil made the dying Greek remember sweet Argos.

Morally justifiable—indeed, morally splendid—as the American action in Korea on behalf of the United Nations may be, and urgent as the need may be to find an honourable way out of the predicament in which she finds herself, what Americans are paying today is one of the normal prices of being a great power, of bearing the burdens as well as enjoying the advantages of power.

Again, I have no intention of minimizing the horror of the Korean war. I was in New York in December 1950, when it was still not certain that the Marines would get out of the trap sprung on them in North Korea—when, indeed, it was not certain that many of them would ever get home. I felt passionately with the American people. And the situation is not purely American. In a year and a half, my eldest son will be in the army and may be in Malaya or Korea. It is a painful story. But it is an old one.

V

Another aspect of the 'you can't do this to me' mentality—which, in turn, is an aspect of the illusion of omnipotence—can best be studied in the writings of Mr. David Lawrence of the *U.S. News and World Report*. To Mr. Lawrence the Korean war, the loss of American lives in it, is not merely painful but unendurable. It must be put an end to, and one of the methods suggested has a real interest—to me a pathological interest. If I understand Mr. Lawrence aright, in order to diminish Communist pressures on the Americans in Korea, Poles and Czechs are to be encouraged to acts of sabotage if not of active revolt, and a 'resistance movement' is to be subsidized, with a view to diverting Russian or other Communist resources from Korea—that is, from the Americans in Korea.

This modest proposal deserves examination. Mr. Lawrence apparently does not pretend that the United States proposes to do anything more to liberate Poland and Czechoslovakia than to encourage and equip saboteurs. He does not pretend that such activities, in themselves, will bring down the Stalinist régime. They will, he hopes, cause such inconvenience that the heat will be off the Americans.

It is obvious that Mr. Lawrence does not know very much about resistance movements, or the means open to a totally ruthless government to repress resistance movements. He may have heard of Lidice, of Warsaw, even of Oradour-sur-Glane. But the meaning of those episodes is lost on him (and on many other Americans). To save the lives of Americans, to relieve this new and heavy but not intolerable pressure on American society, Poles and Czechs are to risk—for themselves and for their families, and if it comes to a pitch, for their countries—total destruction, the execution of hostages, the annihilation of whole villages, possibly the fate of the peoples of the three Baltic states, of whom we do not even know that, as nations, Lithuania, Estonia, and Latvia exist any longer.

These nations, and more especially the Poles, have undergone experiences that not one home-staying American in a hundred thousand, perhaps in a million, can really comprehend. The liberation of Poland, on these terms, might mean the end of Poland. And the Poles are not even promised liberation; merely the satisfaction of annoying the Russians and relieving the Americans. If the United States were in mortal danger, patriotic Poles might be willing to take great risks to aid her, since in American survival 'the only hope of freedom lies'. But she is not in mortal danger; she is in what a Pole who has known first German, then Russian rule, can hardly regard as more than acute discomfort. To ask the Poles to act, at such risks, to diminish this discomfort is something pardonable only on the grounds of invincible ignorance. And it is something that Americans could hardly seriously recommend unless they saw in the situation a denial of one of 'the Laws of Nature and of Nature's God', namely the immunity of the United States from the common ills of this distressed world.

For it should be evident that only if the United States is willing, in a reasonably short time, to undertake, by general war, the liberation of the captive nations, has any American any business urging kinds of resistance which can pay only in the event of a general—and successful—war. Even were the United States to proclaim such a policy, the problem of encouraging resistance is not a simple one. It can be argued, for instance, that the damage done to France by the resistance movement there—from the torturing and burning of victims to the demoralization that some resistance methods fostered —was far more serious than any damage done to the German occupiers. The only justification for disregarding that calculation was a moral one: that if France took no part in her own liberation, she could not, in fact, be liberated; all that could be done was to expel the Germans, which was not the same thing. But even so, the appeals of General de Gaulle and others, and the organization from London of all sorts of resistance activities, were only just tolerable, because they were not only a means of saving English lives but also of saving French souls.

This is not to say that everything possible should not be done to keep alive hope, the Western tradition, the national tradition in the captive nations. A permanently hostile Poland or Czechoslovakia is a double weakness for the U.S.S.R., a possible future military weakness and a present propaganda weakness. But there is a world between the policy advocated by John Foster Dulles and that advocated by those Americans who say, 'This can't go on.' It may, and no amount of asserting that it can't will alter the fact.

When policies are advocated on the ground that they will 'save the lives of American boys', the implication sometimes seems to be that only the lives of American boys really count. It is often forgotten, in this world of short memories, that one justification of Yalta, of the coaxing and bribing of Stalin to enter the Japanese war, was the saving of the lives of American boys. To save the lives of American boys is a high object of policy indeed. It is one of the marks of a democracy, or of a free government, that the military and political leaders can be held to account on that one point. As the Duke of Wellington pointed out, Napoleon could spend his conscripts as he liked, while Wellington might be summoned to the bar of the House of Commons if he threw away the lives of five hundred British soldiers. But that is a very different matter from giving the impression that American lives, as such, are of any special importance; that, as an American friend of mine put it in some unpublished verses:

> Clean-limbed American boys are not like any others.
> Only clean-limbed American boys have mothers.

Their lives are of special importance to Americans, but not to the people of other lands. And there would be widespread resentment over the thoughtless implication that it is the first duty of Poles or Czechs to save American lives.

These are hard sayings and they are negative sayings. But they may not be useless all the same. Only by constant vigilance, prudence, willingness to take the long view and to assess the situation, even in its most unpleasant, frustrating, and dangerous aspects, can American policy succeed—succeed in preserving the freedom of the United States and the freedom of other nations as a means to that end. There are no quick, sure recipes for security and power. The Kremlin hasn't got them; the White House will not have them either. This means that the American people will have to learn a great many new attitudes. (They learn fast, as the history of the world since 1939 shows.) They will have to learn that, even in election years, the world cannot be altered overnight by a speech or a platform. Only by accepting this depressing truth can American power, great, flexible, and beneficent as it is, be used to full advantage.

1952

3

A FRESH APPRAISAL OF THE CIVIL WAR

Happy the country that has no history.

THIS FAMOUS expression of a sardonic view of human destiny may be no more than a generalized version of the old Chinese curse: 'May you live in interesting times.' But I think it is more than that. For the country that has a 'history', dramatic, moving, tragic, has to live with it—with the problems it raised but did not solve, with the emotions that it leaves as a damaging legacy, with the defective vision that preoccupation with the heroic, with the disastrous, with the expensive past fosters.

But there is more to be said than this; the inheritance of a past rich in suffering, in vicissitudes, in heroism adds something to the national assets, even though the price is always high and often grossly excessive. It would be too much to say that the nations that have known no such catastrophes *envy* their less fortunate but more interesting neighbours, but they do feel something lacking. Like the man or woman who has never been in love, they feel that they *have* missed something, including, no doubt, a great deal of trouble and expense.

And perhaps the first thing to say about the American Civil War is that it put the American people, decisively, once and for all, among the peoples who have lived in interesting times and who have paid an extravagantly high price for this experience. It may well be a sign of savagery, but the world picture of America, the American picture of America is deeply different, more impressive, more *attractive* than if it had been just one long success story. I do not for a moment suggest that the American Civil War was a good thing—merely that it was and is felt by the unregenerate (a majority of the Western races now and for as long as we can inspect the past) to be the most moving, interesting, dignified thing that has ever occurred in America.[1]

What is most important in the American preoccupation with their Civil War is not to be exhausted by a politico-economic balance sheet. What is important is the preoccupation, the living memory, the curiosity, the nostalgia. The Civil War is not only refought in an incessant flow of books, articles, and speeches; it is refought hypothetically. If Paris had not run away with Helen, how different the history of the Greeks and Trojans would have been! To want to remake history is to show how much that history means.

But is my emphasis on the American preoccupation with their Civil War justified? Suppose there is going to be a flood of books about the Civil War in the next few years, so what? The publishers know when they are in on a good thing. I am sure they do, but it is naïve to suggest that they have simply invented the good thing. The flood—though varying in volume—has never ceased since the War itself ended. I will go so far as to assert that quite soon the flag that was lowered and raised over Fort Sumter will mean more than the flag that was raised over Iwo Jima. Appomattox will soon mean more, again, than Rheims or the U.S.S. *Missouri* in Tokyo Bay. What songs of other wars (with the exception of 'The Star-spangled Banner') compare with 'John Brown's Body' and 'Dixie' to name only two? Perhaps it was because of the shots fired on Sumter, as much as because of the shots fired on Fort McHenry, that the United States chose its anthem. And if it is only in the South that people still talk simply of 'The War', all over the restored Union I believe that it is still *the* war.

There are, it seems to me, in the experience of nations, ordeals so novel, so disastrous, physically or morally, so dramatic a destruction of hope, the prelude to some long period of humiliation or despair, that they are watersheds in the nation's history. It may be the case of a single disastrous battle, Mohács for the Hungarians, Kossovo for the Serbs, Flodden for the Scots. The history of a nation may be so rich in disasters that it is difficult to make a choice. Thus Ireland has an *embarras de richesses* in this type of experience. It is, however, my conviction that the great famine of 1846–7 was the shock from which

[1] Matthew Arnold, in his high aesthetic fashion, thought that the War, and especially the assassination of Lincoln to the tune of a Latin motto, *Sic semper tyrannis*, made American history quite respectable.

Ireland has not yet recovered (and may not be recovering). For the French until very recent years and perhaps still (I hope not) it was that great *déception d'amour*, 'The Revolution'. For the Germans it was, until this century, the first Thirty Years' War; now it may be (nobody knows, least of all the Germans) the Second Thirty Years' War. For Britain it was (I believe) not the loss of Empire in the Second World War but the bloodletting and faithletting of the First. For the Americans it was the Civil War.

This will be readily admitted by most people if we confine the notion to the South. 'I was born a child of Appomattox,' said Lyndon Johnson, revealingly and rightly. The whole South is a child of Appomattox and of the years just before and the decades after. It is so in fact; it is more deeply so in folk legend and folk memory. Appomattox is the Southern Flodden Field; the Reconstruction is the Southern folk legend and memory equivalent to the Irish memory summed up in: 'The curse of Cromwell on ye.'

That would be enough to account for the careful cultivation of Confederate memories. (I once half-formed the impression that the only books sold in some Southern towns were religious, Confederate, or sexy.) But what of the North? The North won, didn't it? The Northern monuments are not tributes to 'the Lost Cause' but to the saving of 'the last, best hope of earth'. Even the monuments to Lincoln are monuments to one 'who hath outsoared the shadow of our night', to one who now 'belongs to the ages'—as Stanton, for once rivalling Shelley, put it. I think that is too simple a description and analysis of the 'myths after Lincoln', but it can be let stand for the moment.

WHY WAS IT NECESSARY?

But we have to ask ourselves why was 'the last, best hope of earth' endangered? We have to ask what led to the first great political crime in American history—a President assassinated like a tyrant in corrupt and king-ridden Europe? We have to ask why it was necessary for so many hundreds of thousands of men to 'give the last full measure of devotion'. We have to ask the question of what happened to the American dream of manifest destiny, of easy immunity at home, of easy moral, political, and social superiority abroad. For that dream was deeply cherished. True, from 1850 on it was an uneasy dream. Now many, perhaps most, had heard Jefferson's 'firebell in the night'. But it is evident that up till the moment that

Beauregard's guns opened on Sumter, the majority of Americans, North and South, did not believe that it would come to ordeal by battle.

The breed of John Brown and Edmund Ruffin was a minority in every state and section, even in Massachusetts, even in South Carolina. Without saying that there was a general pacific temper (Mexicans and Indians might have demurred), there was a horror of *fraternal* war. There was naturally, also, the simple refusal of the average man and woman to believe that things can really be about to get as bad as they are going to be. In most times and countries, the mass of the people don't believe the man who cries 'wolf' even the first time.

So it was in 1860–1. That is the psychological weight behind Lincoln's words in the Second Inaugural, 'and the war came'. True, Seward had talked of an 'irrepressible conflict' but when the crisis was really upon the country, no one was more fertile in plans and dodges to avert the conflict. Lincoln had talked of a 'house divided', but it is evident from his actions that he did not believe that the division would have to be ended by the sword. (Again the Second Inaugural which puts the burden of explanation and justification on the inscrutable God of Lincoln's political Calvinism is revealing.) Despite the fiery words and the outrages that we now see as the pre-liminaries to the dread and dreaded conflict, despite Bleeding Kansas and John Brown and the assault on Senator Sumner, people didn't see the war as coming, inevitably, with only the date uncertain, as most saw it by 1939 in Europe and many saw it in 1914. What if all the evidence pointed one way? It was too bad to be true. I doubt if Jefferson Davis wanted war, or even wanted secession. It is certain that many Southern leaders, who held out to the end, including the greatest of all, Lee, wanted neither.

'And the war came.' The American people, the rightly favoured children of God, were suddenly reminded of their humanity and mortality. (They were reminded again at Pearl Harbor and didn't like it then either.) 'You can't do this to me' is a slightly irreverent shorthand account of an attitude that was human and general. If the French Revolution was a *déception d'amour*, this was a *déception d'espoir*.

THE ROOTS OF A LEGEND

One thing all foreign visitors to the U.S. before the Civil War noted was the nearly universal self-approbation and the desire to have that self-approbation not so much confirmed, as applauded. The American asked the visitor—Tocqueville, Dickens, who have you—'Don't you think we are wonderful?' but it was a question put in the form of the Latin 'nonne' which expects the answer, 'Yes— and how.' In the Land of the Free few troubling questions were asked—or, if asked, listened to or even tolerated, as Tocqueville noted.

Especially the one black question mark of slavery was not allowed to be put after the rodomontade of the daily Fourth of July oration. Even in the darkening years of the 'fifties, the paean of self-praise was heard round the world. The South was beginning to say 'yes, but'. But my business, at the moment, is with the North that 'won' and yet found the fruits of victory bitter and, in some cases, actually poisonous.

Maybe the traumatic shock would not have been so great or lasted so long if the optimists on either side had been right, if the war, when it came, had been '*courte, fraîche, et joyeuse*'. But the war lasted four years and was the most deadly war between Waterloo and the Marne. The most deadly, not the most bloody, because of more than half a million deaths, most took place not on the battlefields but in the hospitals. (It has been calculated that more Union soldiers died of diarrhoea than died in combat.) But that made the loss less, not more, endurable. '*Dulce et decorum est pro patria mori*' is possibly comforting when the loved son or husband or father dies in actual battle. But it is less becoming to die of the camp-bred diseases, of the aftermath of measles, of typhoid, of pneumonia, of barbarous surgery or witch-doctor medicine. And hundreds of thousands died that way. If the first shock to American complacency was the manifest failure of the sacred Constitution to prevent the conflict, the second shock and, we may be certain, even more wounding, was the human misery caused not only to the sufferers in the fields, ditches, trains, wagons, ambulances, hospitals, but to their kin and friends. John Bright had condemned the recent Crimean War in a famous image:

'The Angel of Death has been abroad throughout the land.'

A far more terrible angel of death was abroad between 1861 and 1865. It chilled the hopes of millions. How many hearts it broke we shall never know. I can remember how the news of the landing on Gallipoli and then of Loos and the Somme came to my small home town in Scotland. So must it have been with the news of Shiloh and Cold Harbor.

So I would suggest as the first reason for the hold of 'the War' on the American memory and the American heart, just this human tragedy on a scale never equalled in American history before or since. (Even *absolutely* the United States lost more lives in the Civil War than in the Second World War and proportionately far more. It lost more proportionately than Britain did in the First World War.)

But, it will be objected, the American people today still devote as much time, thought, and money to the legend of 'The Winning of the West' as to the saving of the Union. They do, but they devote even more time and money to tobacco. There is a great difference between a legend that diverts and a legend that touches and can cause distress as well as joy. I would be the last to denigrate the *'matière d'Amérique'*, or to forget that the United States is the only country since the Middle Ages that has created a legend to set beside the story of Achilles, Robin Hood, Roland, and Arthur. But even the most devoted TV fan is aware that 'the West' is a remote ideal world, not differing very much from science-fiction worlds. Even the sophisticated westerns, with their neurotic heroes and floozies with hearts of stone, are in the Never Never World of fiction. There are many good books on the West, but the representative Western work of art, book, play, TV script, comic strip is fiction; the representative Civil War book is or professes to be fact.

Then there is the mass of devoted amateurs, the Civil War buffs. Is it not significant that the most distinguished living military historian of the War, Kenneth P. Williams, is a Professor of Mathematics? That Carl Sandburg should have devoted so much time and effort to Lincoln? We have *John Brown's Body*; why didn't Benét write on the War of the Revolution? At all levels, here is the great purging experience of the American people, their shame and their pride.

Scale is one reason for the domination of the American historical memory by the War. Americans like things big and this one was big, all right. Compared with it, the War of the Revolution, the War of 1812, the Mexican War were petty affairs. And as for the Spanish-American War, a good Labour Day weekend kills nearly as many people on the roads. The First and Second World Wars and the Korean War are more impressive affairs, but not only did they not kill as many men relatively or absolutely (unless you count the influenza casualties of 1918), they were fought outside the United States. And that is deeply important.

It is not only that the battlefields of the Civil War are more accessible than the Argonne or the Ardennes—not to speak of Iwo Jima or Inchon—but being fought on American soil, they are especially sacred. There is no *less* American sentiment than the one expressed by Rupert Brooke, 'that there's some corner of a foreign field that is forever England'. American boys, if they have to die in war, should die on American soil. (One of the oddest aspects of the Civil War to Europeans was the travelling undertakers who followed the armies and sent the bodies back home.) This was *the* American War, since the soldiers on each side were Americans; and both sides, today at any rate, can take pride in the heroism of the other side. Robert E. Lee is one of the top heroes of the national pantheon, honoured by a memorial in Washington as well as in Richmond. At West Point he is regarded as the *beau idéal* as cadet, officer, and Superintendent. There are millions of synthetic Southerners who, as O. Henry put it, have never been south of Hoboken, and we have recently seen a Congress, controlled by the South, honouring the one hundred and fiftieth anniversary of the birth of Lincoln.

We can be sure that for the overwhelming majority of Americans, the flood of centennial celebrations will bring little bitterness. (That doesn't mean that there was no irony or humour in the recent Virginian suggestion that there ought to be a re-enactment of the First Battle of Bull Run, in uniform, to start the ball rolling.) But we should remember that this 'era of good feeling' dates from this century, that the War left plenty of bitterness at the time, that many things that Americans now share in common pride were then grounds of fierce difference. Then the captured Confederate flags were trophies (that great but not magnanimous soldier, Sheridan, used to ride with a team of orderlies carrying them behind him). When Sumner in one of the few magnanimous actions of his life proposed that they should be given back, he was not listened to and when President Grover Cleveland actually decided to give them back, he had to retreat before the wrath of the Grand Army of the Republic.

It was a long time before Lee became a national hero for everyone, for we must remember that many in the North resented more hostilely the 'treason' of the regular officers who 'went with their states' than they did the treason of the politicians. The West Point officers were a privileged and unpopular class, fed, clothed, and paid from their youth by the Union, the only servants of the Union (apart from Federal judges and of course Navy officers) who had secure tenure. The officers who went South were biting the hand that had fed them. On the other hand, some West Pointers who had left the Army rushed to rejoin it because they felt a special duty to serve a government that had trained them for the service in arms that they could now give. Among them was ex-Captain Grant.

THE WAR OF THE BROTHERS-IN-LAW

But was it a civil war? There has been more than one protest against the title. The 'War of the Rebellion' and the 'War Between the States' are terms of art, each expressing the political and legal view of the conflict that the sides held or professed to hold. It has become common, in this generation, to talk of the 'War for Southern Independence' and that is a just title as far as it goes. But it doesn't go far enough, for this really was a war between citizens of a hitherto united body politic designed, on each side, to establish one view of the character of that body politic. The Confederate States did not merely set up a new government for a new 'country' (I avoid the word nation). They claimed to be the legitimate heirs of the old government in the area they sought to control.

The War was a civil war because it set brother against brother, father against son. Thousands of Northerners (like George Cary Eggleston) served in the ranks of the Confederate Army. Thousands of Southerners served in the ranks of the Union Army. It is hardly necessary to mention the more famous cases, of Thomas, Farragut, Scott serving the Union; Cooper, Pemberton, Gorgas serving the Confederacy. Mrs. Lincoln's brothers fought for the South and two Crittenden brothers became generals in opposing armies. The son of the commander of the Confederate Navy served in the Union Navy. Then, as now, West Pointers tended to marry each other's sisters and the War might be called the war of the brothers-in-law. (After Appomattox, even the unsentimental Sheridan went off at once to see his friends from 'the old Army'.)

And it was not only a matter of soldiers. Slidell, one of the few competent diplomatic agents the Confederacy had, was a New Yorker by origin. Wayne of Georgia stayed on the bench of the Supreme Court and there may be some reason to believe that

Campbell of Georgia regretted having to leave it. It is these ambiguous loyalties and confused duties that mark a civil war. The Lee is
probably the only soldier who has ever been offered the command
of both armies in a war—and when he made his choice, he entered
the conflict in a far more ambivalent frame of mind than that of
Robert the Bruce or Patrick Sarsfield or Charles de Gaulle.

I have always thought that this side of the War is best illustrated
by a story about a personally quite unimportant boy who yet being
the son of Governor Wise of Virginia was in the thick of things. As
a cadet of the Virginia Military Institute, he fought at New Market
and as General Wise's son he was sent on bold and risky rides across
country as the Confederacy collapsed. So he saw Lee on the eve of
Appomattox and Jefferson Davis at Danville just before Davis's last
flight. When the collapse did come, young Wise was sent North to
Philadelphia, but despite his experiences he was deemed too young
to attend a dinner party given by his uncle and had to eat in the
nursery with the other children. His uncle was George Gordon
Meade, Commander of the Army of the Potomac.

Then in the border states, there was civil war of the classical kind.
There were many thousands of men from Kentucky, Maryland,
Missouri in each army. Regiments in the opposing armies bore the
same names and in one disastrous instance wore nearly the same
uniform. Men from the same village met in battle. And in Missouri
(and Kansas) the Civil War was truly civil—that is savage, with
murder and rapine rampant. Quantrill, the Confederate partisan,
might have served with the Black and Tans or the Nazi SS and it
was in this semi-private war that the James Boys learned their trade.
And when we read that Mr. Truman's grandmother would not let
him enter her house in United States uniform, we should remember
what crimes that uniform had covered in Missouri.

Even the geographical distribution of the combatants was not as
simple as it often is made to seem. There were bitter Union partisans
in nearly every Confederate state. Even if the legend of a county
'seceding' from the Confederacy *is* legend, it is revealing legend and
there was an attempt to vote for Lincoln in North Carolina in 1864.
There is an Illinois legend that it was only the influence of Stephen
Douglas that kept 'Black Jack' Logan from joining the Confederate
Army and sent him off to the Union Army instead. There were
Confederate partisans and passionate defenders of slavery as far
north as Vermont, and the Chief Justice of the United States, Roger

Taney, had no sympathy with the cause of the government of which he was the judicial head.

THE GUILT OF CAIN

In any civil war, the question of war guilt is of the deepest importance. The origins of the English Civil War were debated heatedly for two centuries. How great was the guilt (so the Popular party thought) of P. Scipio Nasica who slew Tiberius Gracchus and opened the century of Roman civil wars! In the Second Inaugural Lincoln was to rise above this battle: 'Let us judge not that we be not judged.' But he was outside the usual range of human possibility.

So the American concern with the origins of the War differed greatly from that of a European nation obsessed with the success or failure of its government's policy. There was, to return to a basic theme, the sense that there must be some great guilt somewhere, to account for the ending of the Union (it *was* ended for a time). Each side, in a deeply Christian country, was anxious to throw the guilt of Cain on the other. The leaders of the South were anxious, after the War was over, to explain that they had been right but unfortunate, to refute the charge of treason levelled against them and their region.

The North and its leaders were equally anxious to pin the guilt on the other side, for this was one way—perhaps the only way—to secure the triumph of the Republican party and the great mass of economic interests now clustered round the quondam 'party of moral ideas'. And both sides were composed of Americans, one of the most legally-minded peoples the world has seen.

THE CASE FOR THE SOUTH

Nowhere is the American passion for legality better displayed than in Jefferson Davis's long, often tedious apologia, *The Rise and Fall of the Confederate Government*. Davis had much to tell and a case to plead. By the time he wrote his book, he had moved from being the scapegoat of 1865 to being a hero (if not a warmly loved one) in the South and a highly respectable old gentleman in the eyes of nearly everybody in the North who had not a political or financial interest in 'waving the bloody shirt'. The inside story of the Confederate government, of the President's relations with his Cabinet, with the Confederate Congress, with the generals, with the people, would have been fascinating. The great debates over his policies, over his relationship with Benjamin, his unintelligible devotion to Braxton Bragg, his difficulties with Beauregard, his removal of Joe Johnston, his choice of Hood—themes bitterly debated even before the Confederacy fell—do get some treatment, but there is no revelation of what made Davis tick (and some of the accounts of military disasters are comic in their inadequacy). But there is one theme on which Davis is tireless, the constitutionality of secession and the illegality of the conduct of Abraham Lincoln. The French courtiers who listened to the exiled James II explaining the wickedness of the traitors who had driven him into exile had no need to go further to discover why James II was bound to have been driven into exile. And one feels that the failure of the Confederacy is at least partly explained by this legalistic obsession of Davis.

The real answer to Davis was given by Daniel Webster in 1850 when he asserted that to talk of peaceable and constitutional secession was nonsense, but that for the South talk and practice of revolution was not necessarily nonsense. Yet the South was committed by its leaders (not only by Davis; Alexander Stephens was worse if possible) to a revolution on legal grounds; and even when the Confederacy was doomed, Davis reports how he was shocked at the impudence of Lincoln talking of his loyalty to the Federal Constitution when he notoriously refused to enforce the Fugitive Slave clauses of that document. The same legalistic nonsense afflicted his foreign policy. Palmerston and Napoleon III were given lectures on the nature of the old Constitution which they obviously misunderstood. There was, of course, some political advantage in trying to deprive the government of the United States of the prestige of legitimacy, in refuting the charge of rebellion, but the South was prohibited by its legalistic obsession from issuing an effective declaration of independence.

This is not to say that the South had no case. It did, but many a litigant who has a good case is ill advised to go to law about it. No one knows what the intentions of the framers of the Constitution were in the matter of secession.

Just as even very loving American couples who get married can't quite ignore the fact that divorce is easy and common, the 'People' and the leaders who made up 'We the People of the United States' who entered the 'more perfect union' were willing to give it a try. If they had been told they could never repent of their bargain, they might not have made it.

But this is very different from having a built-in right of secession to be used at any moment one of the high contracting parties thought fit. No government could run for long under this perpetual threat of peaceful dissolution. Nor is this all. Apart from Texas (the only state with a really plausible theory of secession) what right of secession had the new states? They were mostly formed from territory bought by the United States from France or Spain. What sovereignty was Louisiana 'resuming'—Louisiana, a fragment of a territory sold just like a prime field hand? Why should the United States—i.e. the states that didn't repent of their bargain—give up their rights in this great common asset? I think on examination that the case for secession was in practice a case for *dissolution* of the Union. On strict State Rights theory, each state 'resumed' its sovereignty, but why should that have dissolved the United States even if the government of the United States permitted or recognized the secession? What claim on the Indian Territory (Oklahoma to you) had the states that left the United States? What the South was claiming was that when enough states decided to leave the partnership (or agency, for that was a way they liked to refer to the government of the United States), all the assets were to be divided among the partners.[1]

Of course, the South was right in resisting and resenting the imputation of special moral turpitude, in seceding. Talk of secession or of resistance to Federal tyranny had been common form. It was right to recall to supercilious New Englanders their attitude to 'Mr. Madison's War', to recall the Hartford Convention. Since the Republicans claimed to be the true heirs of Thomas Jefferson, it was good tactics to recall the Kentucky Resolutions. It was effective debate to stress the disloyalty of the Abolitionists and their allies. But it was no more than that. States hadn't seceded over the Alien and Sedition Acts, over the War of 1812, over the Tariff of Abominations, over the Mexican War. They seceded over one thing and fought over one thing, slavery.

[1] A curious and otherwise unimportant *obiter dictum* of Davis is yet revealing. He suggests that instead of taking their ships into Union ports, Southern officers in the Navy of the United States should have taken them into Southern ports so that when the division of assets took place, the South would have its hands on them. But this is not a political doctrine of secession. Apart from involving Southern officers and gentlemen in despicable conduct, this course of action recalls a nervous and not too scrupulous director or partner who wants to get his hands on some of the firm's property before the liquidator does.

DID SLAVERY REALLY START IT ?

That this was so, nobody, I suspect, doubted when the War was on. That pathological constitutionalist Alexander Stephens, who was against secession before it happened and not enthusiastic about it even when he was Vice-President of the Confederacy, let the cat out of the bag when he said: 'Our new government is founded on the exactly opposite idea [to the equality of races]; its cornerstone rests upon the great truth that the Negro is not equal to the white man.' This natural and incurable inequality had as its most suitable and—in Southern circumstances—essential embodiment, the 'peculiar institution' of slavery. These were the new 'Laws of Nature and of Nature's God'.

It was about this conception and its institutional embodiment and the passions, fears, interests linked with the Institution, that the war was fought. As Lincoln put it in the Second Inaugural, the 'slaves constituted a peculiar and powerful interest. All knew that this interest was somehow the cause of the war.'

This judgment, which I think few doubted in 1865, has been often challenged since—not only by legalists, but also by naïve realists like Charles Beard. (His limitations as historian and thinker were seldom more manifestly revealed than in his attempt to find an explanation for the War that could be reduced to his naïve doctrine of self-interest.) There has only been one institution in American history that had the necessary emotional as well as (and more important than) the necessary material weight to make so great a war possible. I do not say that the abolition of slavery was the cause of the War, or that the simple defence of slavery was the cause. But the War was about slavery. True, the North fought to save the Union; but the Union was menaced only by the slavery question. The South fought for the Southern way of life, using State Rights as a weapon; but the mark, as Catholic theologians put it, of the Southern way of life was slavery—or so the South thought.

In doing this it raised an issue that would not die. If the South could only exist on the basis of slavery, did it have a right to exist at all ? It has long been fashionable to play down the moral content of the slavery issue. But the moral content was there. It did make a lot of difference whether, like Lincoln, you thought it mattered whether slavery was voted up or down or, like Douglas, professed not to care. (It made a difference to their styles.) The most famous of all

American novels is and was *Uncle Tom's Cabin* and Lincoln had some justice on his side when he greeted Mrs. Stowe with, 'So you're the little lady who made this big war.' No doubt *Uncle Tom's Cabin* is a fantastic picture of the normal working of slavery. But it is not an impossible picture. (The one impossible character is not Simon Legree but Uncle Tom.) Slavery did insult human nature and make possible horrible crimes (one especially horrible occurred in Jefferson's family). And the issue was put in the greatest of American novels when Huck Finn, the American version of Antigone, decides to commit the crime of helping Nigger Jim to steal himself.

It has become customary to argue that only agitators kept the issue alive, that wise men had more urgent things to talk about—tariffs and land sales and railways and the like. This was the argument of a more serious historian than Charles Beard, J. G. Randall. But to tell the past what it *should* have talked about is not the work of the historian. To write off, as Randall does, the men who insisted on talking about slavery as mere mischief-makers is to ignore the role of morals and moralists, ideas and ideologues in history. What we should notice is that every effort to keep slavery out of politics failed—compromises, deals, agreements among sensible men, all failed. Again and again, the American people were summoned to a harmony banquet and each time the Banquo's ghost of slavery insisted on turning up. (I am here reducing to a crude simplification the acute argument of my friend, Professor Pieter Geyl of Utrecht, in the *New England Quarterly*, June 1951.)

Slavery was a ghost that walked and could not be laid by silence or by a national policy of 'togetherness'. This was perhaps a pity but it was also a fact. Because I believe this to be so, I cannot take much interest in the careful, ingenious, almost convincing explanations of how the War could have been avoided. Suppose Dr. Otto Eisenschiml is right in his ingenious guess that it was an accident that Fort Sumter was not evacuated, what of it? The clash would have come somewhere else. True, it might have come in circumstances less disadvantageous to the South, and that has led to ingenious speculation that Lincoln provoked Jefferson Davis, that Major Anderson was left, like the lamb tethered under the tree, to excite the tiger. (The same theory has been used to impute high treason to Roosevelt for provoking Pearl Harbor.) Unless Lincoln had been willing to abandon his conception of his duties as legally elected President of the United States, the war would have come. As far as

Lincoln is guilty it is because, as Professor David Potter has shown, he refused in the period between his election and inauguration to surrender any of his fundamental principles (or dogmas) to reassure the South. Seward might believe that all could be settled by what the Italians call a *combinazione* but Lincoln did not. He did not foresee what kind of war was beginning or, if you like, he was beginning. Maybe if he had, he would have held his hand; I doubt it. He was the toughest of war leaders, inflexible about few things but inflexible about them.

What does it mean to contrast the torpor (or panic) of the last months of the Buchanan Administration or the first month of the Lincoln Administration with the explosion that followed the firing on Sumter? The gunpowder was there; Beauregard applied the match. If Lincoln grievously underestimated the strength of sectional feeling in the South, the South did not understand the forces that moved the North. There was the Union, the flag, the great past, and the great promise of what the vast majority north of the Mason-Dixon line thought of as their country and thought of as a nation. They agreed with Captain Philip Sheridan, U.S.A., 'This government is too great and good to be destroyed.'

There is no need to believe in the legend of an 'aggressive slavocracy' to see in slavery the cause of the War. Whether the North was painting the South into a corner or the South was doing it to her own doom does not really matter. The crisis was there. The South was demanding of the North what it was less and less willing to give—theoretical and, as far as possible, practical equality for the 'peculiar institution'. To get that the South was willing to break up the last unifying force, the Democratic party. If you want the date when the war became inevitable, it was when the Charleston Convention broke up over the nomination of Stephen Douglas. The South wanted more than any possible Northern candidate could now give. As Senator Pugh said:

'Gentlemen of the South, you mistake us—we will not do it.'

That, not the firing on Sumter, was the signal for war.

THE LAST CHANCE FOR THE SOUTH

What drove the South to this extremity? Was it the nature of the slave system that it had to expand or die? That is very doubtful. Was slavery economically doomed unless fresh soil could be secured for it to exploit and exhaust? This too is very doubtful. No doubt many in the South wanted to expand, wanted to revive the slave trade (openly not covertly). But the real cause of the increasing desperation of the South was the pressure of the modern world on an archaic economic and social system. Slavery was both more profitable and more threatened than it had been in the days when Washington and Jefferson thought it an evil doomed—and rightly doomed—to disappear.

But more was involved than that. The South felt the hostility of the world and resented it. It wanted to be approved as well as tolerated (and it wondered how long its social system would be tolerated). There was natural resentment of the moral smugness of New England (and of Old England). Their virtue, it was rightly felt, was due more to geography than to sanctity. The North, if it increasingly tolerated Abolitionist attacks on slavery, showed no signs of offering to share the burden and risks of emancipation. (It would have made no practical difference if the North had offered, but the moral case would have been clearer.) The risks seemed real, especially after the Nat Turner rebellion in Virginia. True, the Abolitionists did not preach servile war. They wanted to convert the masters, not rouse the slaves; but to cast doubt on the rightness of slavery was to threaten the whole Southern system. For the echoes of the controversy were heard in the slave quarters.

Then there was John Brown. It was not so much the attempt of this crazy and murderous fanatic to raise servile war as the way his execution was received in the North that rightly alarmed the South. 'Gallows glorious' indeed! The complacent comments of sedentary literary gentlemen in Concord were ground enough, if not for secession, at any rate for a strong dose of counter-righteousness. If the new Republican party dug itself in, if the Federal administration was to pass into hostile hands, how could the system survive? The new President thought slavery wrong; he would tolerate it as his oath bound him to, but that was all. And the North, in each decade, was getting stronger and more hostile. It was now or never. And indeed if the South had to fight for its life, 1860 was perhaps the last time she could do it with any chance of success. So 'the war came'.

CONFEDERATE ILLUSIONS

In the Southern decision there was a strong and deadly element of self-deception. Less and less had the South permitted reflection on or objective assessment of its position. It had constructed an iron lung outside which it could not breathe. Inside it lived on illusions. It underestimated the political handicap of slavery. So it sent as diplomatic agent to England, to be the Franklin of the new revolution, James M. Mason—known, if he was known at all, as the chief defender of the Fugitive Slave Act. And everybody Mason met in England, including his friends and the friends of the South, had read *Uncle Tom's Cabin* and was on the side of Eliza, not of her hunters. Not until the Confederacy was doomed and slavery visibly perishing, did the leaders of the South think of throwing slavery overboard and even then the egregious Mason in his last and necessarily fruitless interview with Palmerston could not bring himself to utter the fatal words!

There were other illusions. (The North had them too but could afford them.) There was the illusion of 'King Cotton', the revival of the old Jeffersonian agrarian illusion that you could coerce Europe by cutting off supplies. The Federal blockade and the Confederate embargo caused immense distress in Britain and France, but they did not drive Palmerston into intervention and Napoleon III would not move alone. What the South did do was lose the advantage of her greatest asset and cut off her nose to spite herself.

Less commonly remembered is another Southern illusion and a most revealing one. If the North was amazed that the South should fight so hard for State Rights (or slavery), the South was astonished that the notoriously mean-spirited Yankees would fight for anything. The South saw itself as 'The Chivalry'. It was Ivanhoe—and the North was at best Isaac of York, at worst Shylock. Since the North could only be fighting to make money, the War was a plundering expedition. Since obviously it couldn't pay as that, you had only to show this arithmetical fact to the Yankees and they would give up. Alternatively you could promise them a favourable commercial treaty and they could have no object in fighting. This theme is repeated again and again and you can find echoes of it in the last proclamation Jefferson Davis issued to his people. Davis had been answered, four years before, by a retired army officer, U. S. Grant, who wrote to his Southern father-in-law, 'It is all a mistake about the Northern pocket being so sensitive.' It was the old illusion about the 'nation of shopkeepers'; it was dearly paid for.

After the war was over, the pugnacious journalist and contemporary historian of the Confederacy, Edward A. Pollard, in computing the assets left to the South, more than once emphasized her old superiority in the art of politics. Yet all of Pollard's journalism and historical writing was imbued by a contempt for Jefferson Davis which was only exceeded by his contempt for the Confederate Congress. It was as much as anything the political incompetence of the South that ruined her cause. If Fort Sumter was a trap, Jefferson Davis fell into it. If 'cotton was King', the royal weapon was most incompetently used. If British intervention was necessary for Southern success, how badly the South played its cards! Benjamin was as clever a man as Seward but he was a very inferior Secretary of State. Chase was an Alexander Hamilton compared with Memminger. Welles and Stanton, St. Vincent and Carnot compared with the Confederate Secretaries of the Navy and of War (though something can be said for Mallory). What were those Confederate Governors who were not actually Federal assets like Joe Brown and Zeb Vance compared with Andrew and Curtin and the ruthless and unscrupulous and highly useful Oliver Morton? Who cared then, and who cares now, about the eloquence of Senator Wigfall or knows what the Confederate Congress did or left undone? And the comparison between Lincoln and Davis is almost comically unequal. Yet Davis, for all his faults, was probably the best President the Confederacy could have got. How long would it have lasted under a self-satisfied pedant like Alexander Stephens?

THE SOUTH'S STRENGTH

The Confederacy laboured under the fatal disadvantage of its origins. 'In my end is my beginning'—the motto of Mary, Queen of Scots—serves the Confederacy well. Faced with the fact that the War could not be won on the theory of State Rights that justified secession, people like Stephens acted as if they preferred to lose the War rather than their theory (as Jefferson Davis was provoked to remark long after Appomattox). Governors tried to run private wars for Georgia and North Carolina, and the correspondence of Governor Vance with the Confederate authorities is a lesson in political folly. The weak and shrinking authority of the Confederate government was continually threatened by the activities of politicians and lawyers who rightly saw that Jefferson Davis was, in many ways, like the tyrant Lincoln, but refused to see that this tyranny was necessary for the salvation of the South. Congress refused to set up a Supreme Court (as the Confederate Constitution demanded) partly because it might be too 'national' and the immense difficulties of mobilizing men and resources in a backward economy were made almost insuperable by constitutional jurists.

Yet within these limits, the South did raise armies, make a fleet, and, more remarkable, create a war industry and keep it going until the last doomed months. True, this was done wastefully. The fiscal policy of the South *was* bad, both federally and in the states. (Only South Carolina had a good record.) It could have been better but possibly not much better, once the cotton crop was not shipped out. The South was immensely handicapped by its rural character, which in 1861 was innocently seen as an advantage. It was handicapped by its 'colonial' economic position, by its poor transportation system, by its miserably inadequate industrial equipment.

Yet if its handicaps are allowed for, it worked wonders. The South showed, all things considered, more Yankee ingenuity than the North. That it was able to keep armies and a fleet in being should be remembered. And it was in a dilemma. Nothing did Southern morale more harm than the so-called 'twenty nigger' law, which exempted overseers of twenty slaves or more from the Army. Yet it was perhaps the best way of organizing the turnover from cotton production to food production that was absolutely essential. But it fed the feeling that this was 'a rich man's war and a poor man's fight' that finally broke down Southern morale and justified the desertions that destroyed Lee's last hopes.

Were those hopes ever justified? It was the opinion of many sensible people like General Joe Johnston that the South had a good chance of winning that was thrown away. There were two ways in which the War might have been won; by military triumphs so complete that Britain and France would have felt it safe—and so right—to recognize the Confederacy even at the risk of war with the United States. That chance went at Antietam not at Gettysburg. By July 1863, with Vicksburg doomed, no possible victory in the East would have altered the policy of the British government—which was to wait and be quite sure that Jefferson Davis had, as Gladstone had rashly put it a year before, 'made a nation'.[1]

A victory at Antietam might have brought British recognition and might have led to the victory of the Democrats in the Congressional

---

[1] It has not, as far as I know, been noted that this was the one thing that, on Confederate theory, Jefferson Davis could *not* do. The Confederate States were no more a nation than, in their theory, the United States had been. Yet all Southerners kept on talking of 'the country', 'my country'. What did they

elections of 1862. (They were after all won by Lincoln only after a great deal of very sharp practice.) But even after Vicksburg and Gettysburg, the South, cut in two, steadily shrinking in the West, could have won by playing on the war weariness of the North. They almost brought it off (we have Lincoln's testimony for that). But the removal of Joe Johnston and Davis's still more fatal decision to replace him by Hood doomed the South.

Many Southerners must have read Macaulay on Frederick the Great and noted the parallel. Frederick was saved by the death of his enemy, the Tsarina Elizabeth. The equivalent opportunity for the South was the Presidential election of 1864. Had the South still held Atlanta in November 1864, the Northern will to war might have snapped, the summary of the Democratic platform, 'The War is a failure', might have been accepted. The demonstration by Sherman that the Confederate government could no longer protect the heart of the Confederacy began the process of demoralization which made Appomattox merely the QED of the proposition.

Then all the grievances—inflation, semi-starvation in the towns, the inequalities of conscription, the ill-gotten gains of the Snopes family rapidly climbing in the dying planter society—these had added to them the loss of faith in the future of the Confederacy. There were more deserters than men under arms and the eloquence of Davis nerved only the civilians of Richmond. It was touch and go but Lincoln, who supported the long ordeal of Grant's bloody failures, saved the Union as the neurotic Davis lost the Confederacy its last and only chance.

GRANT AND LEE

Grant's failures? I know how much I am running against the tide of current historical opinion when I use such terms. Yet what other name can we give to the campaign of 1864? Where Grant was, was at worst humiliating defeat, at best a bloody stalemate. It was Sherman and Sheridan who kept alive the Northern faith in victory. That Grant was the best Union Commander who had directed the Army of the Potomac is true. That he was a good organizer is true;

mean? It is possible that a Virginian or a South Carolinian exhausted all the meaning of the word when he contemplated his own state. But a citizen of Arkansas or Florida? There was a nation struggling to birth, the 'South'. It did not survive and it could not have passed adolescence if it had lived up to the baptismal promises made for it in 1861.

that he had resolution and clarity of mind is true; that he had an admirable literary style is true and important. He was no Haig or Nivelle or Cadorna. But he was not the equal of Robert E. Lee. Mathematicians, I am told, distinguish between solutions that are adequate and solutions that are elegant. Except possibly at Chattanooga, Grant's solutions were never elegant. Lee's often were.

They may even have been too elegant at times. He demanded and did not get from his raw troops in the early summer of 1862 a perfection of march and battle discipline that Napoleon got from the Grande Armée in 1805 and 1806, Marlborough from his troops in 1704, Frederick from his at Rossbach and Leuthen. But there is the boldness (so unusual in an engineer) before Second Manassas, at Chancellorsville, in the Wilderness, worthy of the greatest captains. And where he failed (as he did fail at Gettysburg) he failed in a curious parallel with Napoleon. Just as Stuart was absent when most needed, so D'Erlon fought neither at Quatre Bras nor Ligny. Just as Lee left too much to the too cautious Longstreet, Napoleon left too much to the foolish aggressive Ney.

Of course, Grant deserves credit for the overall strategy of the Union Armies in 1864-5, for backing Sherman and choosing Sheridan. Had he taken Sherman's advice and remained in the West, his reputation might have gained. It was Grant's opinion that the best of the Union generals (himself presumably excepted) was Sheridan. He was, at any rate, the most modern in his attitude to war. The contrast between Stuart and Sheridan illustrates much in the history of the War. Jeb Stuart was the flower of chivalry. He was consciously the heir of Murat. But he was dead a week after Sheridan took the field as commander of the cavalry corps of the Army of the Potomac. Sheridan was no Murat; he was the ancestor of Patton and Rommel. The brilliant cavalry officer, Charles Lowell, who served under him in the Valley, paid him the highest compliment he could think of: 'He works like a mill owner or an ironmaster, not like a soldier.' Sheridan, who had been a bookkeeper, inspected his army like a businessman taking over a bankrupt firm, and his ruthlessness, while less flamboyant than Sherman's, was more deliberate.

In our modern savage age with memories of Belsen and Hiroshima, Lidice and Oradour-sur-Glane, it is hard to take seriously the repeated Southern comparisons of Sherman and Sheridan to Attila or the march through Georgia to the worst horrors of the Thirty Years' War. But there was plundering and outrage (though few murders and few rapes). 'You can't expect all the cardinal virtues for thirteen dollars a month,' as the soldier said to Sherman. And by his trail of destruction, Sherman not only made the South 'howl', he broke its will to resist. As he said, 'War is hell'; wherever he went, he made it so. If in the degree of destruction caused, the War was only in a minor degree 'hell' by modern standards, it was nevertheless the prefiguration of modern war. 'Unconditional surrender' is another inheritance (if a misunderstood one) of the War.

But it is from the technical point of view that the War is the first modern war. It was modern in the use of railways, of the telegraph, of field works. (Some of the photographs of Confederate trenches round Atlanta or Petersburg could, with a little touching up, be passed off for photographs of the First World War.) Both sides showed astonishing technical enterprise and ingenuity and gave the world the first examples of that American genius for beating plough-shares into weapons that has twice altered the history of this century. (And that would not have done it if the Union had been defeated and dissolved.) The South, as has been suggested, was even more ingenious than the North; it had land mines and sea mines (Farra-gut's 'torpedoes'); it had submarines; and we forget too easily that the *Merrimac* was only the most famous of the ironclads that the South created out of its meagre resources. The North, with far greater resources, was almost equally fertile in invention, and infant American industry was immensely expanded by the War and met all the demands on it. Or almost all. For the ideas were often in advance of the technical resources to execute them, as the vicissitudes of Federal naval architecture showed.

BLUNDERS OF THE NORTH

And there were curious failures to utilize the technical superiority of the North. The Federal cavalry was equipped towards the end of the War with repeating carbines which worked havoc among the Confederates. But there was no general attempt to equip the Union Army with breechloaders. Maybe there was no weapon then avail-able as effective as the Remingtons with which the Turks were to mow down the Russians at Plevna in 1877, but even an inferior breechloader, a *chassepot* or a 'needle gun', would have given the North an immense advantage.

It is less surprising that the Union did not produce a breech-loading field gun. The problem was really one of metallurgy and there was no Krupp steel in America. (Many of the failures of the new Federal warships were due to poor metallurgy.) But it is odder that so much smooth-bore artillery was continued in use since the French had already demonstrated, in the Italian War of 1859, the great superiority of rifled artillery. There was a lack of enterprise here. It is true that Sheridan, in 1870, professed not to think much of the Krupp guns, but Sheridan was not a gunner.

In another way, too, the War was modern. Many of the complaints made against McClellan, Meade, Grant, and even against Lee, for not fully exploiting their victories reflected the belief that all battles should be and could be like Jena and Waterloo, what the Germans called 'battles without a morrow'. But modern war has not been rich in Waterloos or Jenas. It took the unlimited imbecility of Bazaine and MacMahon to give Moltke his deceptively easy triumphs in 1870. (The two French generals were as incompetent as Pope or Hood, nay, as that unending ass, Ambrose E. Burnside.) The Russo-Japanese War and World War I were to be wars like the Civil War in which the complete, quick, and final victory was rare. Old General Scott complained that only Sheridan had what he called 'finish', but Sheridan was lucky.

The War was modern in another way. It marked the end of cavalry in the old sense. There were few or no cavalry charges, foolish and heroic like the Charge of the Light Brigade or the charge of the French Cuirassiers at Reichshofen—or even desperate but not foolish like Von Bredow's 'death ride' at Mars-la-Tour. Jeb Stuart was the last knight, but perhaps the great Southern cavalry chief was the less romantic Forrest. As for Sheridan, he used horses to get his men to the battle, not as missiles in themselves. Few swords and not many bayonets were effectively used in the War and no European army in 1914 had assimilated these lessons of the 'armed mobs', as Moltke called them, who learned so much more of real war between 1861 and 1865 than the Prussians did in their too easy campaigns in 1870. Europe had to learn the hard way in 1914 many lessons learned in Virginia and Tennessee two generations before.

And the War showed the overwhelming importance of industrial power. It was not merely a matter of weapons but of locomotives and wagons, of clothing and tinned food, of hospital trains—and of that ancestor of the world-girdling 'PX', the Sanitary Commission. It may be that the War did actually increase Northern wealth; certainly the North increased its capital equipment all during the War.

It may have been only a catalyst but the War precipitated the entry of the United States into the modern industrial world, made 'the takeoff' (to use Professor W. W. Rostow's brilliant metaphor) come sooner. And by providing such emotional talking points as the crimes of Andersonville, the War made the political job of inducing the American farmer to pay, through the tariff, for the forced-draft development of American industry much easier than it might otherwise have been. The ex-Confederates who began to come back to Washington by 1870 were in a new world, one from which the South was still excluded, except as a colonial tributary.

Before the War, during the War, and after, the North was baffled by the readiness of the non-slaveholding population of the South— that is the great majority of the free Southern population—to fight for 'Southern independence' which, in fact, meant fighting for a slavery system that, many outsiders thought with plausibility, was the curse of most whites as well as blacks.

That there was something in the Northern attitude is suggested by the rage provoked by Helper's *Impending Crisis of the South* in 1857, the only book that got under Southern skins as successfully as *Uncle Tom's Cabin* had done. No abolitionist tract, no bale of *Liberators* was as dangerous as Helper, for the slaves were unlikely to see or read the tracts; but the poor whites might read *The Impending Crisis*. Its message was simple. Helper was no 'nigger lover'. He was basically against slavery because of the harm it did to his own people, the non-slaveholding whites.

Helper and his admirers (who were numerous in the North where his book was a best seller) could point to the indisputable fact that most Southerners had no direct profit from slavery. In 1860, there were '385,000 owners of slaves distributed among 1,516,000 free families. Nearly three-fourths of all free Southerners had no connection with slavery through either family ties or direct ownership'.[1] And if we take as the rulers and leaders of slave society the owners of more than one hundred slaves (and the owners of less than one hundred slaves were hardly the 'planters' of Southern tradition or the whiskey advertisements) there were only three thousand of them.

This, the really privileged class, was less numerous, relatively and absolutely, than the privileged orders in France in 1789. Why was there no rising against a system based on such an inverted pyramid of power and wealth? Why was the contrast between the economic

[1] Kenneth M. Stampp, *The Peculiar Institution*, New York, Knopf, 1956.

and political status of the free farmers in the North and his brethren
in the South not politically more effective? Why without accepting
Helper's exact bill to be sent to the 'introducers, aiders, and abettors
of slavery' (it was exactly $7,544,148,825) did not the majority of the
free population of the South let the slavocracy fight for the system?

THE MYSTERY OF THE SOUTHERN MIND

For one thing, the kind of political arithmetic that Helper and
more serious economists practised exaggerated the rational, calcu-
lating elements in the political reactions of *any* people at *any* time.
Wars are not made on either side by totally rational peoples. As the
Germans used to say, a reasonable army would run away. But the
Northern illusion was made illusory by more than the power of
human folly. It was easier to say that the non-slaveholding whites
were the true victims of the slavery system than to get the whites
themselves to understand that. If emancipation of the slaves was the
only way to the true freedom of whites, the whites—especially the
poor whites—did not know it.

For one thing, the only rag of dignity that a poor white had was
his status as a white man. As long as he was above all niggers, even
prosperous free niggers, the poor white had a way of laying the
flattering unction of superiority to his soul. The numerous class of
free farmers who were not in the derogatory sense 'poor whites'
(though they were not rich) had even more reason to welcome the
boost to their ego that the slave system gave every white from Wade
Hampton down to the most miserable 'cracker'. It is possible too
that the whites who did think slavery an obstacle to the rise of themselves and their families (like the presumably smaller group who
thought it intrinsically wrong) did emigrate from the slave states.
For if it is difficult to think of Tom Lincoln moving from Kentucky
into Indiana under the pressure of conscience or ambition, his son
Abraham might have done so had he come to his majority in a slave
state. Perhaps there was a steady sifting of the white population;
perhaps the majority of sceptics and trouble-makers simply got out.
(The history of the border counties of Illinois, Indiana, and Ohio
suggests that a good many migrated North with a fine stock of
Southern principles and prejudices.)

There is no doubt still a mystery for us in this attitude. The rank-
and-file of the Confederate Armies did not write books, did not keep
diaries, did not write newspapers, were seldom represented by their

own kind in the high command, political or military. So we have to guess why they disappointed their well-wishers in the North. No doubt, if the Southern politician had advocated on the hustings the aristocratic doctrines that justified slavery on grounds that would apply to the poor white as well as to the Negro, there might have been a glimmering of doubt in even the thickest skulls. But the politicians, as apart from the ideologues, were too wise for that. They flattered the Southern masses and not so much imposed on them as 'sold' them the romantic idea of Southern superiority—not only over all Negroes but over all Yankees. 'Farmer and cracker admired and shared more than vicariously in this ideal—shall we call it?—created by the impact of the aristocratic idea on the romantic pattern.'[1]

And when all is said and done, how was the non-slaveholding white—already jealous of the competition not only of free Negroes but of Negro craftsmen hired out by their masters—to know that the emancipated Negro would not be a more formidable competitor? How was he to see that the common interests of the poor ought to unite him with those whom he despised and feared? How was he to see a common class interest, when some labour unions still restrict their membership to 'Caucasians' a century later?

The War, of course, educated a good many. First of all, the natural leaders led and lost. The hostility to Jefferson Davis that was glee-fully reported to the North after the end of the War may have been widespread and deep. The exemptions given to slaveholders, to job-holders, to the people who got into 'the bomb-proofs' as safe jobs were called, bred natural resentment. The suffering inflicted on the families of soldiers by inflation and by the breakdown of Confederate organization shook the faith of others. Yet the South (and the North), if they had only known it, shamed their Revolutionary ancestors and showed more tenacity and courage in the face of Grant and Sherman (or Lee and Johnston) than had been shown in face of Cornwallis.

And this devotion was of long-term political importance. For it meant that the North could not separate the classes of the South so as to win a political as well as a military victory. There was not even possible a Southern version of the Weimar Republic. Even had

[1] W. J. Cash, *The Mind of the South*, New York, Knopf, 1941. I am aware that Cash was not a scientific historian or sociologist but he was what is in this context better, a poet who saw through the poetry of the Southern vision but felt its power.

there been no Reconstruction, the memories of the South would have been 'disloyal'.

If the North was disillusioned by the Southern loyalty of the poor whites, the South was disillusioned by the limited loyalty of the slaves. Lucius Quintus Cincinnatus Lamar told Henry Adams that he ceased to believe in slavery when he realized that it could not stand a war. It didn't. Everywhere that the Union Armies came, the system collapsed. The Christian slaves had no scruples about stealing themselves by the hundreds of thousands. The many authentic stories of fidelity to the Master refer, for the most part, to the house slaves. The field hands had no such feudal spirit. Even the house servants were not totally reliable. The intelligent Mrs. Chesnut keeps on speculating about what was really going on behind the smooth, smiling, servile faces. Sometimes the secret came out. Both Jefferson Davis and Governor Wise suffered the shock of the desertion of trusted servants and, by the last year of the War, the not very intelligent J. B. Jones, the 'Rebel War Clerk', began to suspect the loyalty of the slaves. And the revelation of the fragility of the slave system, of the true sentiments of its four million 'beneficiaries', was an added drop of gall in the full cup of the defeated South.

The ambiguity of the Southern attitude was reflected in calculations of war losses. The 'loss' of the slaves was estimated at from two billion to five billion dollars. But of course this was a loss only for the owners, not for the South; the vast majority of the former slaves were in the South still and were the basis of the Southern economy. They and the soil remained.

What had the South lost? Here we must distinguish carefully and kindly between fact and legend. Just as France is full of families who lost 'their all' in the Revolution (including families that in fact did well out of it), the South has its share of mythical heirs of great plantations wrecked by Sherman's raiders. Whether Sherman did or did not set fire to Columbia or Atlanta, they did burn. (Charleston suffered as much from the accidental fire as by Federal gunfire, and central Richmond was fired by Ewell's retreating garrison, again perhaps by accident.) More serious was the destruction of the South's already inadequate transport system. And the meagre industrial equipment, mostly turned over to the war effort, was mainly wrecked by one side or the other.

Yet at first hearing or at second, it is irritating to find present Southern weaknesses explained in terms of the crimes of Sherman or Sheridan. Was Columbia in 1865 any worse off than Berlin in 1945 or for that matter than London? Is not the cultivation of such memories an obstacle to clear thinking about what the South needs? It is nearly a century since these crimes were committed. Isn't it time they were forgotten?

THE DEFEATED

Third thoughts suggest a difference. If Berlin and London and Rotterdam have largely recovered and perhaps have largely forgotten their dreadful recent history, this is in part due to the generosity of the victorious United States. The United States was not so generous in 1865. What the South needed was Marshall Plan aid. Just as the North refused, before the War, to accept its share in the sin or burden of slavery, it refused (apart from the issue of rations and a little aid given to the Freedman's Bureau) to make any sacrifices to get the stricken South on to its feet. No doubt, it would have been asking a great deal to ask the North to pay more taxes to 'help the Rebels'. 'Reconstruction', however it was organized politically, was bound to be a bitter ordeal for the South since the bills were coming in and the South had to pay them out of her meagre and diminished resources. She needed capital, but what businessman with the immense possibilities of the North and West open to him was going to risk his dollars in the former Confederacy?

It is not a creditable story; yet it is hard to see what, given the conditions of the age, could have been done better. There was first of all the disaster of the assassination of Lincoln. Even he could not have wrought miracles, but his prestige, his resolution, his preternatural political sagacity were such that some of the worst mistakes or neglects might have been avoided. (As Mrs. Brodie has pointed out in her recent admirable life of Thaddeus Stevens, the common belief that President Johnson simply applied Lincoln's policies ignores important differences between Lincoln and his successor.) But even if that honest, stubborn, violent, limited man, Andrew Johnson, had been a wiser man and a better politician, the problem might have been insoluble for that generation.

For Southern illusions did not die at Appomattox. It is an illusion of the conquered that they can determine the use made by the victors of their power. It was useless to demand of the North in 1865 the Constitution or the temper of 1861. Yet the South tried to minimize the Northern victory, notably by making the emancipation of the slaves as nearly meaningless as possible. The 'black codes' are enough to explain if not to justify the worst errors of Radical reconstruction. As Mr. Ralph McGill has recently reminded us (and as we should have expected *a priori*), it was Mississippi that led the South down this path of folly. To expect the North to accept this nullification of victory was a vain thing.

We must not exaggerate the extent of the disaster. Is there much reason to believe that South Carolina was more corruptly governed than New York or Philadelphia? It could afford the graft less, that is all. There was nowhere in the United States the kind of governmental organization, the kind of civil service, the kind of sociological knowledge (if I may risk using that dirty word) that was needed. But as Reconstruction made the 'Solid South' even more solid, so Southern intransigence made 'waving the bloody shirt' profitable and this poisoned the political life of the United States for more than a generation. And as far as the memory of Reconstruction was successfully used (long after Reconstruction was over) to justify such parodies of democracy and world scandals as the present political state of Mississippi, it was one of the most disastrous results of the War.

Perhaps we exaggerate the impact of the War. Perhaps the 'Gilded Age' would have been as base, perhaps a President as incompetent as Grant would have reached the White House anyway. Perhaps in no other way could the American experiment have been purged of the poisonous infection of slavery in the country 'dedicated to the proposition that all men are created equal'. For we must not forget that slavery *was* abolished, the Union *was* saved, 'the last best hope of earth' not debased and destroyed. The price was high and is still being paid. Like the chief captain, the American people can say that 'with a great sum obtained I this freedom'. That is why the War lies so close to the American heart.

To think that on the whole and on nearly all the great issues the North was right is possibly an unfashionable doctrine; it is at any rate an unromantic doctrine. But it is mine. I agree with Augustine Birrell that for once 'the great twin brethren, Might and Right' fought on the same side.

MY OWN SIDE

As a boy, like all boys I hope, I was for the South as I was a Jacobite. Boys are all for Hector against Achilles (and still more against Agamemnon), for Hannibal against Scipio (and still more against Fabius Cunctator). That is right and proper. But 'when I was a child, I spake as a child, I understood as a child, I thought as a child; but when I became a man, I put away childish things'. The issue of the War was fortunate in the sense that it was the least unfortunate issue that was possible. Of this civil war one is inclined to say with Andrew Marvell, 'The cause *was* too good to have been fought for.' But it was fought for and the right side won.

But there is another side to the War and one that it would be wrong to ignore or minimize—the side of glory. There was glory enough for each side. The North has its legends (true legends) as well as the South. There is the desperate and fruitless courage of Fredericksburg; there is the rush up Missionary Ridge; there are the heroic stories of units like the 20th Maine at Gettysburg; there is Sheridan riding on to the field at Cedar Creek and turning the tide of battle like Desaix at Marengo. There is, most impressive of all, the disciplined and despairing advance at Cold Harbor. Here is glory. But whether the South has more glory than the North or not (I think it has), it needs it more and, as is right, cherishes it more. It cherishes the fame of the most Plutarchian (and greatest) American soldier, 'Marse Robert'. It cherishes the memory of Jackson 'standing like a stone wall' at Bull Run and striking Hooker's flank at Chancellorsville. It cherishes or should cherish, with Pickett's attack, the memory of Hood's men advancing to their doom at Franklin. And for the individual heroic actions, their name is legion. It should remember with pride, not that there were so few under arms to surrender with Lee or Johnston, but that there were still so many.

It was the bad luck of the South that the only great poet who commemorated the 'strange sad war' was Walt Whitman of Manhattan. But Timrod's lines on the Confederate dead in Magnolia Cemetery at Charleston may serve as a final text:

> In seeds of laurel in the earth
> The blossom of your fame is blown,
> And somewhere, waiting for its birth,
> The shaft is in the stone.

The laurels have grown; the shafts are all around us. They cannot be too numerous or too high.   1960

4

THE REMOTE REVOLUTION—
A BRITISH VIEW

I HAVE CHOSEN this title in no spirit of paradox. I have chosen it to
emphasize aspects of the American Civil War that I believe to be
true, and, outside the United States at least, to be neglected. That
the Civil War was in its results revolutionary in the South, no one,
I think, doubts. If it was only for a brief period that the 'bottom rail
was on top' (it could also be argued that it was never true, not even
for a few years), nevertheless, the social system of the South was
transformed, positively and negatively; the South underwent changes
that no one would deny were revolutionary if they had happened in
Europe. And the South was left with that apparently inevitable
legacy of revolutions, problems made more difficult along with
problems solved, memories that embitter social life and institutions
along with memories that ennoble and dignify it.

That the Civil War was revolutionary in the North is less evident.
For the Civil War ended in what was formally the victory of the
legal government over a rebellion, over an armed revolutionary
attempt that failed. Nominally, the United States in 1865 was the
body politic that existed, in a mutilated form, between 1861 and the
end of the war. Order and law had been restored. Rebellion had
been crushed. But few people in the reunited states thought it easy,
as simple a matter as that. The old-line Democrats and Whigs in the
North, men like Robert Winthrop of Massachusetts, might wish for
and work for 'the union as it was', but they can have had no hope
of recreating the Union of 1861; at most they hoped for a limitation
of the revolutionary effects of the war. And if in the South men
quoted the promises of the now victorious Republicans, reproached

them with exceeding due constitutional bounds in their exploitation of the restoration of the Union, these were debating points, made to justify resistance to the will of the victors not to deny, plausibly, that the war had done more than restore the Union. True, the South was even more legally minded than the American Union as a whole; the people of the South, as a conscious minority which had attempted a revolutionary course, needed legal support for their position more than the victorious North did. And one can find plenty of evidence of illusion among the leaders of the South, including Unionist leaders like Benjamin Franklin Perry of South Carolina, illusion that the defeated side could tie the hands of the victors by quoting the past words of the victors to them, by insisting that the victors should, with all freedom of action open to them, yet feel themselves bound by the formal premises of their action begun four years and a half million lives ago. Buried in this legalistic argument, in this appeal from Philip drunk with victory to Philip sober with apprehension and bewilderment in face of an unprecedented situation, there was an equivalent of the German protest against the 'Diktat' of Versailles. But it was a less plausible protest than the German protest of 1919 (whose own plausibility has been exaggerated) and it was not listened to.

Nor do I believe that, in their hearts, the people of the South, white and black, doubted that what had happened to them, either the greatest catastrophe in their history or the 'time of jubilee', was revolutionary in its implications. The South of the year of Lincoln's election was not far away in time in the year of his death. The habits of mind of the majority of the population, black and white, had been formed before 1861. But the four years that had passed had been four years of revolutionary destruction. It was not only the ruins of Columbia or Charleston, not only the great scar cut across country by Sherman that made the difference unforgettable and irrepressible.

The collapse of the 'peculiar institution', the failure of the hopes, of the claims, of the ruling class, hopes of preservation of the old order, claims of competence in peace and war, made too great a social earthquake ever to leave anything quite the same. Many southerners, like Lamar, must have reflected that slavery had shown its fatal weakness; it could not stand a war. And the disappearance, in less than a month from Appomattox, of every form of 'Confederate' authority, the absence of all irregular resistance, the passivity of the recently belligerent section in face of the victor, was a revolutionary achievement in itself. The complete effectiveness of federal authority was, less dramatically, present in the minds of the people of the North as well. Putting on one side (but not forgetting) the deep wounds the North itself had suffered in the war (the near three hundred and fifty thousand dead were wound enough), the expansion of federal powers, the millions under arms, the intrusion of federal authority into every part of the economy, the strong hand of the federal government, interfering, often with unconstitutional boldness, in the internal life of the loyal states; all these things underlined the fact that the victory of the North, of the Union, was no mere restoration of the *status quo*, no mere triumph of constitutional legality. 'There are no restorations'; what had been said of European 'restorations' was true of the American restoration. The office that Abraham Lincoln entered into for the second time in 1865 was profoundly and permanently transformed from the office he had entered into in 1861. And the great difference in tone between the First and Second Inaugurals is proof that Lincoln knew this. In 1861 he could still profess to be, perhaps really be, optimistic, believe that North and South were 'not enemies but friends', believe that the two sides threatening war would be touched by 'the better angels of our nature'. In 1865 Lincoln knew better. He knew that his God, a God of a mysterious political Calvinism, had punished, had let sin reap its due reward, and that the Union had now to be remade in conditions in which the optimism of 1861 was empty, in which the healing of the nation's wounds would require almost superhuman magnanimity. There is no need here to stress the catastrophic character of Lincoln's death. The wounds might have been healed earlier had he lived, but the healing would have been a long and difficult job. And all over the Union, even had Lincoln survived, it would have been 'never bright morning again'.

It is possible, just possible, that Lincoln could have given to Reconstruction a moral tone, a practical content that would have given to the forcibly reunited states a true reconstruction to aim at, a carrying forward in peace of the common purpose of the war on the Northern side, and, on the Southern side, a moral equivalent for the fruitless heroism of the struggle for independence which was a struggle to enable the South to contract out of the contemporary world so visibly closing in on it. So it was not to be. The expiation of slavery did not end when the last Confederate soldier or sailor surrendered. The fruits, good and bad, of the revolution had to be swallowed if not digested.

That the Civil War was more than a mere war or even a mere civil war, just as the War of Independence was only part of the American Revolution, is made evident by the character of American interest in it. For it should be noted that the celebration of a Civil War is not always thought to be a politically useful thing. In some countries like France and Germany, good citizens often wish that they had less history, less strife and shame to remember. And in countries where a civil war is commemorated, it is usually a party commemoration, an equivalent to the 'waving the bloody shirt' of the seventies and eighties of the last century in America. That all the American people can safely be called together to remember the Civil War, in a general confidence that what will come out of the four years of celebrations that lie before you will be 'a more perfect union' tells us much about the success of the Civil War as a revolution. There are few unreconstructed rebels today, despite rebel yells in the South. Long after Jefferson Davis did so, the representatives of the defeated side (or cause) can say of the Union: 'Esto perpetua'. That is one thing about the nature of the war. It succeeded, as few wars have done, in the long run for the losers as well as the victors. But the point I wish to insist on here, the need to celebrate as well as the kind of celebration, shows how deeply the war entered into the bloodstream of the American people. It is their great ordeal and triumph. And it is not that to the most sympathetic observer, even to a Canadian or an Englishman or a Scot. It is in that sense that the Civil War is a remote revolution. It is the remoteness that accounts, I think, for the visible imperfections of European comment, at the time of the war, and since. It is this remoteness that accounts for the fact that there is not, military history apart, a single serious, scholarly, original European study of the Civil War as a political and social movement. There is a good deal of military history, some of it good but a great deal of it 'remote', too. There are a number of contemporary tracts and essays of which the most remarkable is Cairnes's *The Slave Power*. There are a number of interesting 'reportages' dealing with both the war and its social and political repercussions. W. H. Russell and Anthony Trollope will serve as samples. There was, later, the work of Von Holst, great in bulk, but possibly Von Holst ought to be treated as an American historian. In any case, I think some of the remoteness from the national way of feeling is observable in his volumes. And it seems to me that this remoteness survives down to the present day. It is still a matter of military history or of not very profound political history as exemplified in Lord Charnwood's *Lincoln*. The European, even the British, view of the war is remote. That may not be all loss, but it is a fact to be noted.

'British'? There may well be critics who will protest against the concentration on the British point of view. There were lively and acute commentators on the war in France and Germany. There are learned and acute European, but not British, commentators today, like my old friend Professor Geyl of Utrecht. But despite such names and such brilliant contributions, the strength and weakness of the British contribution to understanding of the war is of primary importance. We must note the near identity of language (one might have said simply identity of language a century ago), the easy and relevant comparability of institutions, the educational and ecclesiastical links, the steady immigration of people of British stock into the Union, the relative importance of the commercial connections. (England's overwhelming preponderance in the cotton trade had, as its converse, the overwhelming importance of the English market for the South, for the whole Union.) The growth in importance of the British market for American foodstuffs since the repeal of the Corn Laws was important. All these forces made the British attitude to the war of paramount importance.

And it is also important to note that the Americans, still, if you like, 'colonial' in their attitude to British culture, still deferential in their feelings towards the Mother Country (and of course all the more touchy because of that nearly automatic deference), wanted, North and South, British approval and support. Of course there were material reasons for that anxious expectation in Washington and Richmond, in Boston and Charleston. If the British government wholeheartedly threw its influence and directed its policy towards the maintenance of the Union, that was important for the North. If the British government effectively recognized the independence of the South, refused to recognize or actually broke the Northern blockade, was involved by its own policy—or Northern action—in war with the United States, Southern independence was assured. So did Southern hopes rise and fall with the news of the development of the *Trent* affair. So did the rulers of the South get more and more angry, more and more recriminatory as the British government did not insist on what the Confederate government insisted were

Britain's rights, did not break the blockade, but prudently, and with an eye to the future, accepted the international law that the Union was finding or inventing.

But, I think, though I cannot prove the validity of my thought, both North and South wanted the *approval* of Great Britain, of its people and government. That the France of Napoleon III betrayed the France of Lafayette was to be regretted but not to be taken too seriously. That the Tsar approved of the Union was to be noted as possibly of practical importance but not much more. Even the prestige that Alexander II had got as freer of the serfs did not make his diplomatic and moral support a substitute for the active partisanship that both North and South wanted from Palmerston and Russell. The indignation of James Russell Lowell in the second series of *Biglow Papers*, the growing resentment of Jefferson Davis at the refusal of the British government to show a proper sense of dignity and candour in defence of rights whose assertion would have been so advantageous to the South, were not based solely on calculations of how the war would be shortened and victory brought closer if Britain did her duty. They were expressions of a need for approval, understanding, an abandonment of the remote, above the battle, attitude that was noted and resented.[1]

And because of this emotional link, the Americans, North and South, were infuriated by the coolness of the attitude of their kinsmen (for most Americans still thought of the British as kinsmen). But the British could not give either the attention or the passion to the course of the war that both sides thought (rightly thought) was its due.

Seen from Philadelphia, seen, indeed, from London with the advantage of a century of hindsight, it is hard to understand that, from the European shore of the Atlantic, the American Civil War was not always the dominating news story, not the overwhelmingly important political theme that it seems to us it should have been. It was, of course, a great news story. The survival or the dissolution of the Union, obviously, was going to mean a good deal to the future

[1] A minor example of the sentimental or snobbish aspects of the American relationship is given by the intelligent Mrs. Chesnut. She noted that the famous *Times* correspondent, William Howard Russell, showed no interest in the polite Charleston conversation about Thackeray that showed how cultured and up to date the Southern gentry or their ladies were. His interest was in the developing crisis that he was ready and competent to report objectively—which was what neither side wanted from him.

of Europe and especially to the future of Britain. There were dangers and advantages in the triumph of either the North or the South. The possible extension of the warlike habits of Europe to North America was not obviously to the advantage of the nation of shopkeepers. No one could know what the issue of a Southern victory would be. Would there be more than two federations arising out of the ruins of the old? Would Canada, the West Indies, be safer or less safe? These were speculations that should and did cross the minds of statesmen and what we now call commentators.

But we must remember that these spectators had a great deal to think about as well as the fate of the United States. The decade between 1860 and 1870 was full of news, of new political problems, of new and of old dangers. Italy was being forcibly united as the first clouds lowered in the South. That was a good thing for Britain —but not if it meant the threat of a strengthening of the French position, still less if it meant a great European war. From the point of view of mere news, the first battles of the West had to compete with the recent Franco-British occupation of Peking. While the Civil War was going on, there was a series of emotion-charged developments in Europe and some of these threatened more immediate dangers than any to be easily anticipated in North America. The Polish Revolt of 1863, the Danish War of 1864, the Mexican expedition of Napoleon III (if it comes to that), all distracted attention from the battles in Virginia or in the Mississippi Valley, and traditionally the European crises were first-class crises. Out of any one of them might come a new great war, of a remaking of the map of Europe to the disadvantage of Britain or France. Indeed, such a remaking did take place—to the immediate disadvantage of France and the long-time disadvantage of England. It is easy for us to see, looking forward to the twentieth century, that the survival of the United States was a more important event in world history than the creation of Bismarck's Reich, that it was a beneficent result from the point of view of Britain and France, and that it was the most effective comment on and threat to the success of Bismarck's policy. But it is, I think, asking too much to expect that of the contemporary witnesses. The Old World was still the Old World, the New World still just the New. After all, what observer of the prospects of the British Empire at this time thought that it would be seriously affected by recent changes in the internal politics of Japan? Yet, the Meiji Restoration was one of the causes of the end of European empire in Asia. Hong Kong and Singapore were, in time, to fall as easily as the Taku Forts.

A slightly intermittent interest at the time, a slightly remote interest ever since, have been the marks of European and especially of British interest in the war. Even the acute interest in the speedy ending of the war that the cotton trade manifested, in Liverpool and Le Havre, Bolton and Mulhouse, was offset by the continuing economic progress of the North, by the closer intertwining of the British and American economies. It was no doubt a threat to that commercial intertwining that the North was going in so obviously for high tariffs and there were plenty of doctrinaire free-traders, merchants, and intellectuals, for whom tariff protection was a sin almost as evil as chattel slavery. That might be a ground for favouring the South which had tied itself to non-protective tariffs. It was more commonly, I suspect, a ground for crying a 'plague on both your houses'. But I have done enough, probably I have done too much, to explain why we Europeans cannot feel and cannot assess the American Civil War in American terms. If this is an offence, it is one to which we must plead guilty.

It is more profitable, I hope, to turn to the war itself, seen as a social and political phenomenon at the distance of three thousand miles. What was baffling then and what is to some degree baffling now, in the origin of the war, was not the preoccupation of each side with establishing its legal and constitutional right to behave as it was doing, but the evaporation of federal authority over almost all of the South. As federal authority collapsed in state after state after Lincoln's election, some of the truths about the character of American government and society were made plain. You can see the bewilderment at this revelation in the contemporary columns of *The Times* (of London). Europe was, Europe is, familiar with sudden overthrows of government, of the seizure of the levers of command in a few hours, in a few days. Paris had given repeated lessons of the vulnerability of governments; Berlin, Petrograd were to give more. Europe was full of conspirators hoping to provoke mutiny in the army, the assassination of hated rulers, the seizure of fortresses, offices, legislative assemblies. 'To the barricades' was a phrase that recalled failures as well as successes, of revolts that had petered out or had been crushed, in Paris, Milan, Palermo, Warsaw, as well as revolts that had, at any rate, ended a régime for good if they had not turned the social fabric inside out. Revolution meant above all 'the Revolution', the great days beginning in 1789:

> When Death was on thy drums Democracy,
> And with one rush of slaves, the world was free.

The new American revolution didn't look like that in the 'Secession Winter' nor does it look like it now. The slow and solemn withdrawal of state after state, the solemn leave-takings in the Senate, the merely peevish passivity of the Buchanan administration were all unintelligible. Even the country with the closest ties with the United States, the one that was least a police state, most tolerant of political dissent, did not react through its government in so diffident a matter. Toronto and Quebec had not been evacuated in 1837 nor Dublin Castle in 1848. And even today it requires, I think, an effort of the European imagination to realize how sparse, unarmed, dependent on mere popular good will was the federal authority all over the Union, not merely in the South. If this was a revolution, it was at first an unopposed revolution; so it was not a revolution.[1]

Then the obsession of both sides with legality was reflected in the political conduct of the war. There might be bitter complaints about the Bastilles of Lincoln and Seward; in the South itself there were plenty of protests against the tyranny of Jefferson Davis. But elections went on; the press in the midst of a great civil war was freer than it was in most European countries; the opposition was in full possession of its rights. One Vallandigham case did not make the United States a police state; the antics of Governors Vance and Brown in the Confederacy were not signs of the creation of a revolutionary dictatorship. The civilian power, on each side, remained unthreatened despite fears or alleged fears that military dictatorship was sure to result from so great an arming of the nation—or nations —for the English press early used that forbidden term 'nation' to describe the South as well as the North. The near identity of the Constitution of the United States and the new Constitution of the Confederate States baffled the outside observer. The differences in the two texts suggested the refinements of theological controversy rather than the revolutionary clash of two systems of government.

---

[1] The English Revolution of 1688–9 has some, but few, resemblances to this collapse of authority. But General Lord Churchill, going over to the Prince of Orange, was not a real equivalent of General Twiggs philosophically surrendering in Texas.

It was hard in the world of Napoleon III, of Bismarck, Spanish *pronunciamientos*, and brand new Austrian imperial constitutions to assess what was going on in America (except a war), to assess, for instance, the long-term revolutionary consequences of Lincoln's exaltation of the presidency.

Used as we are to the savageness of civil war in nineteenth-century Europe—and worse savagery in the twentieth—the comparative good temper with which the war was conducted from the beginning, the comparative absence, except on the western border, of that savagery and personal feuding under the guise of political duty that has marked civil war in most countries at most times, hid the revolutionary character of the war and hides it still.

Thus, I think, that the average non-American student of the war (like a great many Americans) sees it too simply as the 'War for Southern Independence' and plays down the degree to which it was a civil war, the degree to which families, counties, states, were divided, the degree to which there were crises of conscience, decisions of allegiance, taken in doubt and darkness. Yet this element of division was part of the revolutionary character of the war. Up to 1861 the American people had a common history, a common tradition of achievement, a common treasure-house of glory. The Tories had been expelled after the Revolution; the opponents of Mr. Madison's War in New England were discreet after 1815; the opponents of the Mexican War, from the complete pacifists to figures like Congressman Lincoln, had other things to think of with pride and shared satisfaction. Every society has its anarchist elements, its 'come-outers'. The United States had happily few until 'the War came'.

There is no need to illustrate this aspect of the war, although there is some need to emphasize its expensive results. Mrs. Lincoln's brothers in the Confederate army, Stonewall Jackson's sister a devoted Unionist, brother fighting brother, kinsmen by blood, by marriage, not only fighting each other but doing so in circumstances where to hurl the epithet 'traitor' was tempting, these were not revolutionary conditions in themselves, but they helped to breed revolutionary conditions, or at any rate to make the revolutionary temper more tolerable.

And that is one aspect of the war that needs to be emphasized for the outer world. From one point of view many, most, European countries can very well understand the poisons bred by such divisions, the difficulties put in the way of peaceful collaboration not merely by the memory of death inflicted by each side, but by the ambiguous role each side played as seen by the other. For one side, this was a wicked rebellion, for the other, a monstrous aggression motivated by greed and political and religious fanaticism. It is not paradoxical to say that these wounds last longer than those inflicted by foreign enemies. That this side of the war should not be understood in England is natural enough. Those feuds are long in the English past. But to some degree in Scotland and completely in Ireland, this destructive side of war, this poisoning of the wells of political health and truth, is understood. It is still understood in all of what was occupied Europe; in Spain, in Germany. And it is the reflection on this cost of war and revolution that made a great poet Andrew Marvell, himself committed to one side in a revolutionary civil war, say that 'the cause was too good to have been fought for'.

To inject hate into the veins of the body politic is one of the inevitable 'sins' of civil war, and that injection was performed, necessarily, in America and the poison has not totally ceased circulating. But (and I am not being in the least paradoxical) that poison had very important economic effects, not all of them by any means bad. The animosities caused by the war made possible the creation of a political system that, at the very least, greatly accelerated the industrialization of the American economy and brought about, more rapidly, I believe, than could otherwise have been done, the creation of what has been the American type of society that has so impressed the world (not necessarily favourably) and has so visibly and decisively affected world history.

It would be absurd, of course, to pretend that but for the Civil War the United States would not have been industrialized in the nineteenth century or that something like modern America, an urbanized, industrialized, and, if I may be allowed to coin a horrid word, a 'business-ized' United States would not have come into existence. Even if the war had ended in Southern victory, the fragments of the old Union might have become separately, in time, much like what they are today. Nor do I believe that a different issue to the war would have cured the 'colonial' status of the South, although it might have ameliorated the worst aspects of being a producer of raw materials and so peculiarly affected by what we now call 'the terms of trade'.

But the bitterness of the war, the conviction, on each side, that wrong had been done (naturally by the other side) had extremely important social and economic results. The psychological bias bred by the war provided the political climate that was needed to get American industrialization under way by a forced draught that only politics could provide.

Of course, the first forced draught was the war itself. We have long known, and have recently been reminded by Professor Nevins, that the capital equipment of the North increased during the war, that the economic importance of the Union in world commerce increased, and that the character of the American economy was not indeed distorted, but altered by the artificial demands of the war, by inflation, by the pressure on the labour force, by the imposition, by inflation, of the costs of forced-draught development on the fixed or lower income groups and not on the entrepreneurs whether they were bankers or iron masters or railway promoters. So far, what I have said are the commonplaces of economic history. We have the experiences of America in two great wars since then and the experience of other countries in total or near total war to save us from simple surprise or simple moral indignation. Nor do I assert, or believe, that the take-off, as Professor W. W. Rostow puts it, would have been delayed for more than a decade or so if there had been no war.

But the effects of the war were revolutionary all the same. First of all, time is part of a revolution. If the take-off was accelerated by the war, that is in itself an important if not quite revolutionary result of the war. 'Time is history' as well as 'Time is money' are maxims we ought to have in mind and Time has a price.

But the importance, the revolutionary importance of the war, was the way in which it determined that the nascent American capitalist class would be given the kind of governmental help they needed and, equally important, would not be given the kind of governmental help or interference that they did not need or, more certainly, did not want.

The more that I have reflected on the character of American history in the past century, the more I have been impressed by the unique role of the businessman, by the degree to which American society has accepted his leadership and saved him from most of the practical impediments and social frustrations of his compeers in Europe. Indeed, the word 'compeer' is wrong. The American businessman had no compeers for there was no other society in which his role was so much admired, his totally beneficial effects on the economy taken so much for granted, his claim to be the representative American and to have political institutions that suited this predominance of business, accepted.

Again, I do not wish to say too much. First of all, we don't know whether the blind forces of economic development would not have produced a dominant, unself-critical and largely uncriticized business class such as sprang up so rapidly during and after the war. The American Civil War sowed dragon's teeth and got not armed men but the great entrepreneurs, if you like, the great 'Robber Barons' of the period between the end of the war and the beginning of this century, that is between 1865 and 1901. But what we *do* know is that the rise of this class was immensely facilitated by the war. And facilitated not only by the impact of the war on the economy, if you like by the distortion of the economy by war, but by the elimination, as a political result of the war, of what might have been serious political friction, friction like that which all the other rising business classes had to adjust to, had to come to terms with.

My thesis is this. Thanks to the passions bred by and the interests fostered by the war, it was possible for the Republican party, by the time it had become the party of business, which I put not later than the first election of Grant, to provide the kind of political set-up that Business, especially the new Business itself fostered by the war, needed. It is a commonplace that the American party system was cracking up in the decade before the war and I have myself asserted that the final last drop of water that wore away the stone of union, the last brick of the dyke that gave way, was the division of the Democratic party in 1860. From these, I think, indisputable facts, it could be argued that a new party system was needed, would have been created, and one unit of that party system would have been something very like the Republican party. Of course a Republican party did appear between 1854 and 1856, but it is not only that the 'party of moral ideas' was not quite identical with the party that nominated Lincoln in 1864 (1860 I'll leave alone), but was still less identical with the party that nominated Grant in 1868. More important is the fact that what finally destroyed the old party system was the problem that destroyed the Union and brought about the war—slavery. And if it be said that the Democratic party was wrecked because it could no longer meet the demands of its varying clientele (sectional economic demands for the most part), that, in turn, was due to the slavery crisis that ended in war.

That there would have been some kind of party reorganization even had there been no war, no slavery controversy, I admit. The rise of industry and of the kinds of business associated with industry would have put strains on the old party system that would have forced important modifications in it. For instance the Democrats could not have continued their doctrinaire opposition to internal improvements (as far as that doctrine existed apart from the needs of the South as a conscious section, made conscious by the binding force of slavery). Means would have been found to finance transcontinental railways with federal money and the result might have been another Crédit Mobilier—with different beneficiaries.

But what the war made possible was the perpetuation of economically irrelevant political issues which weakened the natural opposition of the agrarian elements to the claims of the new business class, weakened the position of the older business interests, for example the shipping and importing houses, and by creating an unshakable loyalty to 'the Grand Old Party', enabled the new industrial classes to handle the new industrial masses, making fewer concessions than were needed in Europe and securing the nearly unquestioned dominance of Business for two generations.

Nearly unquestioned; it was, of course, questioned. But how ineffectively whether the questioning came from the depressed farmers or the disillusioned urban workers, from rebel movements like the Readjusters in Virginia, the Greenbackers, the Knights of Labour! I do not, for a moment, argue that there would necessarily have been a 'labour party' or, though here I am more uncertain, that there would necessarily have been an agrarian party. But the role of these two natural pressure groups was made far less important, the price of buying them off or dividing them was made far lower, because there was present, everywhere, the emotion-evoking memory of the war, taken over and used by the business elements dominating both parties, but basically putting their money on and into the natural vehicle of their projects, the Republican party.

I am stating this proposition neutrally. I do not know, no one knows, whether the industrialization of the United States and the form it took cost more, not in cash but in social harmony, in national unity, than it was worth. It may be, I am inclined to think it is almost a rule of history, that rapid industrialization in any country is socially expensive and that a lot of the cost is paid by the farmers or peasants. High tariffs, sound currency, a tax system that encouraged accumulation, all made possible the creation of a business America that might have been much slower in coming to maturity, and might never have come quite in the form it did come, if it had not been possible by 'waving the bloody shirt' (or the 'Stars and Bars') to divert political fervour to the great quarrel of the war. The same or equivalent forces can be seen at work in other countries, notably France. They can be seen in Ireland. They are either part of the long-term cost of the war or one of its beneficial results, depending on how one views business rule in the past or the character it has given to American society.

In two ways, by accelerating industrialization, increasing federal power and so the common market, and by anaesthetizing economic discontent in its political form, the war was revolutionary. But just as the character of the war was misunderstood while it was in progress, so the character of the industrial results of the war was misunderstood or seen in too simple a fashion. We all know how much the cause of the North was identified by 'liberal' and radical opinion, in Europe, with progress and liberation. John Bright and Karl Marx were on the same side. I am aware that the picture of a united working class in England, sacrificing itself to aid a Northern victory and procure the ending of slavery, is a great deal too simple. But it is not false. Lincoln was a hero and a martyr; Bismarck was not—or so the 'progressive elements' thought, although some mixed up the two statesmen and saw in the triumph of the Union and the foundation of the Second Reich the victory of the same good cause.

But Lincoln was the last American hero to be a universal hero—at any rate until the brief apotheosis of Woodrow Wilson. For the forces that had made the United States safe for business and which accounted for the dizzy speed of American industrial progress were not universally admired in Europe. Putting on one side the remaining suspicions and resentments of the conservative forces in Europe, it is more relevant to notice the alienation of the liberal and radical forces. The American political system that had the result I have tried to describe was seen as a boring and futile game. The innocent gratification in his own and in his adopted country's achievement that Andrew Carnegie displayed in his writings was received ironically or scornfully. A scholar like Bryce might note the extension of federal power, the growth of national feeling, but even he minimized if he did not ignore the social transformations of American society in which the war had played so basic a role. Europe, itself, was being industrialized rapidly but not quite at the same speed or in quite the same spirit. The old order was not totally replaced by the new; it was bought over or induced to accept and adorn a mutually profitable alliance. Radical observers like Marx's son-in-law, Aveling, might totally misread the signs of the times in America and see a speedy victory for socialism, a speedy growth of a class-conscious mass of workers. The agrarian discontents of the farmers could be treated as signs of a coming peasant revolt. The realities of the American scene were ignored. More attention was paid to Henry George than his effective weight in his own country justified.

The alienation of the industrial workers from state and society, to be noticed in all the progressive European states, even in Britain, had no real American equivalent where every year, hundreds of thousands of immigrants entered a country that had its recent and unique experience to cut it off from the general trend of European politics.

It would be absurd to reduce the differences between the United States and Europe, the very different reactions to the challenges of industrialization, to the deep psychic shock given by the war and exploited by the political system. There were many other grounds of difference, some buried in what was for the United States ancient history, others rooted in the role of the farmer-owner (it is not necessary to accept all the Turner theory to see that the settling of the West had a part in American mythology and in American fact). These things marked the American experience off from the European experience. If the United States had its terrible experience between 1861 and 1865, Europe, even Britain, knew the burdens of armaments in a way unknown in the United States. And the continental countries like France and Germany endured an increasing militarization that made them very different polities from the peaceful and almost disarmed Republic.

Then, as the war moved more and more into the past, as the Blue and Grey fraternized, as Lee as well as Lincoln became a national hero, the old bitter memories faded away, the old wounds healed. But the institutions, the biases, the political habits that the war had created or whose growth had been fostered, did not cease to have effect because it did not pay any longer tò 'wave the bloody shirt'. The framework of the American political and economic system had been created. The richest and, in many ways, the most advanced industrial society had escaped or evaded the alienation of the mass of the workers from that society that was nearly universal in Europe. The visible sterility of politics had bred scepticism about the value, about the possibility of state action. The state appeared as the auxiliary, or as the ally of business. Politics was partly a game; business was not. All the great political questions, above all the great question of where final political power lay, had been settled. The law expressed by the Courts was almost as much of an expression of business domination as politics was. There were revolts, like the Bryan campaign of 1896, but they were mere revolts, not even attempted revolutions. The economic, the cultural, relations between Europe and the United States were close. In many ways they got closer. One concealed foundation of the European economy was the market for European labour in the United States. But this was not accompanied by a corresponding movement of political ideas, of loves or hates. For many reasons which I cannot enumerate here, this difference was natural and inevitable. America *was* different; America *had* it better as Goethe put it. But one reason why the difference was so visible, so dramatic, perhaps why it was so deep and wide, was the impact of the war, during its course and in the generation that followed it. Had there been no other grounds of difference, the war could not have made them so numerous as they were. But a revolution began in the United States with the coming of the war and, by the time that Revolution had worked out its effects, each continent was in many social and political matters alienated from the other, looking uncomprehendingly across an ocean made wide by very different experiences. In this century common experiences have narrowed the sea that rolls between us. But the impact of the war is not yet exhausted. The American people examining the most moving portion of its past, feeling rather than knowing its profound importance, is re-enacting an experience that none of us from Europe, however deeply our curiosity and sympathy are engaged, can really share. We can try to understand, in that we may have some success. But feeling with you and so allowing for American feeling as a force in the evolution of America is far harder. It is only because I think that an effort towards empathy is called for that I have so rashly committed myself today.

1962

5

AMERICA THROUGH BRITISH EYES

IT IS USUALLY unprofitable to use anniversaries as diving boards for studies of contemporary conditions. Seldom enough does the jubilee or centenary, when it comes round, fit the mood that it is supposed to recall. But there is some utility today in recalling 1851—the year of the first and most famous international exhibition. For in 1851, more even than at either of the jubilees of Queen Victoria, English self-satisfaction reached its height, and the contrast between the Great Exhibition of 1851 and the Festival of Britain of 1951 is a good way of marking the change in the British position in the world and the British view of the world. It is a good way, too, to illustrate the change in the relative positions of Britain and the United States.

In 1851 the complacency of the English was contrasted with the less confident frame of mind of all the other peoples of the civilized world (all Asians, in that complacent age, were excluded from the civilized world). In Europe reaction had triumphed. Order reigned in Warsaw and Moscow, in Berlin and Rome. That is to say, the fine hopes of 1848 had been proved baseless. Barricades were not the way to win freedom, real freedom; that slowly broadened down from precedent to precedent and was not to be secured by any red furies of the Seine. It is unnecessary to stress the change that by 1951 has come over the world as seen from the tight little island. Yet that change and its psychological and material results must be borne in mind if the English view of America is to be understood. First of all, it is no longer a tight little island. All around you in London are proofs of that. The Exhibition of 1851 was built in the pleasant greenery of Hyde Park; the Festival of 1951 is built on what was a

year or two ago a vast mound of bomb rubble, more like a West
Virginia coal tip than an area in the heart of a great capital city. The
catalogue could be continued, but there is no need to do so, for the
change boils down to this. In 1851 the modern world was largely an
English creation. Its makers looked on it and found it good. True,
not the most confident, most optimistic Englishmen, not Palmerston
on one side or Cobden on the other, thought that it was possible or
desirable or necessary to impose the English way on the world.
Certainly it was not necessary. Was not all the world coming to
school in London? Were not the basic lessons of prudential Christianity being taught by direct and indirect means in London, in
Calcutta, in Hong Kong, in Singapore, and, of course, in New York,
Paris, St. Petersburg, Rio de Janeiro? And today? Well, the desire
to teach is there, the conviction that the world needs teaching is
there, but where are the pupils? And where are the ex-pupils to say
politely and gratefully, 'Good-bye, Mr. Chips'?

Surveying mankind from China to Peru, Mr. Podsnap in 1851
might well have rejoiced in his favoured position, and schoolchildren
might well have been taught to sing: 'I am a happy English child.'
Nor was the economic, apart from the political, prospect any less
pleasing to the loyal subject of Queen Victoria. By the adoption of
free trade England had set the world an example that they would be
wise to follow. The way was open to greater wealth and civilization
(in the English mind of 1851 they were united). And it was not only
the rich, the great Whig magnates, the new cotton millionaires, who
thought this. The workers in the dark, satanic mills were themselves
turning away from violence, were accepting the new order, were
producing their own answers to some of its problems in the new
trade unions, the new co-operatives. They were settling down in the
new industrial society that so far had no parallel in the whole world.

*

For, a point not noted enough in the perpetual discussion of 'Anglo-
American relations', a great deal of English criticism, a great many
English complaints are not specifically criticisms of or complaints
about America. They are criticisms of the modern world, complaints
about modern history which are bound to use American examples
simply because the modern world, the world of 1951, so unlike the
world of 1851, is a world dominated, led, largely created, by America.
Karl Marx had to use England as his laboratory for his analysis of

capitalist society because England was then the only full-scale example of capitalist society. And in the modern world of the atom bomb, the movies, the assembly line, the cheap car, modern plumbing, colour film, Marshall aid, bubble gum, the jeep, the centre of power is the United States. Only if you totally like the modern world (and who does?) can you escape the temptation, indeed, the necessity, of criticizing, of abusing some parts of modern society, and the easiest way to do that is to take them in their most representative form, which nine times out of ten will be an American form.

It is this which explains the, at first sight, extraordinary phenomenon that a Swede, an Indian, a Brazilian, an Englishman, none of them Communists or fellow-travellers, may easily and do frequently fall into denouncing the United States, true in inconsistent terms, but with a heart-warming degree of heat. That heat expresses, often enough, no considered judgment on the United States. It merely represents the realization that we are victims of the formidable Chinese curse: 'May you live in interesting times.' The world has been, with brief and illusory intervals, living in interesting times for forty years. During those times by far the greater part of the present living population has been born. During those times fear, disorder, massacre, war, new methods of destruction, all have grown. So has the power of the United States. Q.E.D.

But if the English attitude is a special case of a general attitude, it is a very special case. For it is not only that in many fields American power has replaced British, but, despite all the nonsense talked about it, the linguistic and cultural relationship between England and America is not paralleled in any other pair of relationships. That England has been and is being replaced by America in many areas is evident. Sometimes it is accepted as a mutually advantageous partnership: new blood, new capital, new ideas. But, of course, the arrival of the new, energetic, highly confident rival may not please the old-established firm or its agents any more than the arrival of 'the young, light-hearted masters of the waves', the Greeks, pleased the Phoenicians.

Just because American power is spreading all over the world and because English power (even if diminishing) is still spread all over the world, the points of contact, of competition, of amity, of friction are numerous. If, for example, British oil management is finally ejected from Persia for good and after a year or two the Persians have to fall back on American management, however camouflaged, it will take all the public relations skills of both countries to keep to a reasonable minimum the popularity of the view that for ways that are dark the Heathen Chinee has nothing on the Yank. A good many more instances of the fears, not general, but not confined to a lunatic fringe, which bedevil relations between the two countries could be given, but the Persian case will suffice. It has its comic side, but there it is, a change from the old American picture of the subtle, English aristocratic diplomat with his Oxford accent and monocle, swindling the pants off some simple, rugged, honest, naïve Tammany ambassador.

More serious than this suspicion of the Yankee nutmeg merchant is the very widespread conviction that, for mysterious reasons, Americans are politically erratic, impulsive, ill-informed, dangerous. Part of this conviction is simply a result of an old tradition. Comparatively few Americans had to know so much of the outside world, China or Chile, the Congo or the Caucasus, as had many English people, government people as well as businessmen. It was England, not the United States, that was the 'nation of shopkeepers'. How can the Americans learn, in a few years, the skills that centuries of international dealing have made second nature in the City of London as well as in Whitehall? And both the Americans and the English have something (if I may use an Americanism). For if it is hard for the English to realize, in time, that the old order is going or has gone, it is equally hard for Americans to realize that the old order may be the only order available, that there is not necessarily at hand a technically competent governmental personnel. That may be somebody else's fault, but it may also be a highly relevant fact, not to be conjured away by evoking the spirit of '76. Englishmen think, that is to say, that 'imperialism' is used as loosely, if not as mendaciously, by Americans as by Russians. If asked to repent their sins, they suggest that India compares favourably with China. And since feeling is part of the problem and part of the judgment, few things please the more or less aggrieved Briton more than to see an American discover that a lately oppressed Indian may have a high opinion of his oppressors and even prefer them to Americans. This form of pleasure reaches its height in Dublin where, to mention no other examples, Mr. De Valera's admiration for British administrative and political methods would shock a great many vehement Irish-Americans.

But these reflections are confined to the small groups for whom

Dr. Mossadegh really competes with Messrs. Robinson and Turpin for news value. Much more widespread is the alarm caused by the fine, noisy, rhetorical style of so many American spokesmen. They may be self-appointed but there they are—editors, Senators, preachers of various kinds. First of all, linguistic styles have changed. Oratory is no longer in fashion in England. Even Mr. Churchill, except on very rare occasions, uses fewer flowers of rhetoric than a run-of-the-mill candidate for a state legislature. This means that great, booming statements that are discounted in America are reported and taken seriously in England. And, of course, the intricacies of the American political system are little allowed for, the autonomy of state and national politics, the independence of the Senate, the absence of party discipline in the English sense. All these combine to make the man in the street in London or Glasgow, not to speak of more sophisticated viewers with alarm, genuinely afraid that he may find himself at the tail of a kite whose string is in very unfirm hands. And this prospect pleases him the less that he feels that the results of the kite's breaking away will fall, first and worst, on him. Some firm statements from Senators and publicists remind him too much of the Irish landlord who wrote from London to his tenants in Connaught, 'If you think you can intimidate me by shooting my bailiff, you are much mistaken.' The English are sometimes afraid they have been tapped for bailiff.

*

But to conclude this theme, British policy has always been that of a power that needed friends. (It was, for once, by not making or keeping them, that she 'lost' the thirteen colonies.) In modern times a great many Americans have thought, many still think, that they can go it alone. So they see everything in a bright New England winter sunshine when it is not an Arizona desert of blinding light and shade. We see things in the less distinct colours of a Thames-valley October. I don't believe that 'I can lick any man in the room' is the American attitude, but it is the attitude of some Americans and if (Heaven forbid) it became or could plausibly be made to seem to be the attitude of any American administration, many partisans of the present Anglo-American alliance would reluctantly quote Sam Goldwyn and say: 'Include me out.'

It may seem odd that in discussing the British view of America I have so far concentrated on war, peace, politics, economics, not on more 'human' topics. But, again, it is a sign of the times that these are the topics to which the attention of that minority whose attention is concentrated on any public issue at all, is directed. Nor is this unnatural. We are just getting over a great war fought in common. (We are not sure that *we* are getting over it; every time we get to the top of the hill the delectable mountains are the next range.) We may be moving into a new war to be fought in common. American planes roar over my house every day; my children are now very knowledgeable on types. It would be very strange if the great questions of war and peace were not in the forefront of our minds, apart from the fact that but for American enlightened self-interest, to put it no higher, we should be living at a much lower level. But we don't live by arms aid or by Marshall aid alone, and there was a British attitude to America long before lend-lease, long before the first British child asked the first American soldier: 'Any gum, chum?'

Here it is important to distinguish two levels of opinion. For one form of the old association between Britain and the United States has been a continuous movement of population. Of course, most of the movement has been from east to west and most of the emigrants have stayed in America. But from the days of George Downing (Harvard, 1642) to those of T. S. Eliot (Harvard, 1910) there has been a big return traffic. How big can be estimated from the astonishing discovery made in the late war, that 8 per cent of the population of Britain had visited the United States for longer or shorter periods. This, of course included sailors who had jumped ship and people making brief visits to relatives. There is a great body of people with first-hand knowledge of America whose judgment and memories are no doubt affected and distorted by the press, the movies, the radio, and so on. But they have seen, felt, heard, smelt America. And the America they know is more likely to be Paterson, N.J., or Akron, Ohio, than Palm Beach or Concord or Palo Alto. They are in the main members of 'the working classes'. And it is the working classes who are most pro-American, or least anti-American.

*

Of course, many of them are by political doctrine hostile to 'American imperialism', see in the Marshall Plan some piece of diabolical cunning or some ingenious way of making money by giving it away, a device that only the preternaturally ingenious Yankees could invent. But they are for the American way of life in its visible aspects. And the less politically bigoted workers are for it in more ways than that. They are not worrying about what will happen to European culture if comics, gum, nylons, Coca-Cola, Hollywood styles in clothes, speech, behaviour flood England. Their children are Americanizing themselves as much as they can. There is, no doubt, envy, no doubt resentment, no doubt occasional affirmations that there is nothing the Yanks can do that cannot be done better in England. But the more general attitude is 'nice work if you can get it'. In this they are like the workers of other West European countries, as far as I have been able to judge. And they are like them for the reason I gave earlier; this is an Americanized world and since they have to swallow (to put it harshly) the pill of economic dominance, political leadership, the atomic world, they might as well have the good things too. But this is probably too great a rationalization, for they want the good things because they think they are good, from the movies and the musicals to Coca-Cola.

With the 'intellectuals', the makers and victims of public opinion at a higher level, anti-Americanism is much more common. One reason for it I gave also earlier. The resentment of the old squire at the power and pretensions of the *nouveau riche* is one of the classic themes of fiction and the theatre. It is this class that has had the most conscious stake in the old order now declining—to its loss. But it would be a mistake to put it all down to that, or even to the unfortunate love affair with the Soviet Union from which not all the victims of the thirties have recovered.

For, in addition to these causes for alarm and despondency, there are others. In this American world what place is there for an old culture that may be dying but may also be helped to die? Here it must be noted that nearly all the critical impressions of America shared by this group are based on what Americans tell them through books, plays, movies. The successful American books and plays are not on the whole good sales talk for the American way of life. The artist does seem to be unhappy in America. He isn't, perhaps, any more unhappy than in France or England, but the French and English writers aren't very enthusiastic about their native lands either. The movies, of course, paint a different picture, but then it is a point of honour to dislike or despise American movies or only to appreciate the few which manage to smuggle some gloomy truths past the Johnston Office. Then, and this is important, American literature has not at the moment the great prestige it had before the war. No new American names have really replaced Dreiser, Cather, Lewis, O'Neill, Faulkner, Steinbeck, Thurber. And none of these, living or dead, is optimistic about modern America. Henry James felt at home when he came to London because he knew George du Maurier's drawings in *Punch*. But who could feel comfortably at home in the Thurber world? (I hasten to add that one Thurber, in enlightened British as in American opinion, is worth ten Du Mauriers.) The success of *A Streetcar Named Desire*, the publication, unexpurgated and unmolested, of *Hecate County*, the revival of Scott Fitzgerald, the rise in the market for John O'Hara, these don't make American life a laughing matter, nor the extension of American ways a matter for unmitigated rejoicing. The greatest English poet is an American by origin, but no one would call Mr. Eliot a booster. It is not the thinkers and critics, but the ballad makers who matter, and they are busy selling America to a vast and appreciative audience. Dr. Godhes has pointed out that a century ago there was as much literary piracy in England as in America. Americans pirated *David Copperfield*, the English pirated *Uncle Tom's Cabin* and *The Wide Wide World*, and at the same time as the future of America was being heavily discounted by the heavy thinkers, emigrants by the scores of thousands were risking their fortunes on the endangered ship. So it is today. Americanism is all around us. It is a grave cause for alarm, but Hollywood ties (not it is true of the first virulence) are on sale in the Strand. My records of *South Pacific* have been borrowed from me by a fellow of King's College, Cambridge, home of all forms of intellectual sophistication. The queue for that entertainment already stretches to Bali H'ai. American airmen are back in East Anglia as if they had never been away. We have lots to worry about, but I don't see a British Declaration of Independence casting off the Yankee yoke, even though it chafes at times.

1951

6

THE FIRST ROOSEVELT

THERE WOULD be general agreement that of the occupants of the White House since the Civil War four stand out: Cleveland, Theodore Roosevelt, Woodrow Wilson, Franklin D. Roosevelt. And of these four Theodore Roosevelt is, in many ways, the most interesting as he is certainly the most versatile. He is not the most important. Historical accident, if nothing else, made Wilson and Franklin D. Roosevelt far greater figures in American and world history than Theodore Roosevelt was given a chance to be. Cleveland's career evokes few passions now; his achievements and limitations are as far beyond historical controversy as any man's can be. But there are many devoted friends and tenacious enemies of Theodore Roosevelt still alive and some of the problems he tackled, some of the constitutional innovations he made, are still capable of evoking the uncritical praise or unlimited blame beloved of the first Roosevelt.

Adored and detested in his lifetime, Theodore Roosevelt suffered the automatic denigration that follows so flamboyant a career. His official biography, written largely under his direction, his *Autobiography*, the lush praise of admirers, one might almost say of addicts like William Allen White, provoked a natural reaction. So when Mr. Pringle published the first critical study of Roosevelt, now nearly twenty years ago, it had the effect of pricking an over-inflated balloon. Roosevelt had so managed to impress his view of events on his contemporaries that the application to his record of ordinary critical methods could not but mean the destruction of a legend. The decision of the Roosevelt Memorial Association, the Massachusetts Institute of Technology and other institutions and individuals to make possible a lavish if not quite complete publication of the

Roosevelt correspondence,[1] marks a turn of the tide, a realization that it is time that fresh materials for judgment were provided, that so representative an American deserves serious and respectful, though far from uncritical, treatment.

The task undertaken by Mr. Morison and his colleagues was difficult indeed, for Roosevelt was an indefatigable letter-writer and the range of his interests meant that his letters might be found in the most diverse places. As we expect from modern American scholarship, the greatest zeal and the most ingenious detective skill have been shown in tracking down letters and in making them intelligible. Unfortunately, the editors were faced with a choice that was imposed on them and which, whatever decision they took, was bound to expose them to criticism. By far the most important of Roosevelt's correspondents was Henry Cabot Lodge. From 1884 to Roosevelt's death they were in constant correspondence except when they were physically together and Lodge was the closest of Roosevelt's political friends. Unfortunately, this correspondence has been closed to scholars and the editors have been forced to use the *Selections from the Correspondence of Theodore Roosevelt and Henry Cabot Lodge* published in 1925. The drawbacks are obvious. In 1925, many of the actors in the drama were alive and there was need to consider both good taste and libel. (One may surmise that one or two admitted deletions in the new publication were due to the fact that William Randolph Hearst was still alive when the volumes were in preparation.) Then the *Selections* were edited by Lodge, and it would be asking too much of any man, and much too much of so vain a man as Lodge, to expect a collection of this kind to show either partner to the correspondence warts and all. The editors, therefore, were faced with the choice of ignoring the single most important 'archive', or of printing it in a text whose authenticity they were unable to control. They have chosen to risk the criticisms of the most orthodox scholars and to print the Lodge text. And they have done right. For the Lodge correspondence is the thread on which the rest of the political letters are strung; without it many letters—indeed whole sections—would be difficult to follow. The necessity for this hard choice is not the fault of the editors. Then they have been forced to choose among masses of correspondence, dealing with official and unofficial matters, so as to avoid repetition

[1] *The Letters of Theodore Roosevelt*, selected and edited by Elting E. Morison, Harvard University Press, 8 vols.

and weariness and yet to give a representative sample of each class of letter, to senators or naturalists, hunters or soldiers. Where it is possible to check their judgment (as by comparing the letters dealing with the Navy Department with the Massachusetts Historical Society's *Papers of John Davis Long*), the result is to create confidence in the editors and to renew the conviction that few men had a greater capacity for seeing their own side of a story than Theodore Roosevelt.

Of course there are flaws. Roosevelt was a very bad speller indeed; it took him a long time to learn how to spell the name of Grover Cleveland, who was not merely President of the United States but, for a time, his official chief. So one has every sympathy with his editors, but on some occasions it is handwriting, not spelling, that has baffled them. It may be that 'good' families in Boston and New York in the seventies were so remote, one from the other, that Roosevelt wrote 'Saltenstahl' for Saltonstall. If so it is something for an American Proust to note. But could a resident of Oyster Bay really write 'Seawhaka', or anybody visiting Venice turn San Giorgio Maggiore into San Scorgia Maggiore? And it is probably the editors, not Roosevelt, who have given the credit for Robertson's *Chitral* to Lord Roberts. One letter of Grover Cleveland seems to be misdated (Professor Nevins gives it as 1884; it cannot in any case be 1881). But the editorial work is admirable. It is even admirable in a way that may offend the purists. For the editors, wisely avoiding the pointless note which tells us that Grover Cleveland was President of the United States or that Henry James was a novelist, do tell us that Congressman Grosvenor was not merely a spoilsman, but had a white beard apparently surpassing in magnificence even those of such congressional ornaments as Senator J. Hamilton Lewis or Representative Tinkham. Such information is not strictly necessary, but it livens up the duller, more purely political pages.

Yet there are fewer dull pages in these 1,500 odd than would be the case in the correspondence of most other presidents. As Mr. Morison points out, Roosevelt was not merely a voluminous, he was a good letter-writer. He can even make the knaveries of some obscure spoilsman in Terre Haute or Baltimore exciting. His passion for self-justification and his incapacity for seeing the other side made him a fine, abusive controversialist and his constantly brimming enthusiasm is infectious. When he has a good story to tell, like his capture of the horse thieves in the Bad Lands, we share his boyish delight. It is almost a pity he did not fight a duel with that odd French neighbour of his, the Marquis de Morès. If he had survived it, what a tale he would have made of it. (Morès is consistently spelled 'Mores' by the editors as well as by Roosevelt.) Then the range of the letters prevents boredom. No one reads the Cleveland letters (in spite of some elephantine light verse) for literary charm. But Roosevelt was often charming as well as vivacious. Here is his delight in having a species of deer named after him (it turned out to be only a sub-species, but that news came later). There is the discovery of Frederick Jackson Turner's frontier theory; the discovery of Kipling; the enjoyment of the inspissated gloom of Brooks Adams; the pleasures and miseries of family life; there are speculations on the future of Russia and the uses of wrestling. No president, save Jefferson and John Quincy Adams, had a range like this. And if Roosevelt was not a scholar as his two predecessors were, if he was a good deal of a dilettante, we should not forget the original meaning of 'dilettante'. Roosevelt had what Hazlitt prized, gusto.

But for all his varied interests Roosevelt was a politician, an ambitious politician who fought his way laboriously a little way up the slope and had grave fears of slipping down again when a series of accidents shot him to the very top like a passenger in an express elevator. Through nearly all the political letters in these volumes runs a note of pessimism. For one thing (a point the letters do not bring out), Roosevelt had lost a good deal of money in his ranching adventures, as had nearly all who speculated in the 'Cattle Country', from prudent Scots in Edinburgh and Dundee to the flamboyant Marquis de Morès. He needed to make money by writing; he could not afford a political career out of office. Then he was a New Yorker; he had no safe Republican majority to fall back on as Henry Cabot Lodge had in Massachusetts. New York, he kept on saying, is a Democratic state. It was not quite that, but it was a very doubtful state. And Roosevelt was a very vehement Republican. There is, indeed, something shrill in his protestations of party loyalty. It is commonly said that his branch of the Roosevelt family were dyed-in-the-wool Republicans, while the Hyde Park branch were Democrats. But Theodore's uncle, Robert Barnwell Roosevelt, politically the most active member of his branch, was a firm anti-Tammany Democrat, and died in that faith while his nephew was Republican President of the United States. Roosevelt had to show party zeal to a degree unnecessary to Lodge, with his combination of a naturally partisan mind and a sound Federalist ancestry.

There was an even less agreeable side to the New York situation. Lodge could play ball with the regular politicians, but Roosevelt could not have a real political career without their consent. He was unlucky in his time. There was no direct primary, no direct election of senators, no radio. To get on in politics he had to be a candidate, and to be a candidate he had to get the consent of the bosses, or rather of one boss, Tom Platt. Yet Roosevelt wrote of Platt that he was as bad as his Democratic opposite numbers, Senator Hill and Croker of Tammany Hall. Personal distaste may have had something to do with this. Platt was a drab figure and Roosevelt might have had more tolerance for Boies Penrose of Pennsylvania who was a 'gentleman' and a Harvard contemporary. Yet fate threw Platt and Roosevelt together, with the result that the unsuccessful minor politician became the youngest man ever to enter the White House.

The turning-point was the Spanish-American war. Roosevelt, a frail child, had made himself something of an athlete and hunter by mere force of will, and there was in his admiration for physical prowess (natural physical prowess) something exaggerated, as there was in Kipling. But Roosevelt did not merely dream of shooting moose ('Fit as a bull moose' occurs more than once here; it was not to be a political slogan till 1912). He dreamed of war. It did not seem to matter much what war. War with Britain over Venezuela, war with Spain over Cuba, war with Germany over nothing at all. Mixed up with these militant dreams are protestations of devotion to peace; it is only war if honour is involved, but honour was so easily involved. Made Assistant Secretary of the Navy in 1897, Roosevelt began to prepare for war and, possibly unconsciously, to wish for war. (A comparison of the *Papers* of his official chief, John D. Long, and the Roosevelt letters of this period is very illuminating.) But he found that a great many Americans did not want war, not even after the *Maine* was blown up in Havana harbour. Therefore they were lily-livered cowards. It never seems to have dawned on Roosevelt that some of these cowards were men who had served through a very terrible war indeed, something quite unlike war in the narratives of Kipling and Richard Harding Davis, or that among them was the President of the United States, William McKinley. The war came and Roosevelt, in face of almost unanimous opposition, threw up his important job and joined the volunteer cavalry regiment that the

Press, to his annoyance, insisted on calling the 'Rough Riders'. In similar circumstances his remote kinsman and nephew by marriage, Franklin D. Roosevelt, obeyed orders and stayed on in the post Roosevelt abandoned.

This decision put Theodore Roosevelt in the White House, and it is natural to see in it mere political calculation. But Mr. Pringle is probably right in seeing in Roosevelt the hero-worshipper, now given a chance to work 'upon the plan that pleased his boyish thought'. He had a wonderful time, a 'bully' time, to use his favourite adjective. He led his dismounted troopers up San Juan (or Kettle Hill), himself on horseback, and became a national hero. And the story is told here with that simple egotism that made 'Mr. Dooley' suggest that Roosevelt's book on the war ought to have been called 'Alone in Cubia'. But as Mr. Dooley also remarked, no man with a poor opinion of himself ever got elected governor of New York. Boss Platt needed a candidate who could win; Roosevelt met the bill and did win, though not by much. But to win he had to be nominated, and that meant he had to bargain with Platt, the Platt whom he had detested and despised. From the point of view of applied political science the letters from the Governor to the Senator are the most fascinating in the book and show that the first Roosevelt, like the second, could use all the arts of the charmer when he wanted to. But two years of Roosevelt was enough for Platt and he arranged to put him where he could do no harm, in the empty office of Vice-President. That, of course, is not how Roosevelt saw it, but although *The Autobiography of Thomas Collier Platt* is one of the least reliable of sources, its account of the manoeuvres that made Roosevelt the Republican candidate is nearer the truth than Roosevelt's. There was now, as Mark Hanna said, only one life between 'that madman' and the White House, and a real madman was soon to remove that life.

It is on the threshold of the White House that the editors leave Roosevelt, and their volumes do make it much easier to understand the man who was so suddenly to become a world figure. There are many points on which the letters throw light, but only one need be mentioned. Nothing seems, in retrospect, sillier than Roosevelt's belief, in 1917, that he was fit to command a division on the Western Front, but, apart from egotism and ambition, he had acquired, in 1898 outside Santiago, the belief that there were few things the West Pointers could do that he could not do as well or better. That the German army was not the Spanish army was not clear enough to the Colonel.

In this great mass of correspondence there is a good deal that destroys the simple Roosevelt legend and, at critical points, the editors call our attention to the other side of the picture. The unavailing pursuit of the Congressional Medal of Honour is childish, at best, and Roosevelt's detestation of the 'Mugwumps' is febrile. But, on the whole, he comes well out of the ordeal. He had all kinds of courage, a lively, roving intelligence, a sense of public duty and great charm. It is not unimportant that, meeting Cecil Spring Rice on board ship, he had him as his best man at his second wedding in London, three weeks later. No one could do so much and not do some things badly, but few American or British politicians did so many things so well or have entered great office with such high and worthy ideas of it or such varied talents for making those ideas realities. This series promises to be one of the most important contributions to our understanding of modern American history.

1952

7

UNNOTICED CHANGES IN AMERICA

IN SEPTEMBER 1925 I landed for the first time at New York on my way to Harvard. Now I have just completed a year in which I have spent more than two-thirds of my time in the United States, in every section of the country. I have had opportunity to reflect on the changes in American life that I have noted in over a score of visits in thirty-two years and on the present role of the United States in the world, contrasted with that which I gave it—naïvely but not, I think, wrongly—in 1925.

Then, the United States was already a problem, an example, a hope, a despair, all that she is today. In a few years, M. André Siegfried was to declare that the world would have to choose between Ford and Gandhi. Gandhi is out of the picture now. Nehru's India is not Gandhi's and the competitor of the United States is not a rural, pacific, archaic India, but the machine-minded, materialistic Marxian world.

That the world has changed, and largely for the worse, is obvious; that the United States has changed and largely for the better is what I would maintain. But what strikes me on reflection is the limited character of that change.

If the American scene has changed, it is still very like the America I first encountered in 1925. There is more of it; more Americans, more American things. But the new American things are extensions of the old. Compared with the European, the American is still optimistic, cheerful, energetic—convinced that if not all is for the best in the best of all possible countries, it is on the way to becoming so. He is also convinced, with much justification, that the things that threaten the admirable 'American way of life' come from the outside, convinced, with less justification, that the world (which cannot any longer be ignored) will beat a path in due time to the American doorstep to buy the new mousetrap, 'know-how'.

There is plenty of ostentatious pessimism. Questions are put:
'Why can't Johnny read?'
'Why Elvis Presley?'
'What of the farmer?'
'What of the small businessman?'

But all in all, the American as seen by the visiting and friendly foreigner seems still, by European standards, at ease in Zion. 'Nobody ain't mad at anybody' is obviously untrue; the South is mad and getting madder in more senses than one. But the American is satisfied with the American way of life. There is here—as Father Bruckberger noted in contrast with France—but also in contrast with Britain—a deep sense of the legitimacy of government. No state has less reason to worry about the loyalty of its people than the United States, which does worry so publicly.

Of course, there are problems, but there do not seem to be many new problems. In 1925, the radio was already being charged with the same offences, was deceiving the same hopes, as TV does today. The car and the truck were beginning to unite the whole nation, to urbanize it, to destroy the old deep differences between town and country. The plane, the super-highway have accelerated these changes, that is all.

The impact of the new knowledge on the family, the vogue for psychology, the horror of repression produced the present generation of parents anxious that their children shall have more security. Dr. Spock, Dr. Gesell rule the roost, presumably with good results. But the basic undermining of the old authoritarian, heaven-and-hell family discipline has done its job. Where is the sense of sin today? There has been a revival of religion, but that ambiguous term does not imply a revival of the sense of sin.

There have of course been great and beneficent changes whose speed could not have been foreseen in 1925. The position of the Negro was improving even then, but how slowly! It may be that the improvement has stopped or is about to stop; certainly, it seems to me that the growing tension over desegregation is the most ominous internal sign in America today. But what has been gained will not easily be lost.

Nor will the 'emancipation of women' be undone. Some of the sillier aspirations of the virginal feminists have proved to be unattainable or not desirable or not appreciated. The young American woman today is as convinced as ever Eve was that 'the proper study of womankind is man'. The young American woman wants above all a husband and children, hopes to catch 'the all-American boy', as one of them put it recently to me.

But the days of *Little Women* have not returned. The American woman may not be as powerful as the advertisers tell her she is, but she is out on the world. And all of this was clearly visible in 1925: the general acceptance of contraception, waning of the 'double standard' (how many young women in their twenties, today, know what this sacred phrase means?) . . . these more than the vote changed the position of women—and so of men.

In other ways, American life has changed not at all. There is still widespread acceptance of the educational heresy that all that needs to be learned can be taught. There is still a belief in the power of the law to put down wickedness (hence the absurd and murderous laws on dope addiction). There is still a combination of great generosity with a lack of psychological sympathy or even tolerance of the outside world. Yet some things are happening almost unnoticed. It is to the results of these changes that I now turn.

ALL THE BRAVE YOUNG MEN

In the men's room of the Astor just before Christmas, 1925, I saw the first members of the American Army I ever set eyes on. They were a group of West Point cadets 'on the town'. In those days, the Army was a remote, unimportant, almost invisible government agency. Officers belonged to a curious, differentiated, unimportant class. If they had had the misfortune (as happened to Captain Eisenhower) not to have served in France, they had not even the mildest form of glamour. Even very intelligent members of this professional group, like the future General Gruenther, might spend dreary year after year as lieutenants hoping for death above them to bring promotion. West Point attracted, in the main, moderately ambitious boys of poor or barely prosperous families. There were exceptions; sons of military families like Generals MacArthur and Patton. There were, especially from the South, boys filled with respect for the glory of war. But, all in all, the Army, even the Navy, was a backwater.

On March 17, 1926, Boston (or the Irish part of it) celebrated the coincidence of St. Patrick's Day and the 150th anniversary of the evacuation of the city by the British. I watched the parade with two English friends and we were astonished by its military poverty, by the bad marching of the amateur troops. It was possible to travel widely in the United States and never see any sign of military power.

A few months ago Secretary of Defence Wilson decreed, in his brisk fashion, that officers on office duty in the Capital must wear civilian clothes. This order (later hastily modified) delighted the Washington clothing stores, for it affected between ten and twenty thousand men. That—as much as the contrast between the vast, but now inadequate, Pentagon and the old, comfortably adequate, State, War, and Navy building—illustrates one of the great, under-estimated, understudied changes in American life. Over the past thirty years, the armed services have gradually become one of the most important of American social institutions.

No longer does the ambitious officer contemplate retirement to San Antonio. There are the Waldorf Towers, the board rooms of great corporations, embassies, cabinet offices. There is, in active service, the splendour of Château and Schloss, the viceregal state of command all round the globe. There is the White House of which Leonard Wood dreamed in vain and Pershing did not even dream.

There is—and this is even more important—the presence of nearly twenty million males who have known military life at first hand. They have had an experience that cuts them off from what will soon be a minority of the male population, the total civilians. It has cut them off, already, from the overwhelming mass of women—excluded from this side of male life as completely as from the Tap Room of the Yale Club.

In 1925, there were, of course, some millions of American men who had had some military experience. There was ex-Captain Truman for instance. But few had had much military experience in action (the brief and local character of American intervention in the first world war accounted for that). 'The War' was a dramatic, sporting, exploitable experience for a small minority getting rapidly smaller.

The contrast with Europe was marked. All Europe, as far as I could judge, was shocked to its core by its catastrophe (the first world war, not the second, wrecked the old European hegemony and confidence). In America, it was fashionable to blame everything that the critic disliked in contemporary American life on 'the War'. Prohibition and bootlegging, short skirts and lipstick, the decline of the old-time religion, and the discovery of sex were all imputed to this brief and largely irrelevant ripple on the tide of life. Yet the Model-T Ford had more influence on American social history than the Argonne.

The contrast between Europe and America was made plain enough in the role and antics of the American Legion. Most of the original Legionnaires, in the nature of things, could not have been veterans in any real sense. They had had neither time nor opportunity. War might well seem to them the Big Parade. It was, in the retrospect of their annual get-togethers, a circus. The creation of a privileged class of 'veterans'; the political power of the veterans' vote; the use of the Legion as a political springboard; all were in the tradition of the Grand Army of the Republic. But the GAR veterans were heroes of a war that evoked passionate pride, interest, love, hate. The veterans of the American Legion were 'boys' who had been taken for a buggy ride and wanted financial compensation for being gypped.

A few months ago I had the sociological good fortune to be in Los Angeles during the 1956 Legion convention. Its old high spirits were gone. The press tried in vain to play up the pranksters but the public was indifferent. There was something symbolic, too, in the fact that the new National Commander had served less than ninety days, and 'stateside' at that, in the late war, a war which produced millions of genuine veterans who had fought all over the world.

But if the Legion is on the way out, veterans are not. They number almost tens of millions, and the two new wars—the second world war and Korea—have burned themselves into the national consciousness in a way the first world war never did. The losses of the 1940s and 1950s are not being cynically written off. The fruits of these wars still have to be lived with—the draft, the debt, the Pentagon, the overhanging menace of the H-bomb. 'What price victory?' is the question the American man and woman, veterans or not, ask themselves today.

There may be deep resentment of the fact—but few now deny it —that in the world of atomic fall-out, the United States is inextricably involved. Interest in the outside world may be sulky, prejudiced, ill-informed, but it is genuine.

But this involvement has had internal consequences that seem to me strangely neglected. With three million American young men under arms at any one moment, the armed services are numerically as important as the colleges. Yet how little thought, it seems to me, is devoted to the serious social and political problem of how the armed forces work as educators! There may be scandals like the drowning of the Marines; there may be revelations of excessively slack as well as excessively severe discipline. But the young American male has his life and convenience interfered with by the government in a way that would have seemed preposterous in 1925—or in 1939. It is also surely curious that in all the discussions of equality between the sexes, of the application of the principles of the Nineteenth Amendment, next to no attention is paid to the fact that the law discriminates, and severely at that, against males? But—and the 'but' may explain the neglect of the problem—the tenderness of the American politician for the 'veteran' has redressed the balance; pensions, civil-service rights, job guarantees, special hospital facilities, all make the ex-serviceman, in his turn, a privileged person.

If it be true (Senator John Kennedy is my authority for believing it to be true) that the poor and ambitious boy no longer wants a nomination to the Point, that these nominations are among the least valued parts of a Congressman's patronage, then the United States is faced with a serious danger. For we can be certain that the regular officers of the United States will remain a very important class indeed. If they do not draw on young men of ambition and ability, the results may be disastrous.

Yet how seldom is the problem of military education put high on the national agenda! Willy-nilly, the United States is a great armed power in which the role of the professional officer is of the first importance and it is a role that has been neglected, for example, by political scientists like myself. It is a long way from the West Point cadets in the Astor washroom! For the transformation of an America nominally at peace into one of the world's two great military powers is perhaps the single greatest and most ambiguous change in America.

THE BUSINESS OF POLITICS

I hope I arrived in the United States in 1925 less conscious of effortless superiority than the average Oxford man was wont to display. There was much that delighted me, few things that shocked me. But one thing did shock me. This was the prevalence of what the

Greeks (and my servant at Balliol) called 'idiots'—that is citizens taking no interest in politics. Even then I was far from thinking that politics were all or nearly all. I was quite prepared for poets and scientists to neglect politics for better things. But it was something else again to find historians, economists—even students of government—indifferent. The professionals looked after politics—either because they made a good if shady living that way, or because they had some inexplicable yen for this dull and rather dirty sport.

In 1957, although there are constant complaints about the abstention of voters, politics are not neglected. Politics as a career attract lots of young men and women, and a sense of the importance of political matters—and of government—is as marked as its absence was in 1925. The government is everywhere: it drafts the boys, robs the rich, more and more provides education, pensions, hospitals. The businessman like Henry Ford, who really expected to be able to do as he liked with his own, is dying or dead. Of course, it was fiction in 1925 that the world of business was apart from and above the world of politics, but it was a fiction that many intelligent people professed to believe in. No one believes in it now.

The egghead, still sore after the McCarthy raid on civilization, thinks in too many cases of the present or the recent age as one of black reaction, of tyranny, of enforced conformity. But for millions of Americans who were helpless in face of the great concentrations of economic power which dominated a state like Pennsylvania in 1926, the politician, the New Deal, the labour union have been liberating forces. If there is more conflict than there was in Coolidge's time, it is because deeper things are being debated, greater issues are involved, and things taken for granted in 1925 are disputed today.

We may not think that the Eisenhower Administration shows an adequate sense of the seriousness of the times; we may regard much of its policy proclamations as a kind of 'Miltown', a tranquillizing drug. But compare it with the complete emptiness of the minds, and largely of the hearts, of the business class and its political employees in 1925! It is nearly the Republic of Plato against the City of Pigs!

Think of how little (to put it kindly) President Lowell of Harvard contributed to the public enlightenment! Try to recall the really stifling complacency of Harvard, the House of Morgan, the press, the pulpit in 1925! Even the greatest political figures of that time, like Al Smith, were parochial. It may be, I think it is, true that much of the deep trust that President Eisenhower inspires is like the trust Charles Lindbergh inspired in 1927. But surely it is a sign of comparative maturity to have an Eisenhower, not a Lindbergh, for a mascot?

That American politics are in a satisfactory state I would not pretend. There is always scandal-ridden Illinois to give the 'last hurrah'. Some cherished reforms (like the direct primary) seem more doubtful today. State politics are too often a petty scuffle of local business. And the states—with so much more money to spend, with their archaic constitutions and inequitable distribution of representation —are not very hopeful instruments of social and political devolution.

But even in Illinois, the days of Mayor Big Bill Thompson and Governor Len Small, 'the Kankakee farmer', are over. Where is the Indiana of the Ku Klux Klan? What important Senator could *mean* as little today as Senator Charlie Curtis of Kansas, once Vice-President of the United States? The younger Talmadge is better than his father; Senator Eastland an improvement on Bilbo. Joe McCarthy is an improvement on 'Tomtom' Heflin. If he is more dangerous, it is because he lives in a more dangerous age. American politics, politicians, institutions, have not adjusted themselves perfectly to the atomic age, but they have done a better job than anyone could have thought likely in the days when Coolidge was applauded because he was believed to have said that 'the business of the United States is business'.

THE GULF OF FAITH

Just before I went to the United States in 1925, the 'Monkey Trial' in Dayton, Tennessee, had delighted the European world. Here was the most powerful, richest, most complacent society in the world making a fool of itself over Jonah and the Whale, over the literal accuracy of Genesis. To a continent weakened and, in its heart of hearts, thinking itself disgraced by its recent civil war, the spectacle of William Jennings Bryan, former Secretary of State, thrice candidate for President, floundering over primitive cosmology was funny and comforting.

True, there was a lot of humbug in this attitude. There is no reason to believe that the religion of Bryan was any less sophisticated than the religion of the eminently representative Low Church statesman, Sir William Joynson-Hicks. In my native land, there was plenty of blind belief in the literal inspiration of the Bible and more in an 'impregnable rock of Holy Scripture' (to borrow a phrase from another eminent Christian politician, W. E. Gladstone). Catholics were hesitant in admitting that Darwin was on the whole right and eagerly welcomed scientific theories that seemed to confirm Genesis. The fact was that in my native country, Scotland, no secondary schools (as far as I know) taught biology in any form at all. Tennessee, at least, raised questions.

Yet the European attitude was not totally unjustified if mere scorn was. The United States after the first world war was facing the problem that began to perplex all societies from the late seventeenth century on. Beginning with France, with the undeclared war between Bossuet and Richard Simon, a central doctrine of the Christian faith—the unique and authoritative character of the version of human history given in the canonical Jewish Scriptures—had been continuously and successfully attacked. The old, orthodox view —the blind reliance on the Bible—was everywhere abandoned, amended, dodged. The crisis that Edmund Gosse described so perfectly for the English nineteenth century, in *Father and Son*, which Matthew Arnold noted and lamented in 'Dover Beach', had at last reached America. (Of course Darwin, the higher criticism, *The Golden Bough* had had their impact long before 1924. The conversion of Harvard to Unitarianism was an old story. Washington was no more an orthodox Evangelical Christian than were Franklin or Jefferson. But such scepticism had not yet become general.)

America was going through that crisis when I arrived in 1925. It was revealed not only in Tennessee but in cities all over the land; every big city had its fundamentalist champion, refuting the 'scientists', and millions of honest souls were going through 'an agonizing reappraisal'—to quote the phrase used in another context by an eminent amateur theologian. In every one of the big private universities, in every state university, the conflict raged. If it did not, it was because the skeleton was locked up in the cupboard, but everybody knew it was there.

In 1957, the case is altered or so it seems. A few months ago, at a highbrow party in Chicago, among people 'liberal' in politics and 'advanced' in the arts, I met a brilliant young architect who after exposing his views on the search for God (it was after midnight, 'they call it the Bourbon hour', as the poet might have put it) asked me for mine. When I replied that I was an agnostic, he said in wonder, 'I didn't think you were as old as that.'

The remark was symptomatic. 'Religion' like many other things is booming in America; it is a blue chip. Indeed, one great contrast between England and America is just that. True in England there has been a revival of interest in religion, something of a return to 'the Church' among the intelligentsia. In France, there is certainly a decline in the old Voltairean hostility to the Church. But neither in France nor in England is this revival, or ripple on the surface of the national life, regarded by prudent churchmen as any compensation for the loss of the masses, who are frankly pagan in France—not even using the Church for births, marriages, deaths—and simply less candid and consistent in England.

America is the country of statistics and we have plenty on the rising role of organized religion. Even the most sceptical will have to accept the fact that more Americans are church members than ever before. Even when it is pointed out that it was far less easy to be accepted as a church member a hundred years ago, that it is now no harder to join a church than a political party and much easier than to join a country club (church membership may substitute sometimes for club membership)—when all this is said, the crude figures are still impressive. In other countries there is a steady attrition of the body of believers; in the United States it grows.

The fact is important—but what is the kind of importance? It can be said to begin with, that even conventional adherence to a church, for highly unspiritual reasons, may have important and possibly good results. There is much wisdom in the saying of Elie Halévy that 'many a man has become a good man as a result of a life of hypocrisy'. Many a faint believer may become a real believer as a result of social conforming which involves joining a church. More, the children of these conformist parents may 'get' religion seriously and the need not to shock the children may strengthen the religious habits, as well as faith, of the parents. Belief is a form of habit.

But, it may be asked, is that all? Is there no revival of faith? There well may be, but I should place doubt, rather than faith, high among the causes of the religious boom. Many church-goers are fugitives from the brave new world of progress, prosperity, temporal happiness that shone so brightly under Coolidge. The catastrophe of 1929, the far greater catastrophe of 1939–45, shook that simple faith. The Depression, the war, the concentration camps, the Russian purges, Hiroshima—the list of horrors is long enough to account for scepticism about the liberating force of Marx, Freud, Henry Ford, John Dewey—to name some of the most important prophets of the past generation. Orthodox religion had preached that these were false prophets; and they certainly proved not to be the sure guides that many thought them to be. Since they were wrong (as experience is held to have proved) perhaps the 'old-time religion' was right?

BUT IS IT TRUE?

At any rate the anti-clericalism of Mencken, Sinclair Lewis, and a host of imitators is now old hat. The average man is ready to listen to the professional religious teacher. And this brings me to the centre of the religious problem.

What are these teachers saying? It is surely surprising, even in so pragmatic a country as the United States, that the question is so seldom raised: Is what these teachers are saying, *true*? If it be said that of course it is true, one is forced to reflect on the fact that the denominations often affirm contradictory things.

I do not take too seriously mere denominational differences as such. I know that in Protestant America, men shift their religious adherence in a free, footloose, pioneering way. The ease with which this is done may surprise a foreigner. He may wonder whether it is really a matter of simple, easy choice to be a Unitarian or a Presbyterian or Episcopalian, he may be struck by the lack of narrow denominational loyalty displayed by the families of William Howard Taft and Adlai E. Stevenson I. But I am ready to admit that the representative American attitude is that of the realtor in Texas who built, among other units in his development, a church and who, when asked what denomination it was for, replied that that would depend on who first made an offer for it.

Yet when all this is said and done, there remains the fact that there is a great gulf, an almost unbridgeable gulf, between a Boston Unitarian who believes, said the wit, 'in one God—at most' and a Catholic or a Jehovah's Witness. For the Catholic or the Witness or the good Presbyterian, this world is but a vestibule, its joys, sorrows, ambitions, failures, successes, to be 'seen ever in the Great Taskmaster's eye'. Christianity may be the most this-worldly of the great religions, but it is far less worldly than the world. Its aim can never be reduced to producing peace of mind, to creating national unity, to providing a substitute for Communist faith, to being an extra arm of 'The Voice of America', a remedy for child delinquency, or easy divorce. It affirms views about the universe: is it blind, hostile, indifferent, friendly?

It seems to me to be foolish simply to say that all Church members 'believe in God'. What God? 'We all believe in one God', I am told, is a favourite musical piece of President Eisenhower's. We know, or think we know, what the world of Johann Sebastian Bach meant by that. What does the world—or the family—of Dwight D. Eisenhower mean by it?

A great deal of the present 'religious revival' is, so it appears to me, political in a very wide sense, where it is not the result of a shocked fear of the world in which we all—agnostics and 'believers' —have to live. There is a marked identification of 'religion' with 'Americanism', which in turn seems so often to mean 'the free enterprise system'.

What are the theological implications of the recent insertion of 'Under God' in the pledge of allegiance to the flag? Partly, no doubt, it is a meaningless evocative phrase, borrowed from the Gettysburg address. Partly it is the deliberate association of God with 'the American Way of Life'. How often has it the meaning Lincoln gave it, the submission of the American way of life to the judgment—to the possible condemnation—of the all-judging and harsh God of the Second Inaugural? Very seldom, is my guess.

The good theologians (and America has more of them than she has had for a long time) know this. It is they who are most sceptical of the value of much of what passes for 'religion'. They worry, wisely, about what harm the adoption of the 'Church' as a service organization by a deeply secular society may do to the life of real religion.

That there is a genuine religious revival I do not doubt; that the churches are not in retreat, as they were a generation ago, I do not doubt. I do doubt if the intellectual truce can be kept up indefinitely, in which few people dare to ask, 'Is this true?' And there is a practical test coming that will be, I think, decisive. If five years from now, in those areas in which organized religion is strongest—that is, the South—desegregation *in the churches* is not pretty nearly complete, I shall take the liberty of doubting the existence of a great spiritual upheaval. If the Catholic bishops of the South have to retreat in, say, New Orleans, before a strike of their white faithful, I shall be distressed but shall again be driven to doubt. The belief in God bred by fear in foxholes is not what the United States needs; something tougher, more firmly based on belief in a divine plan for human destiny, will be required—and in great amounts—if the churches are to be leaders not auxiliaries, commanders-in-chief not mere tolerated chaplains.

THE NEW 'SUCCESS'

Along with the religious revival has been a reassessment of values in this world. I should put the rise in the birth rate first among the symptoms of that change. To decide that a couple need children more than a new car, that a child needs brothers and sisters more than an expensive camp or a 'good' school, is a novelty. You can find in people of my generation either wonder and pleasure at the acceptance of the four-child family by their only child, or an irritated bewilderment at such indecently large families. A big family in modern society is seldom a good material investment. Is it not then important that so many young Americans are making this materially unwise decision?

It is linked with other decisions. One is the decision for leisure rather than for ever-expanding income. The man continually striving loses the chance of leisure. His very recreations are driven by a passion to 'succeed'. (Some doctors think that golf kills more executives than it saves.) But the man who settles down today as a lawyer in a smallish town instead of entering a great law firm in Wall Street or La Salle Street may indulge in such 'un-American' conduct in order to get really relaxed holidays, weekends, evenings, the possibility of 'being with the family', not simply a 'good provider'. A divorce, a son going wrong, a wife with a domestic chaplain in the form of a psychiatrist—these, in the new American climate of opinion, are black marks; the man against whom they are noted is not a complete 'success' in his neighbour's eyes.

The whole idea of 'success', the belief in its possibility, strikes a natural pessimist like me as odd. But there can be no doubt that the American concept of 'success' has widened. We should now want to know more about such idols of the twenties as Henry Ford, Harvey Firestone, Thomas A. Edison than that they produced the Model T, the easily changeable tyre, the electric lamp, or even the phonograph.

For the naïve Horatio Alger attitude is less 'smart' than it was. After all, to climb too hard and too obviously is not the best way to get on in the grey flannel world. There, an old-fashioned aggressive 'success' like Secretary Wilson is an anomaly. (An anomaly that provokes, it might be said, some nostalgic admiration. 'I like

Charlie,' said a Washington newspaperman. 'He's the only man in the Administration who doesn't talk about God.') Few self-made men can resist the temptation to give their sons 'advantages' that they didn't have and those advantages often include an education that alienates the son from his father's simple world. Not long ago, I was accosted in a club car by a Midwest businessman who was in desperate need of comfort. His son, sent to an Ivy League college, had refused to enter the business that this man *had made*, for himself but also for his son. What was wrong with life, with business, with America, when a young man with such a chance wanted to *teach*?

There must be hundreds, thousands of cases like that, personally pathetic, sociologically revealing. The businessman may be—I think still is—the representative American figure. But what is the 'businessman' in 1957? It is almost as ambiguous a term as 'God'.

I shall begin by saying that I am not convinced that a new Platonic class of 'guardians' concerned only for the general good now rules American business and can be trusted—so the implied argument goes—to rule the United States. I don't know the solution to the problem of the relationship of the manager to his stockholders, to the public, to the other managers, to God. Perhaps if he put his duty to his stockholders first (as he does not always do), we should be content. But without believing all that I read in *Fortune*, I do think the American businessman is more 'sophisticated', has more sense of social responsibility—or more realization of the advantages of appearing to have that sense—than he had in 1925.

One consequence is that he is less of a bore. He has wider views; he can see his problems in a wider context and even if he is a true-blue Republican, he realizes that politics and politicians have come to stay. So have union leaders. (Few campaigns backfire more regularly than those designed to liberate the American worker from the 'tyranny of the unions'. The wiser businessman knows this, now.)

The American businessman will never again know the free income or the unlimited respect he got up to the crash of 1929. But most of today's leading businessmen haven't known that income and respect anyway. No Administration, however friendly, can afford to be as uncritically friendly as was the Administration of Coolidge. No great manager will ever know the adulation that was lavished not only on Henry Ford but on much less interesting captains of industry.

Yet the businessman in America has a position and rewards that his English compeer does not dream of. A larger portion of American talent and energy still goes into business than in England (or France). There is still more popular admiration for business achievement, less jealousy of its rewards.

But here lies one of the problems of the American future that most interest and perplex me. In a society in which the old unquestioning acceptance of the business 'life of action' is no longer prevalent—in which a great many young men turn away from business not as something disgraceful, but as something dull without being adequately rewarding—will American business 'tick' just the same? In a world in which General Motors has replaced an individual genius like Henry Ford, in which business success is the product of team work, will the businessman get even the present level of cash rewards? If the businessman has to divide not only power but prestige with the politician, the opinion-moulder, will America change a great deal? If there is under way a deep and genuine religious revival, must it not affect America's secular religion of mere production?

A HOPE UNBETRAYED

The new and puzzling aspects of the America of 1957, as compared to 1925, are problems of education—education in a far deeper and more important sense than the discussions over literacy or technology. The new roles of the soldier, the politician, the businessman —these are the new things in a society that in many ways has changed little in its fundamental premises.

There are other changes in American life that are extensions of the lines visible in 1925. There is, for instance, the new position of the Catholic Church, made manifest not only in numbers and wealth, but in a new intellectual tone. This in turn is an aspect of the rise of a Catholic bourgeoisie which may not yet be represented in the higher ranks of the clergy. The sudden popularity of the contemplative life—the appearance of a book on the function of an order like the Trappists—is something new. One could have foreseen Cardinal Spellman in 1925 but not Father Thomas Merton and not the brave testimony of bishops and orders like the Jesuits against un-Christian racial discrimination.

These changes are more and more part of a world trend in which the United States is the leader. Rock 'n roll, colour TV, a host of material and 'spiritual' gadgets reach us in England just after they have burst on you. Sometimes there is no ground for complaint. Billy Graham is better than Billy Sunday. The whole Western world is involved in a crisis of values that does not seem to me any more acute in the United States than in Europe.

The hopes, beliefs, enthusiasms that I brought to America in 1925 have not been deceived. America, today, is a more interesting, civilized, promising society than it was in that year, and the pursuit of happiness is still less of a waste effort there than in any other country known to me. It is not a race that many people win, but Americans, I think, enjoy the race more than we do. It is the fashion in Europe (and even in America) to sneer at the simple optimism of nineteenth-century America, but if it is not 'the last, best hope of earth', where is that happier and more hopeful land?

1957

8

THE END OF ILLUSION?

The heavens themselves blaze forth the death of princes.

THE SHAKESPEAREAN quotation has been in many minds as, in the past weeks, the satellites have woven their patterns in the skies of the world, demonstrating the power of Russian science and the tenacity and competence of the Russian government. The impact of the Sputnik on the outside world has been great; and it has been great and, at the moment of writing, shows no sign of diminishing in the United States. The impact has been doubly felt by me (the personal note is necessary, not intruded for any reason of self-importance) because my main business, in a more than academic sense, has been, for most of my adult life, studying the American people, their institutions and achievements, and explaining and expounding those achievements and institutions to an often sceptical and sometimes hostile audience in Britain and in other parts of Europe. And for the first time I share, not the hostile emotions of the European intellectuals, but some, at any rate, of their fears. For to me the importance of Sputnik is not mainly in its demonstration of something that I did not doubt, that Russian science and technology were now at an advanced stage, but the revelation that has come in the wake of Sputnik, that many dangerous American illusions are still held—firmly; and this revelation has deepened my fear that in the race for the winning of the minds of the world by hope and by fear, the United States may be a loser. For the first time, in my thirty years' study of the American way of life, I am not convinced that it, at the moment, has what it takes to win this contest. I am convinced that it will prove not to have it if there is not a very fundamental stocktaking that will involve the abandoning of some comforting illusions and, indeed, of some totally justified beliefs that were true, relevant, and comforting only yesterday.

The first illusion is the exterior illusion, and it is the less serious of the two. This was the illusion that in all or nearly all matters of technology, of the application of science, the United States was bound to be ahead, that whatever progress the Soviet Union made, it could not, in the next decisive decade or two, overtake the built-in American lead. The visible superiority of the American economic system lay in producing a higher material level of life. Now, I am aware that this is what the world wants. I have no belief in the alleged Asian demand for more spiritual values, no belief that the ostensible contempt of the European intellectual for the American way of life is shared by the masses in any European country (including Russia). There were doubts about the possibility of American methods producing the same results in a very different social environment, about the existence of the desirable social and legal attitudes in the aspiring populations *at any level*. (Most American criticisms of the European businessman's timidity and restrictive attitude seem to be justified.) There might be hankerings for other, quicker, less liberal ways of access to the promised land. But there was no doubt that America had found one of the ways and, for most people, the best way if other less fortunate (or less deserving) people could set foot on it.

This faith has been shattered. It may seem at first sight odd that the material abundance of the American system can lose its prestige by so uneconomic, unproductive an enterprise as launching a satellite into space. But even allowing for the mere superstitious reverence for 'science' that lumps together, as common benefits, penicillin and radio astronomy, new ways of exploiting this earth and new ways of leaving it, there is another reason why the Soviet success impresses the masses and more than the masses in Europe (and I assume, without any knowledge, in other continents). For the Russian propagandists have been quick to assert that this magnificent if ominous human achievement proves that what the Marxists had asserted is true: that the greatest conquests of the human mind are only possible when the limitations imposed by profit, by decadent capitalism, by the shackles a decaying system of property relations puts upon science, are broken. Once those shackles have been broken, the Communist Adam can enter a new Eden in which plenty, freedom, endless expansion of human possibilities will redeem mankind from labour and subjection, the curse of the first Adam. I am convinced, I always have been convinced, that this is mythology, not established fact or even plausible prophecy. But for millions, tens of millions, this has been a hope painfully weakened by the truth about Russia and about the United States made manifest by the human record of each. Now, like an old-fashioned disciple of the old-time religion welcoming proofs that Genesis was right, after all, many of the disillusioned have taken fresh heart. Perhaps all those dreams were not false, not pie in the sky. Perhaps the way to Paradise is through revolution.

If this were all, I, if I were an American, would be distressed but not alarmed, being rightly confident that the material paradise offered by Communism is, in essentials, a backward version of the present American achievement. Time would tell. But possibly time will not be allowed to tell, for the battle for the minds and hearts of the outside world may be lost in the next year or two, not only because of the revival of faith in Russia, but because of the loss of faith in the United States, not in its promise of material well-being, but in its promise of protection. For the Soviet government gains not only by admiration; it gains by fear. Since 1945, respect for American power has been the chief, at times the sole shield of freedom. Now trust in the efficacy of that shield is weakened. Europe is not merely impressed; it is scared.

Again were this all, it would not be a matter of the highest urgency for the American people. It is a political mistake, seldom paying dividends, to alter successful institutions in pursuit of some problematical improvement; you are more certain to do some harm than likely to do any good. 'Things hang together,' as Montesquieu and Hegel both taught us; and the United States should make no serious changes simply to please allies, or reassure neutrals. It should not pay the Russians the compliment of imitation as a hasty remedy for revealed defect. But this is not all, for what the American people have to reconsider are two basic *American* beliefs, both of them plausible, one much more than that; both of them still largely true; but both of them, at the moment, irrelevant or what is worse, acting as blinkers.

The first of these beliefs is the naïve one that all technical progress, or nearly all, is the work of Americans, that Yankee ingenuity, know-how, innate mastery of tools and machines is what it takes to keep on top and ahead in this competitive world. In many fields of activity this is still true. For various reasons, Americans *do* take to machines, perhaps more to machines than to tools, more easily than do Europeans, much more easily than do Asians or Africans. This, combined with the national impatience with precedent, the readiness to do anything at least once, was one of the secrets of American wealth and power. It still is.

Closely connected with this belief is the respect given to the businessman who is, as a representative figure, the man who organizes the great human and physical resources of the United States to produce the 'American way of life'. It is believed, I think rightly, that the businessman is the representative American; every other kind of American is in some way or other dependent on this basic talent, so that if there is a class or an individual to whom the nation should turn, it is assumed to be the business class or the businessman. Even in war, when trust was put, as it has always rightly been put, in the products of the service academies, it has been recognized that the American way of war was one peculiarly marked by the businessman's methods. This was why it was a victorious way of war. 'The battle is the payoff.' In the Civil War and in two world wars, behind the soldier, the G.I. and the General, stood American industry, vast, wasteful, flexible, supremely confident. I think Allan Nevins is right in asserting that the great businessmen (or 'robber barons' according to taste) were the necessary condition of American victory in the second war. And this, I may say, is a truth that I have uttered, written, asserted on radio and TV, in most countries of Western Europe. If I am frightened now, it is because there is a danger that these two American beliefs, each containing, of course, some illusion as well as much truth, may, if left unexamined, prevent the American people and the American government from making the necessary adjustments to an ugly new world, of which Sputnik is only the symptom and not perhaps the most important symptom.

*

First of all, the American people, innocently beguiled by a too nationalist education as well as by complacent advertising, cannot or up to now have not been able to account for any inferiority of the United States, or any superiority of a rival (or even of an ally), except in terms of treason. Faced with a series of Russian triumphs of which the most important was the testing of the first Russian A-bomb, the American people could only account for the Russian achievement in terms of betrayal: Nunn May, Pontecorvo, Fuchs. Or they simply refused to believe that the, alas, so transitory American monopoly of atomic power had really been lost. Thus Mr. Truman, announcing the truth as President, promptly forgot it and expressed doubt about the truth of what his scientists had told him. In doing this, he was acting as a very ill-advised President, but a very representative American. That there were certain things that you *had* to take on trust from experts who were, for the man in the street—and in the White House—as mysterious figures as so many witchdoctors, was an unpalatable, an un-American truth. That in this new world of atomic physics, many of the old and comforting truths were still true but not relevant was a still more unpalatable truth. And most unpalatable of all, there was the truth that alleged American inferiorities might not be due to treason—but to inferiority. That this could be so, the average American simply could not believe any more than in 1914, even in 1939, the average Englishman could believe that sea power was no longer enough. The American people cried 'treason' and turned to the traditional saviours, the businessman and the professional soldiers and sailors.

Unfortunately, the businessmen and the soldiers and sailors were very American. They too believed that America had built-in superiority. They may not have believed that Edison was *the* great world scientist; they knew that many of the technical discoveries on which the American way of life had advanced were importations from Europe (like the internal combustion engine, the most American of devices but not an American invention). But they were accustomed to a world in which, if they got together, they could not fail to win. That combination had been enough to defeat Lee, the Kaiser, Hitler. It would suffice to defeat Stalin. But not only is Stalin dead; the world has changed so rapidly and in ways so novel to American experience that these comforting traditions are actively dangerous, and the best advice a friendly foreigner can give the American people is to run scared.

*

Few things are less profitable than running scared in the wrong direction. And mere 'crash programmes', mere voting of billions, mere stirring campaigns to arouse opinion, even candid confessions of past error are not enough; they may be worse than nothing. They may breed again the complacency that Sputnik disturbed.

For the American problem will not be solved by more of the old

American methods, energy, money, faith, ballyhoo, confidence, the cheerful adoption of novelty. There will have to be a reconsideration of two basic American attitudes: the American 'pragmatic' attitude to education and the American reverence for the businessman, not *in* business but outside it.

In a very deep sense, the crisis is a crisis of education—and not merely of technical education at any level. There is, first of all, the necessity of giving the American boy and girl a more adequate idea of the outside world, of its power and potentialities. An excessively American viewpoint, a concentration on American achievement at the expense of a balanced picture of the world, breeds the illusions that, for the moment, the Russians have shattered. The reality of the comparatively *limited* achievement of America not only in theoretical but in applied science would be a useful counter to the natural but dangerous boosting of the American achievement that marks American advertising. Thus in the 'week of the Sputnik' I noted an advertisement stressing the achievements of American electrical industries (an advertisement with a strongly 'free enterprise' flavour). It listed sixty gadgets for which the American housewife ought to thank the industry. The implication is that she never had it so good, which is true. I reflected that in my house in Cambridge, England, there were only ten of the sixty gadgets, although we have in addition the un-English device of central heating (an American system at that). But more basic discoveries in science have been made in Cambridge (England) than in the whole United States. Oxford is not only a city of 'dreaming spires' (like New Haven), but the great centre of antibiotic medicine. And so it goes. Until American scientific chauvinsim has been tempered, the American public, innocently enough, will not know what has hit it.

Two things have hit it. Despite the vast expenditure on education in the United States, not nearly enough has been spent. Just in time to meet the Sputnik, the Post Office Department issued a stamp to pay tribute to the teachers of America. 'We asked for bread and they gave us a stamp' might have been the reply of the school teachers if they had not been trained to give thanks for next to nothing.

Of course, more money on education will mean less money for other things. It is possible to suggest the blasphemous thought that there are things more necessary than roads, than freeways, that getting around in a car even faster than before is not the main aim or necessity of the American way of life. More schools, more high schools, better teachers, *above all* better teachers, especially teachers of science in high schools, are a first necessity of American survival. Colleges need more money and more teachers and better teachers than the present going rate will get. And, a harsher truth, no increase in pay or status will provide enough first-class teachers for all the boys and girls of the 'bulge' that will soon pour into the colleges. If everybody is to get an 'equal' college education this means that bright boys and girls will not get a good college education, will not be made adequate to compete with the Russians and other Europeans, if there is not an 'undemocratic bias' in favour of brains. It is too late to insist that a college education is a privilege, but not too late to insist that a first-class college education *is* a privilege. And without going all the way with the critics of existing American pedagogy, I share their view that it is intellectually unambitious, that in the pursuit of happiness and 'adjustment' for the young average, agreeable human beings, it neglects the wrong done to the bright boy who suffers more than many teachers realize from not being stretched enough in his school days. These are commonplaces but they are urgent commonplaces.

And in the panic that may well be upon the American people, there is a danger that quantity may be sought instead of quality. 'Engineer' is an ambiguous term. No doubt more engineers are needed, but far more needed are the basic scientists, the men with the original, questing, unorthodox minds, the men who justify Cromwell's dictum, 'the man goes furthest who does not know where he is going'.

This type of man needs more than money, flattery, appeals to his patriotism. He needs a world, a system in which he feels at home. I don't believe that the American academic world has been totally hag-ridden, has been sterilized by what is roughly called 'McCarthyism'. But it is obvious that the world of the late Senator, of his surviving supporters, his admiring columnists and commentators, his credulous victims in many ranks of society, is a world in which the kind of scientist the United States now needs cannot live or does not want to live. Therefore the encouragement of McCarthyism is one of the causes of the present general malaise and manifest inferiority of some parts of American technical achievement. Those who, for any motive, 'let Joe do it' have, if alive, some duty to decorous silence, if dead are entitled to less than wholehearted praise.

At the danger of seeming egotistical, I want to say that I do not share some of the romantic ideas of the necessarily stabilizing effects of the pursuit of natural science on the judgment, its alleged therapeutic effects in breeding souls 'above all pain, all passion, and all pride'. Scientists are politically (and in other ways) as gullible as, possibly more gullible than, the next man. They are not necessarily devoted to liberal and humane ideas. Most American rocketeers served Hitler faithfully; we have seen what the Soviet physicists have done for that odious régime. An acute student of the genus, H. G. Wells, noted the admiration of the pre-1914 English scientists for imperial Germany, where the scientist was given what he needed (including flattery) and where Du Bois-Reymond spoke for most of his colleagues when he said they were proud to be 'the academic guard of the House of Hohenzollern'. All we know about a man when we learn that he is a first-class physicist is that he is a first-class physicist. We may make a guess that he is more likely to be interested in chamber music than in baseball, but we could be and often would be wrong. But first-class physicists are rare, have to be cherished, pampered, flattered, allowed to be queer ducks. They are not the type most cherished in West Point or Grosse Pointe or, indeed, in Congress. But there they are; the necessary men. And at the risk of being thrown out of the union, I am prepared to face the implication that not only is a first-class physicist more valuable and worth more money than a first-class political scientist, but that even a second-class one is. All that I should insist on is the truth that his eminence in physics or the higher engineering does not give his political views any weight outside his narrow speciality. He is not entitled to that kind of reverence any more than is a man who has been getting $500,000 a year as head of a great corporation.

*

For the most dangerous American illusion is that the businessman, as such, is omnicompetent. The American who asserts that what he admires in the millionaire is not wealth but wealth as proof of achievement, is usually telling the truth and making a valid distinction against the mere money worship of Europe. But the achievements he admires may be irrelevant to the problems facing the United States today. They were highly relevant to the problem of defeating Hitler. They are relevant to the problem of equipping and planning the 'conventional arms'. But they are not relevant, they

may be positively dangerous when it comes to the problems of the
new war, the war of H-bombs, of intercontinental missiles, of a
voyage around the outer spaces of the earth or to the moon.

First of all it should be noted that the utility of the businessman
in conventional war was limited. He supplied 'all that and the
kitchen stove', but the decision where and how and when to use the
hardware was, at one level, that of the political heads of the states,
Roosevelt, Churchill, and, at a lower level, that of the military and
naval chiefs, Marshall, King, Eisenhower, Alexander, and the rest.
The businessman was an aid not a boss; he was the hired man (at a
dollar a year), not the employer. For the great questions of policy, of
strategy, the great political 'art of the possible', for the inspired guess
of the soldier of genius about what was 'on the other side of the hill',
the businessman had no special competence. Indeed, he had some
disabilities. For business is more rational, sensible, predictable than
war.

War is uneconomic; it is an anti-economic activity. War is a continuation of politics, not of business; and if war is conceived of as
being a special form of business, that concept leads to defeat. It is a
good thing when a soldier goes about the business side of his business like a businessman. Colonel Charles Lowell was right in admiring that trait in Philip Sheridan (that is what made Sheridan a better
soldier than Stuart). But in battle, Sheridan, or any other great
captain, is something other than a businessman; there is an element
of irrationality and passion in war that is an affront to the business
(and to the academic) mind. 'A reasonable army would run away',
so the Germans profoundly put it. And army morale is maintained
by methods, improved by rituals, that don't make sense to a businessman unless he is a businessman of exceptional width of imagination, unless he is what we call, for the want of a better word, a
statesman. No soldier could be more of a businessman, more con-
temptuous of the 'pride, pomp, and circumstance of glorious war'
than was the Duke of Wellington unless it was Frederick the Great.
But each knew the irrational element of honour, pride, passion, the
fanaticism of discipline or patriotism, none of them qualities of much
use in business, indispensable in war.

More relevant to the present problem is the businessman's
dilemma when faced with the waste of war and of preparation for
war. No doubt there is a place for the use of business talents in pre-
venting waste, in cutting the fat off the military establishment, in

seeing that the soldier can get there 'first with the most'. But a businessman, as such, is no better judge than anybody else of what hardware is needed, how it is to be used, what the final choices are to be. The fact that he has 'met a payroll' is neither here nor there. It may indeed be a handicap.

For meeting a payroll is simply a democratic and dramatic way of saying that a businessman has to keep his company in the black. He has other duties as a citizen, as a church member, as a father, and so on. As a businessman his duty is solvency and expansion, but above all, solvency. Henry Ford had other grounds of superiority over Durant than his ability to keep in the black, but in the rivalry between General Motors and Ford that is what counted. Consequently the successful businessman does not and should not prefer the remote best to the present better or, for that matter, the national interest or the social good to the solvency of his firm. He has duties as a citizen, but he has no duty to ruin his company for the national good unless the case is very plain. I doubt if it often is as plain as that. It certainly would not be plain to me if I were head of a great corporation. The great businessman, like the statesman, has special duties that debar him from exercising some virtues. He has, of course, to keep within the law and within the general principles of ethics, but it is not his business to decide between the good for General Motors and the good for the United States. But the converse is that he should not be asked to choose. As a successful business executive serving his country, he is to bring to his job all the skills he has acquired in his business training. But it is naïve to expect that they will always include or even often include the basic qualities which are those of a statesman.

Thus it would be foolish of a great automobile company to go on producing a rational car when experience (and the success of rivals) has shown that what the public demands is not so much a car as costume jewellery, bustles and falsies, chrome, and gadgets. But the natural and defensible attitude of the business magnate is fatal in the servant of the United States. For the United States needs and must have many things (atomic submarines, missiles, artificial moons, basic research) for which there is no ordinary demand. The welfare, the safety of the United States is not an aggregate of private demands, even of private demands by great corporations. It is something bigger, different, at times hostile to good business practice. And business education—that is, the practice of business—often narrows

the mind, deprives it of that flexibility in presence of the new, the
unknown, the uneconomic that is what the United States now needs.

For the danger in which the United States now finds itself, many
people can but won't claim a share in the blame. If McCarthyism is
one of the causes of the present crisis, 'liberal' gullibility is one of the
causes of McCarthyism. The alleged cure was worse than the disease
but there was a disease. If the Eisenhower Administration disarmed
dangerously, so did the Truman Administration between 1948 and
1950. If businessmen executives starved research, Congress spent
nearly as much money on supporting the price of cheese as on
ballistic research. But the illusion that has done the most damage has
been the business illusion, that government is merely business mag-
nified or, if you like, that government is an inferior form of business.
Motherhood is a messy and inferior method of reproduction compared with the assembly line, but the assembly line is no substitute
for mothers. Paradoxically, small, specialized business is not only
more useful in a crisis like this, but the habits of mind it breeds are
more useful. The mass market breeds the mind that caters to the
mass market and there is no mass market for guided missiles.

It is, I believe, an error to think that what the United States needs
is more business in government. It needs more government (and of
course better government). Some controversies like those over the
Bricker Amendment and over school segregation are too bitterly
funny in the present age to be productive of easy laughter. (It is,
however, one of the hopeful signs of the times that the American
irreverent sense of humour is fully at work.) The mere illiterate
depreciation of the Russian achievement, the vulgar assertion that
the Russians might have Sputnik but the Americans have washing
machines, has nearly died away. Such very different organs of public
opinion as the Hearst press, the Scripps-Howard press, and the
New York *Herald-Tribune* have talked relevant and painfully candid
good sense. As for the others, the peevish columnists who find it
hard to show that the 'Commies stole this one', the rabbinical commentators on the Fourteenth Amendment, the neo-conservatives
caught with their dogmas down, one need only quote an astro-
nomically-minded egghead:

> *Non ragionam di lor ma guarda e passa.*

But the situation is still ominous and it will get worse if the forces
in society, caught short and at a loss, not clear why things have gone

wrong, should rally to defend the old and once-justified way of doing things. It will be disastrous if too much attention is paid to reassuring the public mind. All that advertising prose, colour photography, TV and radio oratory can do to save America has been done. It is not enough. There must be a realization of the existence of war (cold or hot) and of its necessities. Business as usual, the march to battle under the dollar sign will be fatal.

Since the crisis began I have been haunted by an historical memory. I do not believe in the binding historical precedent, in the one clue to the fall of the Roman Empire being the clue to the salvation of the United States. But analogous situations sometimes cast an indirect light, show up our own prepossessions. There was once a great and exceedingly flourishing state, run by businessmen who knew very well how to meet a payroll, with political institutions designed to keep authority in the right hands. (These institutions were much admired by Aristotle.) It was not a society much given to the arts, to speculation, to innovation in anything but business; but it could buy ideas, techniques, as it hired soldiers. It dominated the economic life of its world as the United States does ours. Across its path to more business, to more profits, there thrust itself a backward, rural, conservative state, poor and greedy, convinced that there were more ways of getting wealth than by earning it. This state was even more indifferent to new ideas than was its rival. It sacrificed most graces of life to a dour discipline that made the state the worshipped god. Seeing where its rival's power lay, in the command of the sea that both made possible the profits and guarded them, this rural society set about learning. Its clumsy peasant soldiers were set to learn to row on land. When their ships at last put to sea, they were the victims of ludicrous disasters, some caused by incompetence, some by mere superstition. But they won command of the sea and after that not even Hannibal could save Carthage. Which thing is a parable and no more. But what the United States needs, today, far more than businessmen, is statesmen conscious of the bitter truth that the survival of the United States is in danger—and that in this duel the United States no longer has the choice of weapons.

1958

9

CITIZENSHIP IN THE UNITED STATES

THE UNITED STATES is unique among the nations of the Western world in having not only a specific birthday (Switzerland and Canada have that), but a birthday followed by what can be called a confirmation ceremony in which the newborn child of 1776 was given, in 1787, a charter of powers and a standard of behaviour, and, among the political concepts of that charter, was the concept of citizenship. Constitutional amendments, judicial interpretation have given to the idea of 'a citizen of the United States' a legal concreteness which is not only lacking in the idea of a British subject, but is lacking in the idea of a French citizen, since France has undergone, since 1789, so many revolutions and has endured so many contradictory interpretations of the rights and duties of a citizen.

It is not only a fact that the concept of a citizen is basic in the history of the United States, but there has been from the beginning a concept and problem of dual citizenship, for the citizen of the United States has also been a citizen of a given State (we can disregard the transitory ambiguities of territorial citizenship), and there has been—and is—a conflict of right and obligation between the citizen of the United States and the citizen of the States which together constitute the Union.

Then the American governmental system is openly based on the free assent by the consenting citizen to a specific form of government defined by state constitutions and by the Constitution of the United States. As Lord Acton pointed out, by basing all governmental powers on the consent of the governed, by starting afresh in 1776 or in 1787, the American people, or, if you prefer it, the people of the

States, opened a new era in history in which political authority was delegated from the bottom up, and in which no appeal was made to tradition or to the authority of the accomplished fact.

There is, of course, an element of fiction in this view of American constitutional law. What the colonists did in asserting their independence was deeply conditioned by history, above all by the history of England. Nevertheless, the American, then and now, is, formally at least, a citizen of two bodies politic based on free choice and based on specific legal documents creating and defining rights and duties.

American historical experience has made it difficult for Americans to *revere* any given embodiment of political authority. Even if the American people are deeply loyal to the American way of political life, the creation of new states, the astonishing mobility of the population, the influx, until quite recent times, of great masses of immigrants from Europe, have all combined to make the organization of political consent and political loyalty a continuing problem, not one to be taken for granted or assumed to have been solved in the distant past.

Nowhere has the American genius for practical politics been better displayed than in the handling of this problem. Contrary to the hopes and expectations of the founding fathers, the United States under the new Constitution very rapidly developed a national party system, and there can be few intelligent commentators on the American past and present who do not see in the national parties one of the great sources of nationality, and one of the practical ways of creating political obedience in a society so diversified in climate, racial origin, and local tradition.

Thus sectional loyalties, spontaneously created by geographical conditions and by local and powerful traditions, as in New England, have been tamed by the national party system. Thus the most easily identifiable section, the South, marked off by climate, by its basic economy, by the special character of its population, black and white, has been, except for a brief interval, kept national by the party system. For these reasons, the parties play a role in organizing and defining citizenship and in giving their members an opportunity to fulfil duties and exercise rights that seem, from a European point of view, extraordinary or even excessive. Few things more surprise a European observer of the American political system than the degree to which the internal life of parties is regulated by law. You cannot separate the idea of the citizen and the idea of the party voter. The totally independent voter, the mugwump, is an essential part of the American picture of citizenship, and many mugwumps are the salt of the earth. But it may be safely said that the United States cannot afford too many mugwumps, and that the docile voter who votes the straight ticket is not the 'idiot' of highbrow criticism, but the representative American citizen. Thanks to the primary system, he is not in fact quite as docile or as blind or as tradition-ridden as some critics assert. It could be argued (and I should argue it) that the American citizen has in fact a freer choice of representatives and really a more effective voice as far as the personnel of politics is concerned than has his English or French brother.

Then the American citizen as a mere voter or as a party voter is a member of a society in which every form of organization is tolerated or encouraged and in which every form is in competition with every other form. This truth struck Tocqueville very forcibly and, thinking of a France in which non-state activity was frowned on, he rejoiced. True, in the England of Tocqueville's time, free organization was almost as common and as much a national passion as it was in America; but if English law and custom were very tolerant of private organizations, English law and custom favoured some organizations over others. There was a State Church with important formal and some real privileges; there were State institutions professing to establish standards in the arts and sciences; there were hereditary institutions like the House of Lords. There was an undefinable but real social atmosphere in which certain types of societies were superior to others, and certain groups in society had prescriptive rights to precedence and respect. In America, not only were all men equal, but all societies were equal. George Washington totally failed to induce Congress to set up a national university. John Quincy Adams totally failed to make the federal government a patron of learning and science. The puny remnants of church establishment in New England were being swept away in Tocqueville's time. New colleges, new societies, new social phenomena like the lyceum movement were all in earnest and sometimes in bitter competition for the attention, the funds, and the respect of the average American. Even more than in England, far more than in England, the American citizen had his possibilities of action defined for him by private societies. If it was unrealistic to think of the citizen as exercising his rights apart from the party system, it was equally unrealistic to think of him as exercising his rights apart from the churches, the colleges, the societies for promoting this and that, and even the infant and not very robust trade union movement. More than that, the great wave of feeling rather than doctrine which we call the Jacksonian revolution not only swept away such a centralizing and normative institution as the Bank of the United States; it made political authority more popular but less impressive by the full development of the spoils system, of rotation in office, and of nearly universal election to executive and judicial posts. For it was assumed by Jackson (as later by Lenin) that any citizen could carry out any administrative job, and that the more citizens who got the chance to do this, the healthier the state of the Republic.

There was perhaps more to be said for this innocent view in a pre-industrial age than there is today. But it is quite obvious that a society based on this optimistic view of the potentialities of the average man was very different from that of France, with its professional bureaucracy, or from that of the mainly amateur government of England based on an unquestioned system of social hierarchy. The American citizen was assumed to be able to do more than the British subject. He was also asked to do more.

For one consequence of the democratic revolution in the United States was to impose on the voter a series of burdens unequalled since the civic life of the old city states. Thus the primary system, given the fundamental importance of the party system, was an indispensable reform, especially in a one-party area like the South; but the primary system imposes on the American voter a far greater burden of choice than is imposed on the English or French voter.

When in addition to the mere election of all kinds of public officers from the local dog-catcher to the President of the United States, and the rehearsal of these elections imposed by the primary system, there is added the burden, in many states, of voting on 'propositions' submitted to referendum or on State constitutional amendments, one must have sympathy for the American citizen who, unlike the Athenian citizen, has much more to do than vote and, unlike the Athenian citizen, is not paid for carrying out his political obligations. If it is true, as it is true, that the American does not vote as dutifully as the Englishman or the Frenchman, he has this excuse, that he is asked to vote far more often, and is asked to exercise his judgment in ways from which the Englishman and the Frenchman are totally excused.

If even the American federal system imposed excessive burdens on the citizen and made excessive demands on his virtue and vigilance, until quite recent times it demanded little more than this political service. Federal taxation was light; federal legislation seldom affected the man in the street. Nor indeed were the duties of the good citizen primarily those he owed to the Union. The reform movements of the late nineteenth and early twentieth centuries were primarily state and civic movements. If 'turn the rascals out' was an adequate programme for the good citizen, the rascals were usually in the city hall or in the state capitol. It was quite natural to think of the States (as Bryce did) as laboratories of social and political experiment, and a good citizen might adequately fulfil his political obligations almost entirely in terms of his duty as a citizen of a State. And even that most burdensome function of the state, heavy in England and much heavier in France, the burden of national defence, meant little to the average American. He might never see a warship and might, indeed, seldom see a soldier.

It is one of the truths of comparative politics which it is always timely to recall that political habits long survive the conditions which produced and justified them, and I think it is true that many Americans, even in 1960, live by the ideas and wish for the institutions of the period before the world war of 1914. But there is no chance of getting back to the days of Wilson, and still less to the days of Mr. Jefferson; and the beginning of wisdom for the American citizen today is to realize that his most important duties and his most important rights lie in the sphere of federal government.

There are several reasons for this state of affairs. The integration of the economy begun by the completion of the railway system and fostered by such federal institutions as the tariff and the Federal Reserve System would, in any case, have extended federal power and diminished state autonomy. But the speed with which federal power and federal burdens were increased owed a great deal to the impact of war. The First World War created a national debt on an unprecedented scale. The necessities of war forced on the federal government the exercise of many powers which might, in other circumstances, have remained those of the States—at any rate, for a decade or so longer. Even the attempt to return to 'normalcy' in 1921 was doomed to failure. The decision to go back to a high tariff in a world in which the United States was a creditor, not a debtor, was a decision, for good or ill, affecting the whole of the economy. The decision to commit the federal government to a close control of and support of the railway system was irreversible. The beginning of an elaborate system of grants-in-aid, e.g. for roads, meant that the citizen began to expect to receive from the federal government services he had hitherto demanded from the States. The trust policy of the federal government, effective or ineffective, impinged on the whole economy. And although the Supreme Court oscillated in its decisions about federal economic power, the trend was in favour of the extension of the powers of the Union.

But whatever the possibilities of limiting federal action were in the postwar boom, they disappeared in the Depression. States became insolvent; cities became insolvent. The national sickness was truly national. The policy of relief and redress had to be national too. The trend is visible even in the last years of the Hoover administration. The New Deal undertook to administer a national policy and to enter spheres of legislation and administration hitherto left to the States or to private enterprise, the enterprise of business or the enterprise of charity. Despite the serious efforts made to enlist the States as partners of the Union, efforts that were in detail often successful, power passed irretrievably to the Union. The citizen, whether he liked it or not, was now enmeshed in the federal system, and it was not often that state government mattered as much to him as federal policies did. He asked for more from the Union; he got more. But the federal government also demanded more. The social security number became not only a proof of the benevolence of the federal government, but a mark of its intrusion into the centre of the citizen's economic life. And the income tax and the other tax burdens laid by the federal government eclipsed those laid by the States at least as much as federal services eclipsed those offered by the States.

Again, war accelerated a process that was going on in any case. The degree to which the federal government had undertaken to manage the national economy in the First War was immensely increased in the Second. The citizen got used to being organized and ordered about by the federal government. For a great many of the problems that now afflicted the citizen, the only political remedy, if there was one, was in Washington.

For example, it was very largely by federal legislation and federal administration that the trade unions became organizations of the first order. The unification of the economy tended in any case to bring about a unification of the labour market, but federal legislation (demonstrated in wages and hours legislation) put the power of the federal government behind this unification.

Inevitably, this extension of federal power affected both the theory and the practice of citizenship. If the federal government did not, as yet, regulate elections in the States, the courts banned some forms of state autonomy, e.g. the white primary. The most enthusiastic defender of States' rights, if he reflected in cold blood on what the voters wanted, knew that in many cases they could get it only by federal action, or possibly by federal and state action in collaboration. The basic and minimum conditions of social action by government authority were laid down by the federal government, and if state government in many places remained healthy and interesting, it was no longer true that States could determine by themselves how much or how little they would do in the general field of social security and social legislation. The farmer, dependent on a parity payment, was no more independent of federal action than the worker, enrolled in a union fostered or supported by federal legislation, and relying on unemployment payments in part determined by federal policy. The federal government took not only the cream, but much of the milk of tax revenue. And peace turned out not to be quite peace. The Cold War not only meant an almost intolerably high level of federal taxation, but it meant the perpetuation in peace of military conscription, the exercise of a sovereign power that no State had ever claimed.

And the States themselves, however much they might protest against federal usurpation, were in fact affected by the climate of opinion and by the range of federal action. Few States, even in the fields in which they were still effective, could take a hands-off position. Both as a federal voter and as a state voter, the elector came to expect much more from political action than he had done as late as the beginning of Wilson's first term. And in such a world the citizen had new duties, new obligations, new rights, for which the traditional doctrines of the Fathers provided an inadequate guide.

That those doctrines would be inadequate would not have surprised the wiser Founding Fathers. Few of them would have been surprised at the new stresses and strains imposed on a Union far greater in area than any they had foreseen and far more implicated in the affairs of the outside world than any of them could have feared. That the traditional liberties of the Americans would be in novel danger in this new world, these prudent men would have foreseen; that they could be preserved by a mere blind faithfulness to the customs of the ancestors neither Hamilton nor Madison would have believed for a moment.

What are some of the necessary adjustments that must be made? One is implicit in what I have already said of the new impact of the government, state and federal, on the citizen and on the economy. It was natural and perhaps it was also right to assume in the great days of the makers of 'Big Business' that the businessman was the representative American, the most useful American. There is a great deal to be said for this view and there was more to be said in the past. It was natural to see politics and politicians as auxiliaries of business, not as equal partners and still less as masters. Of course, it was a fiction, even then, to think of business as operating in a vacuum. The world that it transformed was a world defined by law and deeply affected by the policies of the federal if not of the state governments, by tariffs, by land policy, by railway policy, by monetary policy. Business and businessmen did not neglect politics; they used it.

Even in the golden age, the role of the political order was basic. The greatest business magnates could not have worked their wonders in a less great and less rich territory than that of the United States. The long immunity from external war, the complete establishment of the authority of the United States as a result of the Civil War, these were political preconditions of the creation of the business empire. So was the American climate of opinion that both rewarded, materially, on a scale unprecedented in history and gave credit as well as cash, admiration as well as prodigious fortunes. It provided also the necessary auxiliaries, the hundreds of thousands who aided the captains of industry, the millions who were more or less content with the social and political system.

Already, the primordial importance of politics had been insisted on by Theodore Roosevelt. If he did nothing else as President (and of course he did a great deal), he insisted that the government of the United States was not simply another type of corporation, doing business with J. P. Morgan on equal terms. It had a greater power and a greater and nobler responsibility than any corporation, however big, could have.

That this was true ought to have been evident but it was one of the curious 'archaic' features of the twenties that an attempt was made to return, in more than in foreign policy, to simpler days. It was a time when President Coolidge said that 'the business of the United

States is business' and although he probably did not mean what the public crudely assumed that he meant, his dictum was revealing. It was the age in which Henry Ford I got an adulation that none of his predecessors in the business world had ever known and was, despite his manifest unfitness, seriously talked of for President of the United States.

But that dream world came to an end in 1929 and the basic importance of the political order was brutally insisted on. Perhaps the economy would have recovered by itself in the long run; but, as Keynes put it, 'in the long run we are all dead', and the American people were not willing to wait for a recovery that not all could be confident they would live to see. Something quicker was wanted and only government, only the federal government, could provide it. The impact of the new 'social service' state has already been dwelt on. What needs emphasis here are the direct political results and their impact on the rights and duties of the citizen.

In the first place, there is a neglect of what was the most important service performed by the politicians during this disastrous era of faith shattered and hope daily dwindling. This was the preservation in the mind of the average American of trust in the general benevolence of the American way of life. It might not be giving all that it had promised, but somewhere in the system there was a remedial power. And that power was political.

I do not think that this truth can be effectively denied, yet there is in the American attitude to the politician an ironical admiration that allows for the need for politicians, but does not insist on any automatic admiration or formal respect for them (the slightly sneering character of the word is itself significant). There are good historical reasons why this should be so. If Jackson was right and any citizen could fill any job, or nearly any job, it would be very foolish to expect, and indeed undesirable to achieve, a general atmosphere of respect for politicians as such.

But if this is so, it does not follow that a casually superior attitude to the function of the politician is equally natural and equally admirable. Yet the belief that the politician, the employee of the State, of the Union, is necessarily an inferior type of American to the go-getter who has 'met a payroll' is a dangerously widespread attitude among Americans who regard themselves, with a fair degree of justice, as good citizens. A politician is not thought of as being serious, as a businessman or a professional man is. Again, there are historical explanations of this attitude. The spoils system was not likely to produce an official class marked by technical competence. More important, the belief which once had some justification, that the politician was not performing any fundamental functions, justified contempt both for the function and the functionary. If what he did didn't matter very much, it didn't matter very much who did it.

The consequences may be, indeed are, serious at more than one level. It may not matter a great deal that rural government in many areas is still unreformed, the province and the perquisite of the 'court house gang'. But as the economy gets more and more integrated, the inefficiency, the archaic character of local government at that level will lead to its atrophy. And a respected system of local government at the grassroots has been basic to the American concept of citizenship. The immediate business of the community *should* be done by those in immediate touch with the people affected. The local community *should* produce the local leaders; but if those local leaders are visibly inadequate for the demands of this age, the grass is poisoned at the roots, and the result of the poisoning is the replacement of the county or the town by the State. And it is not quite impossible that there may be replacement of the town and the county by some federal office.

The same problem can be found at all levels of the governmental system. The claims of a candidate for office are often enough weighed in very different scales from the claims of an applicant for a private job or the claims of a businessman for leadership in the business community. It should of course be plain that for many political jobs, the rational grounds for election or appointment may not be the same, cannot be the same, as those which are valid in the business world. The candidate whom the critically 'good' citizen can vote for with hope and confidence may inspire that hope and that confidence by qualities very different from those of a successful corporation executive. Even in these days of public relations and of the importance attached to the public image of the firm, the place of persuasion is higher in politics than in business.

The politician must organize consent and support where a businessman, however politely, is giving orders. And so the politician must be pardoned many tricks of the trade, many examples of bogus geniality, many exhibitions of democratic 'friendliness' that a businessman or a professional man has neither the time nor the need for.

But a society in which the politician does nothing but organize personal popularity, win personal support, gain consent for trivial or private issues is not a healthy political society and voters who tolerate or encourage so mechanical and empty a conception of the democratic process are not good citizens.

It always mattered a bit that mere play actors, mere playboys, could sometimes have their theatrical talents rewarded by high office. In the political America of today there are few jobs that the good citizen can afford to treat frivolously, even if only because every job so treated involves the whole political system in some degree of discredit.

It is true that the States are not so effectively autonomous as they were, that forces whose power cannot be evaded reduce their freedom of action. But the States are still political organizations that for good or ill affect the lives of the citizens and often can make or mar the political health of the community. It is therefore unfortunate when so great a representative and so great an executive office as that of governor is won by demagogy or allowed to go by default to some exploiter of frivolous issues treated as part of a game or of grave issues treated as part of a melodrama. It is one of the misfortunes of the segregation issue that it makes the second role so tempting and so profitable, makes the still small voice of reason so hard to hear, and permits the weakening of the prestige and long-term efficacy of the most important state office.

I am assuming that it is desirable to keep as much life in the state system as possible. In a country the size of the United States, with such varying regional needs and traditions, a failure of state government can only result in the extension of federal bureaucracy. I say federal bureaucracy rather than federal power, since because of the size of the country, federal power could only be exercised bureaucratically. It could not be exercised by and through Congress. And whatever technical advantages such a system might bring about (and some state government is so much behind the times that I can conceive of some advantages accruing from a federal assumption of power), the politically disastrous effects would be great indeed. It would mean the overloading of the federal system to a dangerous degree and what is more to the point in our context, the exclusion of the citizen from a determining voice in many fields of political action that concern him deeply.

But the enemy of the preservation of effective state power and so of the opportunities open to the citizen for service is not only the demagogue, not only the exploiter of an inflammable issue. It is always dangerous to the health of the body politic when the claims to authority are palpably fictitious. And in American state government, there is another deeply embedded weakness that will more and more undermine the moral claims of state government to respect and already has created a class of second-class citizens. It is notorious that, in most States, the allocation of seats in one house and in some States the allocation of seats in both houses defies the principle of 'one man one vote'. That principle is not absolute. There is a case for weighting representation to secure the rights, even the privileges, of groups that might be threatened by a rigorous system of arithmetical allocation of seats. This principle is enshrined in the system of election to the Senate of the United States and, to a lesser degree, in the system of electing the President of the United States. It is true that the letter and the spirit of the Constitution are both sinned against by the refusal of many States to redistrict, but the House is reasonably representative all the same and the President does embody the choice of the majority of the American people in a way that makes the office a force for national union.

In the States, however, there is no such redress for the inequitable allocation of seats, sometimes reflected in the system of election for governor. It is not a matter of protecting a small minority from the aggression of a majority but of securing the minimum rights of the majority. And as it is the rural counties that gain by this system and as the most urgent problem of American politics today is to find institutions suitable to an urban society in a technological age, these absurd systems of representation are not only among the chief obstacles to efficient government, but by the obstacles they put in the way of effective political action they serve to depress the civic spirit of even the most tenacious and the most worthy voters. A state power based on a rotten borough system is a weak reed to lean on in the war for the preservation of the local basis of American government.

Equally important, in the not very long run, will be the continued evasion of the federal Constitution and of the spirit of American constitutional principles inherent in making the right to vote a matter of race. It would be absurd not to notice that the failure to secure to every American citizen the right to vote on the same terms as his neighbour is a weakness to America in the cold war. I am more concerned to stress that it is a weakness in the theory and practice of citizenship in the States, as well as a constant temptation to and a constant justification of federal intervention. For the arguments that are used, today, to justify the practical exclusion of the Negro from the ballot in a state like Mississippi prove too much. They deny the democratic premises that men (and women) should have a voice in the making of the laws that they must obey. The implication that one group can be trusted to look after the needs of another ignores not only the fact that they may not know and may not feel the needs, but that a third outside party may be, on these terms, a better judge of needs and legitimate feelings than any of the parties immediately concerned. A defence of States' rights based on a denial of equal suffrage is a dangerous weapon indeed for the preservation of local autonomy!

In the same way, the use, the threat, of violence, the encouragement of an attitude of inflexible resistance to what has been declared the law of the land, however tempting, is not only an example of dangerously bad citizenship, but an occasion of it in others. Civil order is a seamless web, torn at great risk and hard to repair.

It is easy enough to point out how absurd it is for people of Maine and Texas to vote for the same national ticket for reasons that have nothing to do with current issues, but a lot to do with the dramatic and traumatic historical experiences of a century ago. The independent, intelligent, honest elector whom we have been taking as our norm is often baffled when he casts his national ballot for a ticket of which he knows little. He helps by his vote to produce a congressional majority whose effective authority will be in the hands of committee chairmen of whom he knows nothing, chairmen who can ignore the party platform on which, formally, the presidential candidate has run. There is nothing to be said for this system except that it does elect Presidents who have adequate moral authority; it does make possible a fairly effective minimum of authority in Congress so that some business can be done; and that it has, save in the case of one catastrophe, always succeeded in keeping the people of the United States from asking passionate and profound questions that might wreck the whole system.

Yet the artificial character of the American party system presents problems for the citizen and for the Republic. The existence of 'solid' areas, not only the Solid South but the Solid North-east, has distorted politics, since it has meant the crushing together in the same party structure of voters with widely differing, indeed deeply opposed, points of view, interests, and sentiments. Tempered by the primary system, the one-party States have managed to get along without any finally fatal disasters and, indeed, were only state politics involved, the situation might not deserve much attention. But state politics are involved with national politics and it is the American citizen who is bewildered, at the national level, by the ambiguous character of the national verdict. It is one thing, and a dangerous thing, to insist on a rigorously doctrinal party system operating uniformly all over the Union and another to accept without question a party system that has *no* grounds of unity except historical tradition.

Yet there are signs that the old purely historical, purely sectional party system is giving way to one more adapted to the needs of modern America. In an age when there are not only Republican Congressmen from the South, but when the sole Congressman from Vermont is a Democrat, there is no need to despair! More important still, the spread of the modern industrial economy over all of the Union makes the survival of the old sectional attitudes less likely even if, as far as they still survive, they are still more anachronistic. The car, the truck, the bus, the aeroplane all work for a more perfect union. And what is the role of the citizen in this more perfect union?

It is surely to cut himself free from the old automatic allegiances. As long as 'talking for Buncombe' pays off, so long will politicians on the national scene talk local bunkum. Yet the number of times that, in contemporary America, there *is* some overwhelming local interest that the politician must and should promote at any cost, is small. The habit of considering the federal politician simply as a local agent is, in many cases, a traditional survival that has not any very deep roots even in material interest. To send and keep on sending a man back to Washington because he serves local interests with blind fidelity and never lifts his eyes, or his nose, from the claims of his district, is to abdicate the responsibility of a citizen in a world where the efficiency and prestige of the American governmental system are important items in the world's balance sheet.

This is not to assert that the voter should pay no attention to local issues. I have already suggested that in state and local politics he ought to pay more, be more selective, more ready to provide the conditions under which alone local government can flourish. More than that, the solution or non-solution of local problems not only affects the total health of the United States, but affects its position in world opinion. A good PTA is an asset, as is a good hospital system or a good library system. The rising tide of youthful violence is not confined to the United States. But the United States is the great exemplar and failures there are heard round the world. No one can be content with a system in which future citizens, not all of them, by any means, underprivileged, so often show an automatic reliance on violence. And in a society so threatened and so plagued, again the seamless web of public order is torn, for whatever motive, at a very great risk. The political education that the future voter receives at home, the degree to which the boy or girl is encouraged to be law-abiding or to express his passions, his most sacred feelings, if you like, in violence, is basic to the problem of effective citizenship in the modern world.

There remains one last duty of the citizen and of his political representative, his duty, the duty of all Americans to the world. One of the most remarkable and encouraging features of the modern world has been the readiness of the American people to recognize and accept duties outside their own boundaries. Looking back at the troubled years since 1945, when the American people learned that the most complete military victory did not necessarily bring peace, bearing in mind the long hold of isolationism on the American mind, especially in the mind of the American as voter, as elected person, one is entitled to be both surprised and deeply impressed by the acceptance by the American people of the new role history has imposed on it.

It is easy enough to show, and it is often a comforting exercise for a European to indulge in, to assert that in being generous in money and goods, in undertaking new burdens and new obligations not enumerated in the bond of the United Nations, the American people has been pursuing its own enlightened self-interest. It has, but how many nations are always capable of pursuing their self-interest or seeing it or having enough self-control to postpone immediate gains to long-term aims? Certainly in the past, the American people, like the British or the French, has not always shown this selfish mini-mum wisdom, to its own loss and to that of the world.

That Americans have done so now should be a matter for un-reserved rejoicing. But it is my conviction that they have done more than that, that had they only been concerned with their self-interest, they would not have seen it so clearly. There has been among the motives for American international good citizenship much more than a prudential desire to restore the world to health, since a sick world is dangerous, more than a desire to find and keep militarily useful allies. There has been what the Quakers call a 'concern', a belief that the American people should not pass by the wayside. No doubt the thought that the Soviet Union might turn up performing the role of the Good Samaritan to some degree influenced the Americans, but they were more moved by the tradition that insisted that they *should* be Good Samaritans. And they were also moved, I believe, by a feeling, possibly justified, that in the aftermath of the First World War they had not lived up to their own highest ideals or highest wisdom.

Be that as it may, in the United States of today, they are few among the American citizen body who deny all responsibility for events in the outside world, or simply pass by the victims or potential victims whom the world provides in such embarrassing quantities. Despite outbursts by bodies like the Daughters of the American Revolution, there is a widespread acceptance of the fact that a citizen's duties do not stop at the high-water mark. In *some* way, the American citizen today has extra-national duties. If the American citizen is also a citizen of the world, he has a duty to keep his own house in order, perhaps to give it newer and more 'contemporary' furniture. Only so can the United States teach by example the fundamental truths on which the nation is based.

But there is a further problem, not solved by the American voter setting his local political house in order. Measures as well as men are needed, policies as well as honest and broadminded executants of them. And here the duty of the good citizen is patience. This is an un-American virtue but one that is deeply necessary. The story of the United States (except for the catastrophe of the Civil War) has been a success story. And it is natural for the American voter to want quick results. It is natural but dangerous.

It is dangerous, for the voter may be tempted to succumb to a new form of demagogy, to accept recipes for quick success or to despair if quick success cannot be promised. For the very moral candour and passion that, more than self-interest, have made the American people ready to bear the great burdens imposed since 1945, have dangers. It may not be wrong to see the outside world in black and white, but it is wrong to expect the outside world to see itself in black and white. The moral fervour which Americans bring to political principles (as apart from their often excessively tolerant attitude to political practices) may have its roots in the evangelical tradition. The errant nations should accept conversion and testify to it in word and deed. They, alas, will seldom do so and not often enough for the United States safely to build a policy on it!

If this diagnosis be true, then patience is the most important virtue the American citizen can display (after a conviction that he has a duty to the outside world). For if he does not display it, he will be unjust to his leaders, to the President, to the Secretary of State, to his Senator and Congressman who may well have learned in Washington that things are more complicated than they seem to be at home. The domestic virtues of wanting quick results, of disliking secrecy, of insisting on (and too often settling for) the acceptance of grand moral principles, are less visibly virtues on the international scene. There, very imperfect solutions are all that can be hoped for and the pursuit of perfection can end—and usually will end—in deception and disillusion.

And disillusion is one of the great dangers facing the citizen and weakening the effectiveness of the politician. Perhaps, in the past, it did not matter that the politician offered a new heaven and a new earth. No one really believed him. Just as it is wrong to expect pure or mere business methods to be adequate for the purposes of the political world, it is wrong to expect even American politics or American business to be simply exportable to a market willing to operate on American lines.

The American citizen as a world citizen will have often to be content with small successes, with successes to be hoped for rather than for successes immediately realizable. He will have to learn to put up with bad manners, ingratitude, incompetence. And, of course, not all of his political agents will be wise, upright, or lucky. The virtue of patience does not exclude the duty of realistic criticism and of democratic scepticism. Many but not all of good American political habits will be usable in the outside world. But the failure of the outside world to meet American standards will not absolve the American citizen of his duty to that outside world, or make it any less true that a concept of citizenship that does not extend beyond the frontiers of the United States is sterile and self-defeating today. Of course, this truth is not only for the Americans but for the British, for the French, for the citizens of old and new nations, still earthbound by dangerously exclusive national or doctrinal coils at the very moment that man is about to take off into space.

1960

10

THE UNIMPORTANCE OF BEING ADAMS

A SIMPLE WAY to outline the aims, limitations, and success of the most famous of American autobiographies is to contrast it (as we may be sure Adams did) with its only American rival, *The Autobiography of Benjamin Franklin*, and with the *Confessions* of Jean-Jacques Rousseau. Compared with the lucid, lively, humorous and self-satisfied narrative of Franklin, a 'success story' if ever there was one, *The Education of Henry Adams* is full of shade, of emotion suggested rather than expressed, is allusive, and, at times deliberately, or so one may think, obscure. And, the point is hammered in a hundred times, it is *not* a success story. It is indeed, on the surface, the story of one who failed because, trained to be at home in Franklin's world, he had to live in a world transformed by the new science and the new technology.

Compared with Rousseau, Adams is or purports to be discreet and is evasive. Rousseau boasted of his candour and made a great virtue of his exposure of his own nakedness. We need not take the proclaimed candour too seriously; the truth that Rousseau tells is the truth of the artist, not of the mere noter of pathological or scabrous detail. But Adams openly and covertly ignores many sides of his own life. And yet, the 'Education' has more in common with the 'Confessions' than with the sober and surface narrative of Adams's fellow-Bostonian, Franklin. For Adams is a child of Rousseau, of the romantic movement. He knows the importance of feeling, the image he draws has, like modern life, a wavering edge, is an unequally lighted spot in the dark penumbra of mystery with which human life is surrounded. Even that theme wherewith Rousseau excited, shocked, and titillated his readers, sex, recurs in a muted form again and again in the 'Education'. Success and failure in handling this divine force is a test and an assessment of an education —and Adams suggests that not only his education but that all of his male friends failed—to the damage of themselves and also of their superior, the American woman. It is not for nothing that he twice quotes Lucretius: *Quae quoniam rerum naturam sola gubernas*. And the companion book to the 'Education', *Mont-Saint-Michel and Chartres*, is a prose hymn to the successor of Venus, the Virgin. Franklin was at home in his world. Adams, no more than Rousseau, was at home in his. His report on the world as he saw it, felt it, resented it, is the report of an artist. That artist was also an historian, a journalist, at times a rather pedantic scholar. But here, in the 'Education', he is an artist, moving with the artist's freedom and licence among the mere data of his life. He is, if not quite as free with mere fact as a novelist, yet an ocean away from the sententious historian of the 'Administrations of Jefferson and Madison', not to speak of the Harvard professor who, so his mock Latin epitaph ironically boasted, had explained the mysteries of sac and soc and the other arcana of Anglo-Saxon law. But if it is essential to read the 'Education' first of all as a work of art, it is also essential to read it as a *document pour servir*. It serves in two ways, as an illuminating view of American history seen sometimes from the inside, sometimes from an exceptionally good position on the sidelines. And it is a statement of the predicament of modern man in the late nineteenth century, assailed in his long-accepted certainties by the impact of science and of sociology, of Darwin, Comte, Marx. Adams's ancestors of the eighteenth century had moved from the certainties of their ancestral Puritanism to the newer certainties of the Enlightenment to the truths declared to be self-evident by his great-grandfather's friend and fellow revolutionary, Thomas Jefferson. But few truths were self-evident in the year 1900, the year when Adams confronted the dynamo (six hundred years after the ideal year in which Dante found his guide), and in feeling his preparation inadequate for this world of flux, Adams was merely stating, with his own accent and his own point of view, a nearly universal dilemma, of having to live 'between two worlds, one dead / The other powerless to be born'.

As much as a member of the Russian intelligentsia, Adams was seeking a doctrine, a practice, and as far as his life was a failure at all, its defeat lay in the inability to attain a world view that could be clung to and serve as a plan of action. It would be easy enough to find parallels in all countries for the situation of the author, in Japan and India as well as England and France. But the peculiar flavour and value of the book can only be appreciated if it is realized how American the book is and yet what an exceptional American Adams, merely as an Adams, was bound to be.

It would be easy to write off the 'Education' as a kind of parody of Oscar Wilde and give it the sub-title (not of 'An autobiography', for which there is no authority) but 'The Unimportance of Being an Adams'. But before that is done, it is well to begin by stressing what *was* the importance of being an Adams, and that takes us, as the 'Education' does on its first page, to Boston, to Massachusetts, to New England, to the United States of which the Adams family were among the handful of founders. Family pride can be ludicrous, it can be crippling, but it can also be fortifying, a guiding light, a barrier to surrender to 'the contagion of the world's slow stain'. It was all these things for Henry Adams.

The Adams family is one of those dynasties like the Broglies in France, the Russells (or Stanleys of Alderley) in England who combine a great role in history with an astonishingly high level, generation after generation, of intellectual competence and achievement. Samuel Adams, a close kinsman, was one of the makers of the American Revolution, an original party organizer, a pioneer in agitation, something (but only something) of a Lenin. The great-grandfather, John Adams, was one of the makers of the Republic; one of the four drafters of the Declaration of Independence, first minister of the successful rebels to their quondam King, first Vice-President and second President of the United States. He was also a political theorist of distinction, a man of eager ambition, utter probity, and of great if intermittent magnanimity. His son, John Quincy Adams, was Minister to Prussia, to Holland, to Russia, Senator from Massachusetts, Secretary of State, and Sixth President of the United States—and a man of more originality of mind and more wide-ranging curiosity than his lawyer father had been. And he was a man of limitless political courage, ready to make enemies on all sides in obedience to his conscience. He showed this by consenting to serve in the lower house of Congress after he had held the great office of President, because his neighbours wished him to do so. And there, in the House of Representatives, he fought the encroaching power of the slave states and the slave system as his father had fought the encroachments of King George III and the English Parliament. Had the Adams family been Roman patricians, no great house could have equalled their ancestral images, no house could have had more pride in its *fasti*. If pride was a family fault, it was also a family support; it was not the mere vanity of the Guermantes but something more like the pride of the Metelli.

But Henry Adams not only belonged to the greatest American family (there were no legitimate descendants in the male line of Washington, Franklin, Jefferson, the only founders of the Republic to be compared with John Adams), he was a Bostonian. True, the Adams family had their home, their roots in the little town of Quincy (now a Boston suburb), but Charles Francis Adams, the father of Henry, had married a daughter of Peter Chardon Brooks, the greatest of Boston merchants, and it was in Boston he was born, in Boston that he was 'christened by his uncle the Minister of the First Church . . . Had he been born in Jerusalem under the shadow of the Temple and circumcised in the temple by his uncle the high priest under the name of Israel Cohen, he could scarcely have been more distinctly branded.'

It is no light thing to be born a Bostonian, but to be both a Bostonian and an Adams was indeed a heritage that was goodly but might also be damaging. For Boston, as it was to be said, was not only a place, it was a state of mind. For two hundred years, its Puritan founders had seen it as a light unto the gentiles, and though the light that shone from it had changed a little, it still saw itself as a city set on a hill. That Boston was 'the hub of the solar system' was, so Oliver Wendell Holmes the elder put it, the deep belief of the true Boston man. And it was one of the handicaps of Henry Adams that he could neither believe nor wholly disbelieve this. Of course, it was an absurd belief—not even Athens in its prime had lived up to the true Bostonian's idea of the importance of his city— but there was something in it. There *was*, for the Boston of Henry Adams's youth was both a highly integrated society and one open to all the winds of doctrine.

It was a society marked by the rule of what on the continent of Europe is called a 'patriciate', by families wealthy or not so wealthy, but cultivated and serious in their approach to life. It was a society with its characteristic institutions, above all Harvard College, then two hundred years old and a much more serious centre of original learning even then than one would gather from the 'Education'.

Boston had been founded by men at the very opposite extreme from jesting Pilate, men who cared deeply about God's plans and God's will. They were no longer so certain that they knew either in the detail that their fathers had known them. The primitive faith of the founders had been affected, or, if you like, corrupted by the Enlightenment, then by German philosophy mediated through France. But there remained a deep conviction that duty could be known and should be unflinchingly followed. And when men differed over their duty, they did not differ lightly nor, it must be said, always amiably. The righteous and self-righteous Senator Charles Sumner, who plays such a part in the 'Education', was only an extravagant specimen of a common and, in some ways, admirable type. A much more admirable and less representative specimen was Charles Francis Adams, the father of Henry. He was a 'conscience Whig', one of those who protested against the alliance of the 'lords of the lash and the lords of the loom', the rich owners of the slave cotton plantations of the South and the even richer owners of the new cotton mills in the drab new towns round Boston.

Henry Adams was connected, too, with the Bostonians who thought that the great issue of slavery should not be stressed, not be pushed to extremes, with such ornaments of Boston Society as his uncle by marriage, Edward Everett, the Greek scholar who was to be Minister to England, Secretary of State, President of Harvard (the order is ascending). Boston was a divided world, but it was united in the primacy it gave to conduct, to learning, and to service of the state. Money was a good, a highly desirable, a necessary thing, but to make the pursuit of money or even the pursuit of happiness, laid down as a fundamental right by Mr. Jefferson, the chief end of man was to betray the spirit of Boston.

It was a limited world, but not as limited as we now tend to think. Boston was a great port, enriching itself by trade with the Orient, above all with China; that was one window on the world. It was an exporter of men and institutions to the new West; that was another. Perplexed by the impact of the new learning on its traditional faith, it was hospitable to new prophets like Kant and Charles Fourier and Carlyle, and to the Vedas. It sent studying pilgrims to a Germany still marked by Goethe and, more gingerly, to an Italy made living by Byron. Where Boston differed from the Frankfurt of Goethe's youth or the Geneva of Rousseau's, it was in being far more hospitable to new ideas, far more conscious of what was going on in

London and Paris than of the bustle of often petty business in Washington and New York. A young man born into so great a family in the Boston of 1838 might well think that 'the lines were fallen to him in pleasant places', that his was indeed a 'goodly heritage'. The 'Education', briefly summed up, is the story of a lifelong apprenticeship to the fact that the world could ignore the standards, the ranks, the assumptions of Boston, that nothing was stable, not even the natural precedence of the Adams family.

Put that way, the 'Education' can be represented as a peevish book. Why should the world stand still, why should a young man of Boston, even an Adams, be prepared for inevitable success in a world being changed by the railway, the steam loom, cheap steel and the dynamo, to leave aside great external events like the American Civil War, great movements of the mind like Marxism, the 'higher criticism', the destruction of Newtonian physics? The impression of undignified self-pity can be seen in another light if we reflect that Adams was an artist and a romantic artist. And from the vast body of letters, memoirs, commentaries that this highly literate family has produced and provoked, it is evident that in his old age Adams painted in his shadows in the fashion of a mannerist artist. He had a happier and, even in his own eyes, a more 'successful' life than he could bring himself to admit.

The 'Education', we must remember, was not destined for general publication but for a small group of Bostonians who would know, without having it stressed, when Henry Adams was being wholly serious, when he was playing with paradox, when he simply wanted to *épater les bourgeois*. The first readers knew, too, that much was deliberately left out, as irrelevant (for the 'Education' is only in a narrow and special sense an 'autobiography'), or omitted for reasons of decorum or protection against too painful memories. Thus Adams dropped twenty years of his life out of his narrative and that period covered his marriage which ended in the catastrophe of his wife's suicide. All that he writes on the superiority of American woman, on the failure of American man should be read in the light of this private tragedy, so private and agonizing that for long after he was dead the fact of suicide was kept from print. Adams was a man whose private life had known a disaster greater, more painful, perhaps more humiliating than the disappointments of his public career.

What were these disappointments? His father, then serving in Congress like his father before him, was sent as Minister to England at the outbreak of the Civil War. It was a post as important, as decisive as any his father or grandfather had held, for English intervention could have saved the southern Confederacy as French intervention had saved the infant United States. Henry Adams does not exaggerate the greatness of his father's services and all that need be said of the brilliant account of the war years in London is that we know that the young secretary of the American Minister enjoyed his life more than he lets us see in the 'Education'. From one point of view, this is the most successful part of the book. Adams was a privileged witness at a great event in history. True, his caginess, his desire to emphasize his inadequacy mar, to some extent, his account of the only period in his life when he was a constant witness to the workings of power, to the ways in which the world was governed. He does imply that he learned Oxenstierna's lesson: *quantilla prudentia regitur orbis*—with how little wisdom is the world governed. He was, more than he allows to appear, a passionately committed American and he found English indifference more trying than English hostility. He neglects the relevant truth, that the English ruling class had a lot to worry it at this time, apart from the doubtful destiny of the United States. There were the designs of Napoleon III, harmless and impotent (but Palmerston and Russell didn't know that). There were the problems caused by the unification of Italy and the rise of Prussia. There was the ambiguous policy of Russia, so quickly recovered from the defeat of the Crimean War. We can now see, Adams could see when he wrote the 'Education', that the survival of the Union was more important than any of these events that, naturally enough, seemed so important to Palmerston (who had been Secretary at War during the administration of Mr. Madison) or to John Russell (who had ridden the lines of Torres Vedras with Wellington in 1810 and had talked with Napoleon at Elba). They *ought* to have known better, but was it proof of especial turpitude or stupidity that they didn't? But, recollecting times past, Adams didn't forgive either, especially not Lord Russell, who was, Adams thought, so two-faced. Minister Adams did not feel towards Lord Russell as his private secretary came to feel and would not have done so, we may guess, even if he had known that Russell had been, for a moment, more belligerent than Palmerston. 'Pam's' Anglo-Irish frivolity and worldly wisdom saved him from the errors that his more serious colleague fell into. But after all, being a Russell in England was the nearest thing to being an Adams in Boston, and

Minister Adams recognized this fact. And Henry Adams was more valuable to his father and more valued by him than the 'Education' suggests. Despite his interesting later role as an eavesdropper and as a chronicler of the Washington scene, Henry Adams was never as much at the heart of things as in his years in the London legation. This was, in a real sense, 'his proudest hour', and perhaps some of his rather tiresome self-deprecation came from the feeling that so brilliant a start had led to so little.

But there is more in the account of English life in the 'Education' than war and politics. Adams enjoyed London more than he admitted. He made at least one lifelong friend, Charles Milnes-Gaskell, and some of the happiest hours of Adams's life were spent 'on Wenlock edge'. But again the caginess is to be noted. For the most dazzling friend that Adams made at this time was Lord Houghton, 'whom the Gods call Dicky Milnes', the most effortlessly superior ornament of London drawing-rooms, 'the cool of the evening', the first biographer of Keats, the patron of the young Swinburne (whom Adams does mention), and the man who, through his ownership of the greatest erotic library of modern times, revealed to Swinburne, the Marquis de Sade. It is impossible to believe that Adams knew nothing of this side of Lord Houghton—or that it excited no curiosity in him. Horror, too, like that his great-grandmother Abigail had felt at the sight of the Paris ballet dancers, but interest also. For this was a part of life that Boston either knew nothing of or preferred to ignore. Be that as it may, when Adams left London, his wander-years were over.

The shock of the return to America is brilliantly conveyed. It 'was never bright confident morning again'. And it can be held (I hold this view) that the most important part of the 'Education' is the record of disillusionment with the victorious Union.

The Civil War had cost six hundred thousand lives and many thousands of millions of dollars. It had done away with the great national sin of slavery. The Union, to quote Lincoln, had known 'a new birth of freedom'. It was natural, if innocent, to assume that the reborn nation would live up, morally and intellectually, to the legacy of the war. It was natural and human to assume that it would welcome the services of all its public-spirited young men—especially if they were members of the Adams family. Adams had a double disillusionment; he found that he was not wanted and he found that the war, far from ennobling the American people, had made it morally lax, had given opportunities to gamblers and what it is not too severe to describe as business bandits. For that world, the education given by Boston was not merely useless; it was harmful. Again and again in the remaining chapters, we are recalled to this grim fact. Even those most fitted for the new technological world like Clarence King fail, fail to secure wealth, fail to secure power, fail (though this is omitted from the portrait of King) to secure private happiness. Adams became, or asserts that he became, what the French used to call an *émigré de l'intérieur*.

If we are inclined to think of the representative American as being complacent, we should remember how critical of their country, of a business civilization, of mechanical politics so many great Americans have been. The epoch that Adams detested and describes was called by Mark Twain, who also despised it, 'the gilded age'. Henry James took refuge from it in Europe. But it is as well to remember that Adams darkened the picture. A man of his temperament and interests would have found it hard to attain the seats of power (if that was what he really wanted) in any age. For here was a born critic rather than a born leader. Nor was he always a just critic. He sneers at St. Louis for daring to put on a great exposition. But St. Louis, new and raw as it was, had a highly cultivated bourgeoisie, largely of German origin but with New England exiles like Mr. T. S. Eliot's father among them. It was the centre of Hegelian studies in America and had, in its great bridge, an architectural triumph at least as worthy of interest and admiration as the churches and houses built by Adams's friend Richardson. Nor was Harvard University quite as sterile socially as Adams claims. He might have learned much had he stayed there longer, from William James and from the young George Santayana.

Indeed, the alienation of Adams from America was only partly a result of discovering that it no longer was enough to be an Adams. It was part of that alienation from the bourgeoisie and from commercial standards in life and politics that marked nearly all the great literary artists of this time. Ibsen, Tolstoy, Flaubert will serve as examples. Again, Adams was an artist and an anarchist and even if all that he says is true, there were other things to be said. He could look back and make us look back with nostalgia to the simpler, less opulent, more stable days of his childhood in Quincy, of his first visits to Washington. But that peace and confidence was gone or going everywhere.

To that change Adams, like every great artist of the age, was a witness. He had always taken a competent amateur interest in the sciences and he was acute enough to know that the old simple scientific truths were as much threatened as the old religious and political truths, that Henri Poincaré's defence of Euclidean geometry was made in a very different spirit from that in which his mathematically minded grandfather, John Quincy Adams, had revered 'science'.

Adams was not a scientist or a philosopher but an historian, and he had shown in his writings a mastery of the techniques of historical scholarship. But that was no longer enough. What did history enable one to predict or even to guess about the future was the question he put himself. What were the historical equivalents of the 'laws' that scientists were discovering? He asked and got a dusty answer and his own answer, set out in no very clear fashion at the end of the 'Education', satisfied neither its author nor the historians whom it challenged. By this time, Henry Adams was much under the influence of his brilliant, original, contentious younger brother Brooks, and both brothers, at the very height of complacent belief in progress around 1900, doubted if progress, as apart from change, was likely. But while Brooks with his more combative, optimistic, and aggressive temperament knew that an age of iron was opening but thought that the United States could triumph in the struggle, Henry took a more pessimistic point of view. No more than he had managed to, would the United States successfully adjust itself to this new world. Again, this pessimism is partly 'an act'. But the correspondence of these years is in places very depressing reading. Adams spent more and more time in France (in that justifying Tom Appleton's famous jest[1]) but the letters he wrote from Paris show how limited was his curiosity, how pedantic his taste. Little that was living in French culture appealed to him. (No one reading these letters would imagine that, physically at least, Adams was in the Paris of one of the greatest explosions of artistic genius in history.) There was in his correspondence with Brooks an unattractive and rather stupid strain of anti-Semitism. There was plenty of that in the Paris of the Dreyfus affair; it is a pity that Adams drew no other spiritual nourishment from France than that! Of course, in the letters, as in the 'Education', there are brilliant guesses and deep insights that are more than guesses. The roles of Russia and China in the world that was being so painfully born are foreseen, no doubt 'as in a glass darkly', but with real prophetic genius.

[1] 'Good Americans, when they die, go to Paris.'

There are other brilliant guesses in this and in other writings of Adams, but they are not what makes the book a classic as it has been recognized to be ever since it was given to the public in the time of disillusionment that followed the First World War. Adams had turned from American history to the human situation, first to the human situation in the thirteenth century when the Virgin had her palaces like Chartres, where the weary and bewildered could be comforted and the human mind had its ordered system of knowledge in the *Summa* of St. Thomas. What could the new twentieth century offer? Adams asked science, asked technology and got no answer. But that the demand for a form of unity as systematic as that of the thirteenth century was deeply felt, the success of Marxism shows. Adams would not have welcomed the new *Summa* and its political and technical embodiment, but nothing that has happened in Russia and the world would have surprised him. For the background of our present perplexities, the 'Education' is an indispensable document.

But it is more than that; it is a great work of art and in its first half, at any rate, a nearly perfect work of art. Adams spent a great part of the last years of his life in France and he fell more and more under the influence of French ways of thinking and writing. The stylistic effects are beneficial. There are evocations of the past worthy of Proust, brief but admirable statements of human experience worthy of La Rochefoucauld; portraits worthy of La Bruyère or Saint-Simon. Adams did not live to see the sudden flowering of his literary fame, a flowering so brilliant that it is a natural temptation to regard the whole history of the great family as culminating in the author of *Mont-Saint-Michel and Chartres* and *The Education of Henry Adams*. Adams had not set his ambitions so high. He had, he tells us, 'sought the orbit that would best satisfy the observed movement of the runaway star Groombridge, 1838, commonly called Henry Adams'. And we find the following of that runaway star more interesting and more profitable than we should have found tracing his life had he become a President of the United States like one grand father or a millionaire like the other. He speaks to us as mere Presidents and mere millionaires cannot and he speaks for an American attitude that we tend to ignore, for that critical side of American life that knows how much more the human heart needs than mere material goods and the vulgar success that Henry Adams, to our profit, escaped.

1961

11

ANGLO-AMERICAN
RELATIONS:
RETROSPECT AND PROSPECT

FIFTY YEARS AGO occurred an event that is now totally forgotten in
the United States and Great Britain and only faintly remembered
in Canada. The event was the Taft Administration's successful
negotiation with Canada of a reciprocity treaty that was, by the
standards of the age, enlightened and likely to benefit both contracting parties. But this proposal for what would have been a close
integration of the American and Canadian economies ran aground
on two shoals, one Canadian, one American. In Canada, the Conser-
vatives, threatened in their high tariff privileges by the treaty, combined with the extreme 'Canadien' Nationalists of Quebec to attack
the Laurier Administration as betraying Canada. (They had very
different ideas as to what kind of Canada was being betrayed.) In the
United States, Speaker Champ Clark briskly announced that the
treaty, formally only economic, would in fact lead to the annexation
of Canada by the United States. In the Canadian general election,
Sir Wilfred Laurier was defeated, the treaty went down with him,
and whatever danger (or hope) there was of Canada's being assimilated to the United States ceased to threaten.

The episode is important not only because of the great role Canada
has since played in mediating between Britain and the United States,
but also because it underlines one of the problems of Anglo-American relations today—the refusal of a great many Americans to notice
the changed character of the former British 'empire', their innocent
assumption that anybody who *could* be an American wants to be one,

that people are panting everywhere for liberation from the imperial yoke, that every year, all over the world, it is 1776 again.

I do not think I underestimate or overestimate the importance of the survival of the revolutionary legend in America, the role that the ghost of George III plays in American mythology or demonology. But one of the permanent difficulties in Anglo-American relations is the lingering belief that the British still slumber, no doubt restlessly, under the royal and feudal yoke. And this belief, still living fifty years after 1911, points up a fact many or most Americans ignore— that by 1911, the United States was no longer seen by any European country, at least by the masses in any European country, as a liberating power. It was seen as the stronghold of high capitalism and, as socialist propaganda spread, as an enemy to the liberation of the workers.

It had not always been so. Long after the Civil War, when most of the British workers showed that they shared Lincoln's belief that the United States was the 'last, best hope of earth', the legend of the great Republic still lived, the image still shone. But by about 1890, the legend was less and less believed in, the image tarnished. The last American who made an impact on the British radical movement or movements was Henry George. And shortly after his landing in England, the official song of what was to be the Labour Party, 'The Red Flag', contained a reference to the Chicago anarchists—or martyrs. A few years later, many boys in Britain were getting their first impression of the realities of American society from Jack London's *The Iron Heel*. Aneurin Bevan got his first (and last) impressions that way. I got my first but not my last.

So there was a built-in clash: the Americans seeing themselves as predestined liberators, the more active-minded among the British workers seeing the United States as a brutal and exploitative society. There were, of course, important exceptions to this general condemnation. For the United States was still 'America the Golden' for tens of thousands of emigrants, even if Canada, for a short time, rivalled her neighbour. The tradition of a society where the streets were paved with gold did not die out entirely under socialist polemic. The 'Uncle from America' still came back to dazzle his poor relations who had stayed at home. His opulence (often the result of hard saving) *did* impress the more restless boys and girls. After all it did not take much opulence to dazzle the inhabitants of a village in the West Highlands or Connemara. Emigration took off some, if not all

of the edge of the new anti-American sentiment, although many of
the returned emigrants who had tried their luck in America and
failed to make the grade gave an embittered account of life in New
York slums (worse than Glasgow's they improbably reported) or in
the Pennsylvania coal-fields (worse than the Rhondda). But the
century-long movement west meant that in the British working
classes every family had cousins in America; they exchanged photographs and letters and the American cousins at times came back to
visit the ancestral home. British and Americans might not like each
other but they knew a lot about each other, the British naturally
knowing more than the Americans.

At the political level, there were comparatively few grounds of
difference or quarrel. True, the course of the Mexican Revolution
brought friction, because, by a curious reversal of present-day roles,
the British were the stout supporters of the *status quo*, of Díaz and
then Huerta, against the much more intelligent foresight of the
Wilson Administration. For the President realized, better than his
advisers, that the time of troubles that began with the revolt of
Madero was not a mere series of *pronunciamientos* but a revolution.
But if Wilson in one way caused friction (in a good cause), he
lessened it in another by forcing the repeal of the differential Panama
Canal dues, giving the world an impressive example of American
good faith.

Then came the watershed, the war of 1914. It was a watershed
because, as we now can clearly see, Great Britain began her imperial
decline, even in the moment of formal victory. And the balance of
power was redressed, the German challenge to British power
defeated, by United States intervention. No British government
could ever again act in deliberate hostility to the United States. This
was noted and, by many old-fashioned people in Britain, resented.
By immense sacrifices, Britain had saved Europe; at the last moment,
the Americans had stepped in and easily and cheaply carried off the
real prizes of war. (The losses of the war of 1914–18 have been used
to explain so many faults and feeblenesses in British politics,
1919–39, that few noted that the United States suffered greater
losses, relative to population, in the Civil War. But Britain in 1919
was more in the position of the South in 1865 than of the
North.)

The war produced new causes for friction as in the long, and at
bottom, sterile controversies over the blockade. Not many people in

Britain noted that the American government did not press its claims or actively interfere with British naval methods. Indeed, a later source of conflict was to be the acceptance by so many Americans of the view that the Wilson Administration betrayed American rights and pushed America into the war to save Britain's bankers. But with the sound of the guns in Flanders booming in London streets, it was hard to be objective. And Wilson's peace moves were seen as giving aid and comfort to Germany, as examples of moral smugness and indifference to moral duty. What moral duty? Well, there was the duty to 'save civilization', identified with any cause that the British government and people espoused. And there was a lingering feeling that the United States owed a duty to her mother country. She ought to have entered the war voluntarily as the other dominions had done. For to many simple-minded people in Britain, the United States was no doubt formally independent, but bound by duty to the imperial isle. (This sentiment could be found lingering as late as 1939.) As the pressure of war grew worse, the casualty lists longer, the immunity of the Americans was resented. It hadn't mattered so much when the boys were to be home by Christmas 1914, but by the bloody summer of 1916, tempers were frayed. American entrance into the war eased the strain but the simple American assumption that they and they alone could and would finish the war was resented. All British children were brought up, as I certainly was, on a tradition of 'Yankee brag'. The Yankee might come from South Carolina; he boasted just the same. And (so I was told) the impression made by the fresh, aggressive, credulous American troops in France on the battered and resigned veterans of the Somme and Passchendaele was ambivalent. It was nice to be so confident but 'wait till they've spent a winter in the line'. (The Australians, I was told, were peculiarly ironical on this subject.) The Americans didn't spend the winter in the line. The Germans collapsed, and after the age of dangers came the more irritating age of difficulties.

There is a lot more to be said for the Treaty of Versailles than it was fashionable to admit thirty years ago, but a treaty which left everybody dissatisfied, both victors and vanquished, must have had some defects. One of the defects was that it provided ground for exacerbation between the victors, notably between Britain and the United States. To the Americans, the British with their insistence on seizing colonies and demanding reparations were the old imperialists of American tradition. Soon they were the people who had taken the simple Americans for a ride. On the British side, the Americans were the people who had prevented the making of a 'sensible' peace treaty, who had made promises that anyone with a knowledge of the realities of international life (which the Yankees notoriously hadn't) would know were impossible of fulfilment. And they were, worst of all, the people who, walking out on the treaty they were responsible for, refusing to join the League of Nations they had set up, had the cheek to send in a bill for war debts! It is not necessary to discuss the validity of the charges and counter-charges; it is enough to note that they were made and believed in. The American saw himself as a man who had been played for a sucker by British propagandists, and the Englishman saw Uncle Sam as Uncle Shylock.

If we add to this smouldering fire of mutual suspicion and resent-ment such ill-advised attempts to redress the balance of payments as the Stevenson rubber scheme in which the British government was a partner to a conspiracy to keep up prices, like a great American business executive of our times, we might expect permanent alienation. But the surprising thing about Anglo-American relations in this period is that the friction did not produce fire. Despite the formal abdication of American responsibility for the peace settlement, despite the nervous drawing away of American skirts from the League of Nations like a pious matron passing a brothel, America did act in Europe. There was a considerable and possibly unwise injection of American capital into Germany. There were the Young Plan and the Dawes Plan. There was the Washing-ton Naval Treaty of 1921 by which Japan was the real gainer, but which did mark the end of naval competition between Britain and the United States. And, despite later friction over cruisers and scandals over lobbyists, it was assumed in practice that Britain and the United States would never be at war.

At another level, an old cause of political difficulty lost most of its importance. The establishment of the Irish Free State, followed by a disillusioning civil war, reduced to a low point the temperature of the oldest ethnic pressure group, the Irish. It is usually said that the American-Irish were uniformly hostile to the foreign policy of the Wilson Administration, and many of them were, but many in America —and many in Ireland—were sympathetic to the British war effort until the savage reprisals after the Easter Week rebellion of 1916 destroyed the old Irish Parliamentary party and discredited its

American advocates. (But for the fact that he was an American citizen by birth, Mr. de Valera might not have survived to be one of the most respected elder statesmen of the Western world.)

The Irish, as we all know, were particularly prominent in politics and were, despite that self-pity on which Mr. Galbraith has recently commented, much more assimilated to the dominant Anglo-Saxon culture than most other ethnic groups. And they were rising in the world. They were soon to produce a very popular and remarkable candidate for the presidency of the United States, the shadow of things to come. If they had continued to harbour resentment of British rule in Ireland it would have paid politicians to exacerbate the 'ancient grudge'. The 'Friends of Irish Freedom', the Irish lobby of the time of the Troubles, included such diverse figures as Mr. Doheny, the multi-millionaire of the Teapot Dome, and his Nemesis, Senator Walsh of Montana. After 1921 this mattered little. The old professional managers of the Irish question like John Devoy lost their audience. Ireland drifted away from Irish-America, each misunderstanding and perhaps disliking the other. A constant irritant if not a real poison was removed from the American body politic.

More important, much more important, was the new immigration policy of the United States. That most seriously affected countries like Greece and Italy; for them it was disastrous. But it affected Britain and Ireland, too. No longer could you just hop on a boat and be 'off to Philadelphia in the morning'. Although the British quota was the largest and the Irish quite large, they were quotas, quotas that meant to discriminate, as the 'national origins' provisions showed. The Statue of Liberty still stood but the inscription was now ironical.

Then came the Depression. Soon the United States was losing more by emigration than she was gaining by immigration. This had important effects in Britain. It cut down sharply the personal connections between the industrial populations of Britain and America. People in the Bridgeton district of Glasgow no longer thought automatically of seeing what it was like in Paterson, New Jersey (their favourite American city). The close family ties, which have been ignored in many accounts of Anglo-American relations, between the workers in both countries, grew slacker. Fewer people in Britain knew America at first hand. Yet the ties remained important. In 1940, a very careful investigation in which I was concerned as an official, showed that 8 per cent of the population in Britain had been in the United States at some time in their lives, and of course this 8 per cent was overwhelmingly working class.

The Depression killed for ever the vision of 'America the Golden'. All that Jack London or Upton Sinclair had written was proved to be true. Already the Sacco and Vanzetti case had shown, so all Europe thought, the ugly and murderous side of American society. (My mother, no radical, welcomed me back from Harvard in 1927 with joy that I had left that 'murderous country'.) The returning emigrants brought back stories of the collapse of American society, of the absence of social services, even of the 'dole', that shocked many and confirmed the dark suspicions of more.

The doubt of the values of the American Way of Life that the Depression deepened had not been bred solely by the Depression. In the twenties, contemporary American literature had a high prestige value in Britain and a wide circulation. But the admiration and interest went to debunkers like Sinclair Lewis, to mockers like H. L. Mencken. They made America interesting but not particularly admirable. In a lighter vein they carried on the tradition of Jack London, Upton Sinclair, and Theodore Dreiser. And what had been said of the prosperous twenties helped to explain, so many people in Britain thought, the disaster-ridden thirties.

But the New Deal to some extent reversed the tide. In the drab and stagnant world of Baldwin and Daladier, Franklin Roosevelt shone like a good deed in a weary world. A great deal of the interest in the New Deal was provoked by the contrast between the dazzling innovations of Washington and the treadmill politics of London and Paris. But there was a demand for a serious study of the New Deal which produced a number of good books and a more serious treatment of American news, even in the less serious British press. Of course, the character of the American economy had been studied in the boom years. One successful book, *The Secret of High Wages*, was soon discredited by mounting evidence that the secret had been lost. The interest of the thirties was partly in bold experiments like the TVA, and partly in the overturning of so many of the traditional American ways of life, ways that most people in Britain disliked or distrusted. But this interest in the New Deal, this fascination with the personality of F.D.R., created another strain. The American conservative in London and the American clubs that invited British lecturers did not welcome proof that F.D.R. was admired in Britain.

Even today, many Americans try to shake the faith of the British in F.D.R., but it is hate's labour lost.

Then the New Deal was soon overshadowed by the threat of war. War came in Spain, was visibly coming to Europe. Loud American adjurations to stand up to the dictators from the western shore of the Atlantic were received with irony by many on the eastern who saw no signs that the Americans were going to do any of the standing up. On the other hand, the increasingly numerous enemies of appeasement thought they had an ally in the White House. It is historically doubtful if this was so in the way the anti-appeasers meant it, but it put heart into them all the same.

'Then the war came.' With the Second World War, Anglo-American relations entered on a new phase. What had been an off-and-on love affair, with spats and reconciliations, became a shot-gun wedding. In the desperate summer of 1940, the mass of the British people and, of course, the new war leader Churchill, knew that American support was all-important. That, possibly, accounted for the muting of the criticism that had been so rampant in the first part of the First World War. But there was more to it than that. The American desire to stay out of war was sympathized with, if it was not thought a practicable or dignified policy. And I think it only candid to say that the news of Pearl Harbor was received with something like relief. (I know it cured me of a very bad cold.)

With American entry into the war, the whole pattern of Anglo-American relations changed. The British noticed that the United States was at war at once. It had been a year after the declaration of war in 1917 before the American Army was seriously engaged. The American Navy was never seriously engaged at all. It was different from December 7, 1941 on. And although the Pacific war was never adequately reported in the British press, the Americans were recognized as real combatants as they had not been in the few months of active fighting in 1918. With the arrival of the G.I.'s, Grosvenor Square became Eisenhower Platz and every village was filled with 'Yanks'. All things considered, the difficult job of adjusting to the invasion of a small island by millions of foreign though friendly troops was well handled. (The American Provost Marshal for the London district did a magnificently intelligent job.) There were difficulties and incidents of course. Sex reared its ugly head and many Americans were shocked or professed to be shocked by the sexual freedom of England and by the small role played by organized religion.

American race prejudices shocked many genuinely and some arti-
ficially. A story went around London that a reporter who asked a
villager in Somerset what he thought of the Americans was told,
'We like them a lot. They've got such lovely voices and nice manners
and they're so kind to the kids, but we can't stand the white bastards
they brought with them.' (The origin of the story was finally traced
down to an ingenious young man in the American embassy.)

Battle brought the armies and the people together. The British
War Office found that the British soldiers who served with American
units liked and trusted them far more than did the troops who knew
of the 'Yanks' only by repute. And, as a substitute for the dwindling
emigration, came the continuing flood of G.I. marriages. Sometimes
the American bridegroom told a tall tale about his economic and
social status at home, and many a bride longed for the two cars, the
automatic kitchen, the smart social life she had seen in the shiny
magazines or in the movies but failed to find as the wife of a semi-
skilled worker in a small Midwest town. But the marriages were—
and are—a bond.

With the ending of the war in Europe a new epoch set in. It bred
friction. For the Americans it meant the boys coming home, the
rapid dismantling of controls, the return to the normalcy of abundance, and the continuation of the great war boon of full employment.
For the British, it meant a continuation, indeed an increase, in
restrictions. 1947 was worse than any war year. I went to America
at least once every year and, as I usually flew, the contrast between
the glitter of New York and the drabness of London was continually
brought home to me. But the British, cooped up in their little island,
could only hear rumours of the golden age across the Atlantic. There
was resentment based on two beliefs or prejudices. The first was that
American wealth was seized in some way from the British. The war
had undoubtedly impoverished us. It had apparently enriched the
Americans. So American wealth was resented, American aid accepted
grudgingly. I quoted, at this low tide in Anglo-American amity, the
story of how Napoleon answered the question of why the brothers
and sisters he had made kings and queens and princes and princesses
were so ungrateful: 'Because they think I have cheated them of their
share of the inheritance of our father the late king.' That was one
attitude.

Another was born of the politically dominant philosophy of the
late forties. The Labour intellectuals, as a group, knew little of

America and had doctrinaire reasons for disliking what they knew or thought they knew. They had sincerely believed that it would be easy for a 'Socialist' Britain to deal with Communist Russia and hard to deal with a 'Capitalist' America. Since it wasn't working out like that, someone must be to blame, presumably the Americans. On the other hand, in America there was a great deal of real or feigned alarm at the dangers of a Socialist Britain. Some Americans talked as if the adoption of 'socialized medicine' almost offset the crimes of Hitler. The visible decline in the strength and in the world position of Britain distressed many old-fashioned British patriots and alarmed others who thought the Americans were too brash and inexperienced to play the role that Britain had played or was thought to have played.

But at a higher level, this nonsense had no effect. The great and magnanimous gesture of the Marshall Plan was estimated at its true value by the Labour ministers who had to deal with realities. The increasingly visible and depressing truth about the aims of Stalin awoke all but the most credulous from illusions about the Socialist lamb and the Communist tiger lying down together. Subsequently there has been no real danger of the two countries drifting apart on any serious issue. There was alarm over a possible American use of the atom bomb in the Korean War and a very inadequate sense of the sacrifices the American people were making in that remote conflict. But the shot-gun wedding held.

There were other grounds of friction. There were many aesthetic characters who, deeply disliking modern popular culture—rock 'n' roll, the movies, 'I Love Lucy'—damned them all as 'Americanization'. They refused to note that they were part of a world culture common, in increasing degree, to all the highly advanced industrial powers, undermining traditional culture in France as well as Britain. The Americans were simply the richest and most advanced example of this culture in the twentieth century, as Britain had been in the nineteenth.

And for reasons that are not wholly clear to me, contemporary American literature has not recovered the general prestige it had in the twenties. There are British admirers of Mr. Salinger and Miss McCullers, of Jackson Pollock and Aaron Copland, but these artists do not arouse any widespread knowledge or admiration. One exception has been the American musical. Almost all the successes of New York are successes in London, and when they are failures it is

usually due to bad casting. And veterans of the London stage aver
that they have never seen anything like the first night of *Oklahoma!*
in the drab year 1947. The audience were entranced to find it was a
beautiful morning *somewhere*.

Nothing is likely to change the general *aigre-douce* relationship
that has undergone such tests and trials. But there may be important
changes for the future. If Britain enters 'Europe', the possibly
illusory 'special relationship' with the United States will lose much
of its plausibility. With the evaporation of the British Empire, some
old American suspicions may die. Already there is more appreciation
of the fact the imperial record was not all black, at worst tattle-tale
grey. There is a wider acceptance on the British side that the
Americans are not just another brand of 'colonials'; they are a very
different but not hostile people. There is too, in Britain, more
willingness to take the United States seriously. Thus there is far
more study of American history, of American social conditions than
there was, far more readiness to admit that possibly the Yankees can
teach as well as learn. The trickle of Rhodes scholars over the last
fifty years has now become a flood into the White House, and it is
beginning to be rivalled by the increasingly large number of British
students who are passionately eager to visit America, like the Clerke
of Oxenforde, ready to learn as well as teach. (When I insisted as an
undergraduate at Oxford that I wanted to do post-graduate work on
American history at Harvard instead of accepting the much more
respectable project of continuing my studies of medieval history in
Vienna, I was regarded as a maverick. That attitude is now almost
if not quite dead.)

Whatever backward lookers of the Left or Right may think, the
omelette has been made. NATO, 'Europe', the North Atlantic community as an ideal and already a bit of a reality, the common if not
totally admirable new technological society that we both share,
impose on us a need for mutual understanding. And the menace
from Russia imposes on us the discipline of danger. Since Britain
and America are highly moralistic countries, you will criticize us over
Suez and we you over Cuba. But the die is cast. Neither country can
be really independent and no complaints can alter the ineluctable
fact of American predominance and leadership. The nearly common
language, the largely common political traditions and vocabulary are
still a great bond, although the average Briton now realizes that most
of the American people are no longer of British descent. 'In the

Archey Road,' said Mr. Dooley, 'when a man and wife find that they simply can't go on living together, they go on living together.' So it is with Britain and the United States. But as any observer of life knows, many a marriage of necessity or of *convenance* ends as an affectionate and reasonably trusting partnership. So I believe it is and will be.

1961

12

THE AMERICAN PERSONALITY: A CRITIQUE OF NEW WORLD CULTURE

I AM CONSCIOUS of the dangerous position in which this paper places me, for I am venturing to speak on a topic which, it is quite certain, is better known to many people in the audience than it is to me. And I am venturing to speak on a topic that is peculiarly difficult to treat objectively, scientifically, for it must involve—it does involve—so many judgments based on nothing more substantial than taste.

It will be prudent of me to begin by defining and limiting the field, sown with mines, I am about to traverse. I shall not attempt to define the American personality with any degree of psychological precision. I am no expert in either social psychology or pathology. I am incapable of competing with the modern masters of group and individual psychology. The most I can attempt to do is to set out the observations of an historian who has read a great deal about and visited a great deal in the United States. And I ought, perhaps, to add that I have read a great deal in the mass of European accounts of American life from the classics of Tocqueville and Bryce down to the latest hit-and-run report from the casual and possibly malignant as well as ill-informed visitor.

I ought to go on from here to try to define both what I mean by 'personality' and by 'culture'. I don't mean the personality of all Americans or most Americans or even a least common denominator personality which would be the residuum, the minimum 'Americanism' of any American. I want to discuss the total personality of the American state, of American society, its communal American character. What, to borrow a word from Cardinal Newman, is the 'note' of the American community? Has it more than one? Has the note, or notes, changed in the past century or even since I first came to this country nearly thirty-six years ago?

Then I must try to define what I mean by 'culture'. I shall use it in two forms, as an anthropologist does when he describes the whole structure of a society (doing it, I think, more successfully when dealing with a primitive society of which we know little, than when dealing with a technically advanced society of which we automatically know a great deal, either by being members of it or being, as in my case, a frequent visitor—even what one may call an occasional dweller in it). I shall also try to describe 'culture' in the narrower sense, in what has been quite a long time the most common use of the word, the use we make of it when we talk of somebody as 'cultured' or 'uncultured'. (The last word is, I am told, a really offensive term of abuse in the Soviet Union so that if I am making a mistake in using culture to exclude as well as to include, I am in good or, at any rate, in numerous company.)

There is, I know, a verbal contradiction. There can be no such thing as an 'uncultured person', even in the Moscow or New York subways. We are all marked by at least one culture; we cannot escape this fact. We may be marked by two cultures, as an immigrant is bound to be; no matter how much he wants to throw off the culture in which he was bred, some of the habits of mind, speech, manners, biases, will stick to him. Neither Carl Schurz nor Alistair Cooke, great American figures as they became, completely got rid of the German and English cultures in which they were raised. (I am not for a moment suggesting that they tried to do so or should have done so.)

I shall begin by trying to state what I think to be the 'note', the historical culture of the United States, but my main theme will be culture in a narrower sense, the culture by which we mean the arts, practised and appreciated, the sciences, the religious and moral ideas, even the cultural institutions of the community like the press and television as well as the colleges and seats of learning and research. Even this narrow field will provide me with enough chances to make a fool of myself.

Then I should like to define, not too narrowly, but still to define, what I mean by the 'New World'. I am not talking in geological terms. Australia is, I understand, in this sense, an older continent than either America or Europe. By 'New World' I mean simply a society in which the most of the population are recent immigrants, most of the institutions and habits traceable to origins in another geographical setting and their transit to this 'New' world can be examined in a far brighter light of day than can, for example, the transit of the Greeks into the eastern Mediterranean or the Anglo-Saxons into Britain. America is 'new' in that demographically and socially, its culture has grown and developed in a nearly empty land, and behind the highly visible past of the settlers in that empty land, stretches a fairly visible past in Europe and a less visible but not invisible past in Africa. All Americans except the Indians are immigrants or children of immigrants, from Jamestown or Plymouth Rock to the latest arrivals landing at the New York piers or airports. Part of the problem of 'American culture' is that it is not just that. It is American culture based on a European culture and that European culture has been growing, changing, adapting itself to the phenomenon of the new American culture since the seventeenth century. Lastly, I should like to set down my dogmatic belief that something like a common culture, a common North Atlantic culture is coming into being, maybe is already here, and much that is said in praise or blame of contemporary American culture is equally applicable to European culture, is true of Rutherglen as well as of Podunk.

What then is the problem of the 'American personality'? On what grounds can one criticize the idea of a 'new world' culture? By 'criticize' I hasten to say I do not necessarily mean to comment on adversely, simply to examine with as few prepossessions as possible and to examine in the light of criteria that I am willing to see applied to my own country.

Let us begin by assuming that Crèvecoeur was right; that the eighteenth-century American was a 'new man', the product of new social forces and of a novel environment. What were the forms of that novelty, and is the American of 1961 still a new man? In what did not only Crèvecoeur, but La Rochefoucauld—Liancourt on one side, Franklin and Jefferson on the other, see the novelty of the American which, of course, involves his difference from the European? The novelty lay surely in the fact that the American had already attained that freedom from artificial restraints, from the chains of an irrelevant and oppressive past to which so many Europeans were aspiring. It was not, I hasten to add, a matter of worshipping the noble savage. None of these writers did that even if, like Jefferson, they took what we should call both a humanitarian and anthropological interest in the Indian. It was the white American, the recent child of Europe, who embodied the gains of the new society, even if these gains were mainly negative gains. It was these gains that provoked Goethe's famous poem. It is a little odd that no one, as far as I know, has noticed that the famous lament of Henry James in his life of Hawthorne, his list of things the American literary artist had to do without, including Ascot (a race track not simply a tie), the whole feudal past that was poorly represented even in Salem, is in a sense a reply to Goethe. It was *because* the American wasn't so burdened with the past, had no such *damnosa hereditas* to live down or live with, that Goethe declared: 'Amerika du hast es besser.'

Here, in the new and empty world (the emptiness is part of the picture) lay the possibility that man, or at any rate European man, could stretch his limbs, test his powers. The French Revolution was welcomed because it promised an end to the old iniquities; the American because it revealed a country in which they did not exist and a country resisting (I don't attempt to justify the history) a wicked attempt to export to the new world the follies and crimes of the old.

Such was the novelty of the New Man, the American, such his symbolic role. I have not the time and, I fear, not the capacity to defend this view of the American and of the American Revolution. I may briefly state my belief that the European and American faith was as well justified as any widely-held, necessarily simplified view can be, that, in the eighteenth century, the American *was* a new man, the American Revolution a real breach with the past (as Acton argued against Bryce), that it was, as Franklin and the other intellectuals of the Revolution believed and hoped, *novus ordo seclorum*, a new order of the ages. And the basic question is, can we so describe, so believe in the United States today? Has the American national personality, seen from the outside and even from the inside, changed?

It is certainly a popular doctrine that it has. We are asked to notice and regret the disappearance of the 'inner directed man' to use David Riesman's useful phrase. We are asked to note—and to regret—the decline in democratic feeling, the pursuit of status, the increasingly visible class lines and class barriers. We are asked to note the decline of the 'common school' system, as more and more of the prosperous members of society cease to use them. We are asked to consider the implications of the decline of the American farmer, diminishing in numbers yearly, becoming a capitalist entrepreneur —and a political dependant—instead of a representative of the new race that attracted the notice of Crèvecoeur and the political adoration of Jefferson. The Americans may be, to use Professor David Potter's admirable phrase, still 'a people of plenty', but the plenty is not merely the abundance of good land or even of minerals and other raw materials that attracted the admiration and envy of Europe a century ago. The American affluent society, to quote from Ambassador Galbraith, is not the affluent society of the time of Tocqueville and Bryce. Texas may be the new frontier but it is a very different kind of frontier from that whose passing Frederick Jackson Turner predicted more than, in his famous essay, he observed. I could add to the new views of American society that are continually being put on the market, a market that seems to have an insatiable appetite for self-examination and is, in its present temper, a glutton for punishment.

Must we abandon, therefore, the old picture of the American personality and look for a new American, and if we do—what kind of an American? It is easy enough to construct from the abundant literature on the subject what the new American is like. He is not only no longer the independent, nearly self-sufficient, upright, egalitarian farmer of the legend; he is almost the opposite. He does not seek independence in business, not to speak of farming. Entering on a job, he has, as a young man, an eye on his retiring pension. Instead of the adventure of being his own master, he wants a place on the corporate escalator. He does not resent, he tries to exploit, the increasingly undemocratic social structure. He seeks not the approval of his fellow citizens for his independence of character, but for his passion for adjustment. Far from being a zealous political democrat, he is a bad voter, devoting little time and next to no thought to affairs of state, permanently afraid of conspiracies to upset an American way of life that seems in far more danger than it was during the Revolution or the Civil War. 'The embattled farmer' has become the nervous, conforming inhabitant of suburbia or exurbia. He is no longer confident that he has built the ideal political mouse-trap and that the world will beat its way to his door. He wants security, not adventure.

I have not the time nor the capacity to assess the justice of this inverted view of the modern American, of the alleged change in the American social personality. (I put entirely on one side the large psychological, psychiatric and psycho-analytical literature on what is wrong with the American man, woman, child, family.) I have read of the financial rewards of those who go through high school as compared with those who never got past grade school. I know the computed value of a college education. I know of the pursuit of security, the sense of danger in a strange new world.

But I wonder if we are not facing a false dilemma. First of all, the ideal picture of Crèvecoeur, of Jefferson, was an ideal picture, not, perhaps, so much a myth as that of the noble savage or of 'the West' of Buffalo Bill and Sitting Bull. You can find some of the materials for Riesman's analysis in Tocqueville; you can find a lot of Vance Packard's analysis in Francis Grund. The Adams family, for a century past, have made what it is hardly too harsh to call an industry out of predicting that the day of wrath has come. And it is quite a long time since the triumph of 'the Heathen Chinee' led to the speculation that civilization was a failure and 'the Caucasian played out'.

What has happened inside the United States in the new world has happened outside it in the old world of which the new is a child. As the president of the Massachusetts Institute of Technology has recently reminded us, our most difficult problems at the moment come not from the mass of change but from the speed of change. If the American is bewildered in this world moving in unknown directions, at a speed unprecedented in history, so is the European. Both are better off than the member of the nascent nations of Asia and Africa (not all of which may survive their birth pangs) who, overnight, are having to adjust to our changes of the past and our changes of the present, from the world of, at latest, the Middle Ages, to the world of outer space. This may not be much comfort; indeed, in another context, it might be an additional cause for alarm, since the Americans will have to lead as well as stumblingly try to find a path for themselves. The most they may be able to say is 'in the country of the blind, the one-eyed man is king'.

But it is something to be one-eyed. If the American cannot recover that innocent complacency, optimism, conviction of divine favour, which he owned yesterday, it perhaps only shows he has rejoined the human race. And he has rejoined one particular section of it, as well as the whole race. He has rejoined the old world from which the new world came or, to be more precise, both the worlds have been thrown together in a novel fashion, so that it will soon be risky, without adding many important qualifications, to talk of the American national character—or of the English or the French. It may even be dangerous to talk of the Russian national character, of the Soviet national character as the irresistible forces of modern technology assail and alter us all.

Perhaps I should modify the word 'irresistible'. The forces are not totally irresistible; their power can be used for good and evil, their impact modified in various ways. But however that may be, we are all in the same boat in the western world, parts of a world we have, as societies, made but which none of us planned. It is inevitable, even if regrettable, that the unique character of the American and of the American experiment (if the adjective was ever justified) is over. The United States as a body politic, as a society, is no longer something to be studied in isolation.

But it is worth studying as a special case of a bigger society and I am prepared to agree with Max Lerner that it is entitled to be studied as a 'civilization', even if we do not see it as an isolated civilization. More than that, it is worth considering how far it is safe to assume that the old 'notes' of American society have vanished. It is not only that we can see much of the present America in the America of Andrew Jackson, but we can see much of the America of Jackson in the United States of today. At this point, I am bound to be even more impressionistic and dogmatic than before. Yet, speaking as an outsider who has been closely observing this society for most of his life, I think I can still see in the personality of the American body politic, much of what was to be seen at the time of the Revolution, what was to be seen down to the beginning of this century.

This is a country which, in comparison with those European countries I know best, is egalitarian in temper; a country in which what I may call economic and political hope springs eternal; in which a possibly uncritical belief in national and political institutions is potent; a country in which envy (a point Bryce noted) is far less than in Europe a political force; a country in which past political and social resentments play a smaller part than they do in so egalitarian a society as Australia. A great deal of the traditional image of the traditional American is still usable. This is no doubt in part true because the belief in the image affects the conduct and produces a possibly false surface conformity with it.

But I believe it is deeper than that, that inside the general western technological civilization, this people of plenty had still a very different character from that of the peoples whom it leads, for whom it serves as an examplar. It is still a 'new world', still marked off from the old world in important and, on the whole, helpful and hopeful ways. America—Americanism—is not a myth, nor a mere survival of a dead social and historical order like the Holy Roman Empire. And since this is so, America is worthy of the most intense, critical, scholarly study not only by outsiders but more particularly by Americans. The assessment of their inheritance is one of the most important items on the American agenda. And if a foreigner may be permitted the impertinence, I propose to devote the rest of my remarks not so much to making my own assessment as to discussing the dangers of too excessive a concentration of interest on the uniqueness of the American and the American way of life. Again, I am aware that American historians know of more than one frontier, know more than one society that is a child of Europe, look hopefully, perhaps too hopefully, for parallels in Australia, Latin America, Siberia, as hopefully, perhaps, as some of the students at Johns Hopkins in the heyday of Germanic historiography looked to Tacitus to discover the origins of the New England town.

But what I want to discuss, in a mood of mild deprecation, is not the isolation of American history from the history of the North Atlantic countries—or of the whole human race for that matter. I am concerned with a much narrower field of cultural history (cultural being taken in its narrow sense), concerned with certain problems of what are now often called 'American studies'. It is my belief, to be short and possibly rude, that too much effort is being put into the study of American literary and artistic culture, or rather that it is being too much studied in isolation from other literary or art forms in related cultures. I am quite well aware of the dangers of laying down absolutes, of erecting personal or national taste into universal canons of interpretation. I am also aware of how rash it is to inspect the cultural inheritance of another society and recommend that some prize exhibits be relegated to the attic if not to the junk heap. Yet, rash as is the enterprise, I am about to risk it.

It seems to me that in the study of the American past there is now disguised as a genuine aesthetic treasure-trove, what is often merely interesting because it 'casts light' on an American society we are studying for quite different reasons. As long as we approach the artifacts and the literary remains of the American past as historians, read dull books, dull sermons, estimate the comparative worth of various minor artists and architects because these laborious studies aid us to comprehend the American past and present, all is well. It is only in romantic travel books that an archaeological expedition always brings up things of intrinsic interest. Most relics of the past are relics of a very limited human success in the now very old war of man with his environment. Many monuments of the past are magnificent without being beautiful. I often wonder whether Rome was not greatly improved by being ruined and I note how small in bulk the great Greek architectural legacy is. Alexandria and Babylon may well have been far more vulgar than New York seems to the supercilious European visitor and I have no doubt that Nero would have been dazzled by it. What little we know of Carthage makes us hunger after Dallas or Sydney. There is nothing, that is to say, novel in the American situation as I see it, in the fact that not many relics of the American past are intrinsically beautiful or interesting. They are important because they are part of the American past. They should be studied as such, but that study should not be palmed off on the young as an aesthetic experience. It is right to point out how interesting and illuminating is the great range of historical styles to be seen within a few blocks in the centre of Indianapolis. There is as much variety as there is in the same area in Siena. But Siena is capable of giving rewards to people who arrive with no historical background and go away with none. The interest of Indianapolis is historical (and, of course, human); it is not artistic. I could give many more examples but one is enough.

Less obvious, but important, is the question of scale. In Boston, in New York, in Philadelphia, in Charleston, are buildings of grace, beauty and charm. They are also of great historic interest. There is no great harm in mixing the two as long as we don't transfer the interest that Independence Hall has as an historical relic, comparable to Westminster Hall or the relics of the Roman Forum, to the building as a building, compare it with the Sainte-Chapelle or the Parthenon. (I choose these examples to show that by scale I don't mean mere size; I mean scale in the history of human architectural achievement.) But size *is* something. Restored Williamsburg is charming, elegant, but, its historical background omitted, it is not impressive if compared with contemporary building like Compiègne or the Dublin Customs House or the château of Saverne, still less if it is compared with Versailles.

The student of American arts and architecture ought to be constantly reminded of this question of scale, asked to compare the work of the best American architects with that of Wren or Fischer von Erlach or Cameron. If he does, he will discover that not till the late nineteenth century do we get architecture and architects in America who are interesting in the history of achievement or taste, not because of the light they cast on American culture at a given period, but because of the light they cast on the human achievement at any period. I could multiply instances and I hasten to point out that if the American achievement was not of the first order, it was due, in part, to the limited resources of the new country and, equally important, to the distribution of those resources. Compiègne, Chatsworth, Peterhof, Saverne, all represent the reverse of the medal, the absence of the 'new man' of Crèvecoeur who had much better things to do with his country's resources than to waste them in sterile splendour for the glory of immoral tyrants like Catherine the Great or immoral bishops like the Cardinal de Rohan. And, of course, the same explanation applies to the absence of what the French call 'le luxe pour Dieu' which gave the world the great eighteenth-century baroque churches of Germany and of Mexico.

The America of Franklin and Washington had no time or patience for such extravagances. We may think that America was right. But we should not deceive ourselves, confuse the issue, by getting young Americans to misjudge the scale of American effort and the degree of American success. They should be made to realize, for instance, that elegant and clean as Franklin's Philadelphia was, it was not nearly as elegant as the Dublin or Edinburgh or Nancy of Franklin's maturity. It is right to insist on the modernity and cleanliness of Philadelphia, but if the young American is to be given means of judgment he must be reminded of the limitations of Philadelphia in the age of the Enlightenment. (I think I can say this as I myself am a most loyal son of an important secondary city of the Enlightenment and I should reluctantly have to admit that Glasgow, in the eighteenth century, was not only smaller than Edinburgh but a lot less magnificent.)

I could say much the same of the treatment of painting, of furniture, and the like. It is proper, it is edifying, to go through Fairfield

County or Bucks County looking for Paul Revere silver or Trumbull or Stuart paintings but if, by accident, you found a Chardin or a complete silver service designed for Madame de Pompadour, you would be wise to suppress your patriotism and buy the foreign stuff.

I conclude with remarks about a field in which I am very much at home. The American colonists from the beginning—from John Smith and Governor Bradford—were literate. You have an unparalleled archival treasure house. Some of the early annalists were good writers. Taylor, if not a great poet, is an interesting one, but until Franklin there is hardly an American writer who, intrinsically, from the light he casts on the human condition, is of real importance. Jonathan Edwards was a man of great acuteness and of great stylistic merit, but if we reflect he was a contemporary or a near contemporary of Johnson and Burke in London, overlapped with Swift in Dublin, with Hume in Edinburgh and Adam Smith in Glasgow, we can see the dangers of introducing a young American undergraduate to the intellectual life of the colonies without reminding him constantly of the limitations of the colonial culture, of its colonialism. It is not merely a question of being out of the main stream of things. Vico was out of them in Naples. It is a matter of being imbedded in a society that was developing its unique character and was sacrificing much to the achievement of that new man, the American.

From Franklin on, the case is altered. We have Americans in the front rank of literature, in learning, in the sciences. And if we do not mix up, in our teaching or writing, two orders of importance, perhaps stress too much Jefferson's scientific interests and achievements, confuse Cooper's very real merits as a writer with his much greater importance as the creator of an American legend that became a world legend, no harm is done—or no harm is done that is not in a sense self-correcting—for America had become mature enough to produce its own critics and its own corrective forces.

Yet the danger is not totally done away with. I seem to have read some books, long and short—novels, short stories, verses and the like—whose interest is purely historical but which have been revived out of piety, which may be all right, but with an implication that they are still worth reading, not for the light, often disconcerting, they cast on life in Georgia or on the literary antecedents of Mark Twain, but for their contribution to our knowledge of and ability to handle the human situation. I do not for a moment deny that this kind of literary archaeology can dig up treasures. Taylor is an example and

Melville is a more impressive one. (I hope I may be pardoned the truth that the Melville revival began in England not America and was not animated by cultural patriotism.)

I could multiply examples but I have taken up too much of your time. To go back to the beginning: I think the novelty, if you like, the unique character of the American experiment, of the new man, Homo, Americanus, is an historical viewpoint eminently capable of being defended and eminently capable of casting light on the situation of the American today. I should be the last to defend the old, naïve political idea of history or to deny that we can't begin to understand American civilization if we exclude the arts, the crafts, the techniques of American society. But it is an easy and a dangerous step to move from discovering what made American society what it was to evaluating the end product in purely national terms. And it is particularly easy to do this in the cultural field, where the American achievement, until recent times, was limited and parochial in many arts and where general standards may be abandoned in a fit of patriotic enthusiasm for a book or a work of art that today is only what French historians call a *document pour servir*.

There are works of art which have a double purpose of the first order. You can read *Anna Karenina* for the light it casts on the social conditions of Russia after the emancipation of the serfs. You can read *Huckleberry Finn* for the light it casts on the social conditions of the Mississippi Valley on the eve of the emancipation of the slaves. But it is not the best way to read either masterpiece. You may read an author like Howells with a pretty even balance of interests, use a painter like Remington in two different ways. No harm will be done as long as the teacher of American history remembers that that is what he is teaching—not the history of the human mind as represented in masterpieces of art or literature. The young American needs to be told and shown what society bred him; he also needs to be shown and told of the greater society of which that society is a part, to be reminded, for instance, in Detroit, that the internal combustion engine is not an American invention. Historians of the next generation should explain both the success of Elvis Presley and of *My Fair Lady*. It will do no harm if they, from time to time, drop a hint that Mr. Presley is not Chaliapin and *My Fair Lady* not *The Marriage of Figaro*.

1961

13

THE CATHOLIC POLITICIAN

THE UNITED STATES is a Protestant country. This will seem to most Americans something so obvious as not to be worth stating. But it is worth stating because the official theory of the United States is one of complete religious neutrality. Yet in practice this official neutrality means that the United States has a religious bias, and that religious bias is towards some vague, undenominational Protestantism.

Arthur M. Schlesinger, Sr., has said that anti-Catholicism is the oldest and most permanent of American prejudices. There are historical reasons for this, and they greatly affect the position of the Catholic politician. Whether the average American Protestant likes it or not, or is conscious of it or not, he regards the Catholic office-holder, in any serious office, as an anomaly. True, the United States is committed officially to the view that all denominations are created equal, but I think it is impossible for an observant foreigner to move around the United States, as I have been doing for nearly forty years, and not realize that this formal equality conceals a real inequality. An American who belongs to any of the Protestant denominations is accepted as being automatically a suitable candidate for high office. No Catholic is. President Kennedy may have broken this tradition, but a great deal of the respect and admiration he has won is rather like the admiration Dr. Johnson commented on when he spoke of women preaching: it is based on surprise that a Catholic can be President of the United States without immediately revealing his subservience to a foreign priesthood.

There is, of course, something absurd in this gratified surprise. In the Western alliance, of which the United States is the leader, nearly all the effective heads of state from General de Gaulle and Dr. Adenauer downward are Catholics. Only England has a Protestant

THE CATHOLIC POLITICIAN 165

chief (I mean the Prime Minister, not the Queen, who is, of course, Protestant by statutory definition under the Act of Settlement). And in none of these countries, not even in England, is the notion of the Catholic ruler as extraordinary as it is in the United States, for all of them have visible and, historically speaking, recent Catholic pasts. Even in my native land, Scotland, the Catholic past is not very remote in time and is visible in many ways. To give an example, the eminently Presbyterian University of Glasgow still confers its degrees by apostolic authority, and when it celebrated its five hundredth anniversary ten years ago, its first act was to send a Latin address to the heir of its founder, the Pope. And at the coronation of Queen Elizabeth II a large number of the great ceremonial offices were held by Catholics who had a hereditary right to take part in this once Catholic ceremony. These historical relics do not necessarily mean that there is not a great deal of anti-Catholic feeling, and in Catholic countries like France and Italy a great deal of anticlerical feeling and outright hostility towards the Catholic Church. But the Church is there. It always has been there. It always will be.

In the United States it is very different. The United States was made by Protestants and cast in a Protestant mould. The founders and the major part of the population had a lively hatred of Catholicism. It does not matter whether Benjamin Franklin was right in believing that his ancestors had nearly been victims of Bloody Mary in England. The important point is that he *did* believe it. The so-called Scotch-Irish, the Ulster Presbyterians, hated the Pope as much as they hated the King of England. Many of the early German settlers, like the Palatines and the Salzburgers, were genuine victims of Catholic intolerance in Germany. And when the United States framed its Constitution and got its character, the Catholic Church was seen not only as hostile to the principles of free inquiry, of Protestant private judgment, but as a dying institution. It was treated with contumely by 'Catholic' sovereigns like the Emperor Joseph II, and two Popes were taken captive by the triumphant and anticlerical French. To men like Thomas Jefferson and John Adams, both enemies of the 'priests' (by which they meant the Protestant clergy), the thought of a Catholic President would have been not so much odious as absurd. And I am convinced that this feeling of absurdity is an important part of the American makeup today. Of course, there are lots of Catholics in the United States, but they are meant to be hewers of wood and drawers of water, certainly not the rulers, even the elected rulers, of their betters. So any Catholic office-holder, from dogcatcher up, has two strikes against him: he will be regarded with automatic suspicion by the Protestant majority and regarded with another kind of suspicion by the Catholic minority. He will have to walk delicately between the two suspicious groups.

*

The Catholic Church in America is a church of immigrants, and its great expansion from almost nothing came in the nineteenth century and continued until World War I. The two great immigrant waves of Irish and Germans were followed by lesser but very important invasions of Italians, Poles, south Slavs, Bohemians, and the like. And all of these came into a country which was only formally prepared to receive them. Of these groups, by far the most important was the Irish. They were probably not much more numerous than the Germans, if they *were* more numerous; but they were politically far more talented, and they set the role for the Catholic Church in American public life. They were politically more talented than the Germans, although less literate, because they came from a country which, though it had many just claims to being called 'the most distressful', was fantastically badly governed *under parliamentary forms*. The Irish Catholic immigrants knew by experience at home what elections were and what party organization was. In Daniel O'Connell they had had one of the greatest democratic leaders of the nineteenth century, and they brought to the United States political experience which made them very quickly an important political force.

But it was a political experience of a distorting type. They had no reason to like the political organization from which they had fled, and they very soon discovered in America a degree of hostility which seemed familiar to them. If the burning of the Charlestown convent and the Philadelphia riots are still alive in the memory of American Catholics of Irish origin, it is because they are linked in ancestral memory with much more odious happenings in Ireland, with the whole history of the Penal Laws. Even if Protestant America had given a more cordial welcome, these Catholics would have been suspicious with a suspicion bred by centuries of disastrous experience. In fact, they had living and more recent memories of religious persecution than had the New Englanders or the Scotch-Irish.

An American Catholic, especially if he is of Irish origin, is bound to receive with irony many of the protestations of devotion to religious freedom, many of the declarations of hostility to religious persecution, with which the American Protestant is so lavish. A man of great independence of character like John Jay Chapman could, in all innocence, preach to the Irish slum dwellers of New York a kind of political anti-Catholicism based not only on liberal theory but on ancestral Huguenot memories with no consciousness of how absurd his preaching seemed to the Irish Catholics of Manhattan. They had had their own revocation of the Edict of Nantes, the breach of the Treaty of Limerick, of which it is likely John Jay Chapman knew nothing and his hostile audiences knew only a passionate but not seriously wrong historical version.

As I have said, the tone of American Catholicism in its political aspect was set by the Irish. And by the historical experience of the Irish, their priests were leaders in politics, as in everything else, to a degree unknown to any other country in Europe. In the two great civil wars of the seventeenth century in Ireland, summed up for the Irish Catholic in the names of Oliver Cromwell and William III, the old Catholic aristocracy was almost entirely swept away. The Catholic middle class almost disappeared, or survived, as did the families of Edmund Burke and General Wolfe and of John and James Sullivan of New Hampshire and Massachusetts, by turning Protestant. Only the priests were left as leaders. The British government recognized this, and after it abandoned hopes of converting the 'mere' Irish to Protestantism, it used the Catholic bishops and priests as an instrument of government. The great seminary of Maynooth was established by the British government to produce a loyal and useful rather than a learned clergy. It did not produce a very loyal clergy; but it bred a habit of political activity, which the Irish priests took to America and which their flocks were prepared to accept.

It is impossible to understand the automatic political activities of a prelate like Cardinal Spellman without remembering the background of the American Catholic clergy. Historically speaking, the American Catholic clergy may have started as children of the great French seminary of St. Sulpice, but they have been for more than a century children of the great Irish seminary, St. Patrick's College at Maynooth. And the American Catholic politician, whatever his ethnic origin, is sure to have to deal at every stage in his political career with priests and bishops who are children of a system in which a priest had to be a political leader to defend his flock.

It is not surprising that this natural and traditional role should be misunderstood and disliked by American Protestants, and, indeed, by Catholics of a different tradition. The fact remains that, until this century, perhaps until this decade, the American Catholic politician has had to deal with a Church accustomed to a degree of political loyalty unknown in Europe outside Ireland, unknown even in Poland or Bavaria or the southern Netherlands. This, it seems to me, rather than the dogmatic views of the Catholic Church on its role in politics, is the force that keeps alive the traditional American suspicion of Rome. It is less 'that old sinner the Pope' than the more visible and noisy prelates of the Irish Catholic tradition who explain, if they do not justify, the pathological anti-Catholicism of so many Americans. But of course there is a rational and defensible suspicion of political Catholicism which goes far beyond the experience of Irish Catholics at the hands of Protestants, back to the creation of the Catholic doctrine of church and state personified by great figures like St. Gregory VII and Innocent III and great thinkers like St. Thomas Aquinas.

*

If the political experience of the American Catholics has been formed mainly on Irish traditions, the fact remains that an adjustment between church and state, between the Pope and the secular power, has never been easy, in the Roman Empire or the Holy Roman Empire, under Napoleon or Bismarck, not to speak of Stalin, Hitler, and Mussolini. The United States is committed to a neutral view (at any rate, between Christian denominations); it is committed to denying preference to one denomination rather than to another. God is not in the Constitution, and all religions formally compete on even terms. In this competitive world, as Tocqueville noted, the Catholic Church has done very well for itself, but not on its own terms. As that honest man, the late Monsignor John Ryan, pointed out, the Church has not given up its claims to supremacy, and what toleration is given to Protestants or Jews is given of favour, not of right. True, in most European countries and in the United States, this doctrinal rigidity has little if any political significance. But the difficulty is real if not normally important. The United States is dedicated to a certain set of propositions about the religious role of the state (or the political role of the church), and the Roman

Catholic Church is dedicated to a different and, in some instances, opposed set of doctrines. No Pope, certainly not a sagacious Pope like John XXIII, is likely today to insist on making a doctrinal fight, but equally certainly no Pope is likely to make a formal withdrawal of the doctrine of the intrinsic superiority of the Holy See over all competing ecclesiastical authorities, or of its right to assert its own views on great matters, even against the omnicompetent state.

A clash, if a clash there must be, is most likely to come when the Church and the adored national state clash. The possibility of a clash is always there. And so the Catholic politician must move carefully; he may think that the survival of the papal claims of the Middle Ages is simply an archaic nuisance. But he cannot say that these claims are archaic nonsense; he can only act as if they were. And he is always in danger of being pushed into a corner by some dialectician who wants him to harmonize his unconditional allegiance to the United States with the claims of his Church. Put that way, it cannot be done.

But the Protestant voter who is not just out to make debating points, who may have genuine intellectual difficulties compounded of many unrecognized inherited prejudices, is puzzled by the role of the Catholic office-holder. And I think that his first ground of bewilderment and alarm comes from the apparent docility of Catholic politicians in face of the prelates, in face of the undemocratic pretensions of the bishops (the kissing of episcopal rings, for instance) and the role played by a Pope who is always a foreigner. The Catholic politician, it is thought, is not, or not always, a free man. What is whispered to him in the confessional? What attention does he pay to the pronouncements of the bishops? How far is his mind conditioned by an exclusively Catholic education? There is a sense in which a Christian is never free to be just a secular statesman. He may seek answer in prayer or from a pastor, but he cannot put the material well-being of the state before everything else. Nominally Christian statesmen have done so in all ages. But while the Protestant politician wrestles with his conscience alone, or seeks counsel from his pastor, the Catholic politician is a member of a church with a large body of political doctrine, and its rulers are not at all shy about laying down the law.

*

How much of this laying down of the law does the Catholic politician have to pay attention to? If the Pope speaks *ex cathedra*, which he very seldom does, the Catholic politician has to believe in the doctrine laid down—but the American voter is not concerned with doctrines like the Assumption. He is concerned with practical issues in which the Catholic politician is thought of as being too docile; with matters like education, birth control, divorce, some delicate problems of medical ethics, some issues of free speech and free publication. Here the leaders of the Catholic Church do set themselves against majority opinion. They may be defending an old Protestant tradition, as in opposing Sunday trading, but they are a pressure group which orders more than it argues, and the people it orders are the Catholic politicians. True, Protestant ministers, in the South especially, may be as dogmatic in laying down the moral law that the state is not enforcing; they may even be laying down the same law as Catholic bishops. But they do not do it, as a rule, so dogmatically, and even if they do, 'This is a Protestant country.'

Here again, the Irish background of the dominant tradition in American Catholicism works to the disadvantage of the American Catholic politician. As the late George A. Birmingham, the Irish (Protestant) novelist, pointed out a long time ago, Ireland is one of the few countries in which ecclesiastical leaders have what we now call a captive audience. North and south, Catholics and Protestants listen to what is said by bishops, moderators, and the like. No doubt the really faithful do so in France or Italy, but the number of really faithful there is small. In Ireland, it is nearly the whole population. In England, Anglican bishops, convocations, church congresses issue declarations, pass resolutions, but few think that the mass of the semi-pagan English population pays much attention. In America the case is altered, for judging by the printing of sermons in the press on Monday mornings, there is still a general market for clerical utterance. But this may be an editorial illusion, and it may be an illusion that even the faithful Catholic accepts the episcopal letter read from the altar or printed in the diocesan newspaper with a complete and docile faith. Yet an American bishop brought up in the Irish tradition may assume that the silent respect with which his letter is received is the same as fervent assent. And so he may be tempted to issue too many statements and utter them in too peremptory a tone. The Protestant voter will not realize with what ironical weariness some of these manifestoes are received or how lacking in real force they are.

The Catholic politician may resent the matter and still more the manner of the episcopal declarations, as many Catholics resented the tone of the pastoral letter of the bishops of Puerto Rico in the campaign of 1960. But he will be reluctant to say so. Any public resentment will be used against him, not so much by the bishops or by Protestant rivals as by Catholic rivals who will be anxious to show their zeal and may profit by a show of religious indignation. Above all, the politicians would like the clergy to keep their mouths shut or to stick to safe generalities. A politician's motives may not be very creditable. If he is in the South, he no more wants an episcopal declaration against segregation than do his Methodist brethren. He may not want to stop Sunday trading (Sunday sellers and buyers are voters).

The clergy are often right, often courageous, often saying something that needs to be said, but from the politician's point of view, the clergy, especially the Catholic clergy, especially the Catholic clergy bred in the Irish tradition, want the state to promote morality, positively and negatively, more than even the most upright politician (who has to get elected) thinks is practicable or wise. The practising politician knows too much of human weakness, of the limitations of the law, of the incompetence or the venality of the enforcers of the law to wish to erode the authority of the body politic at any level by too ostentatious enforcement of the moral views of the clergy, *any* clergy.

After all, the great lesson of wisdom in this field was taught not by or to Catholics but by and to Protestants. Prohibition was the equivalent of Catholic crusades against birth control, and some Catholic politicians have been known to wonder if Cardinal Spellman and his brethren ever ponder the damage done to the Protestant establishment by the follies of the campaign to make America dry. The law could not make America dry. It cannot make it pure, and the effort to do these things may make the last state worse than the first. And again, except in a few areas, the Catholic politician has to remember that 'This is a Protestant country.' If the Catholic Church gets the reputation of being Meddlesome Matty, as in many places it has done, the sufferers will be the Catholic politicians—as well as the bishops. And the Irish Church, with its strong Puritan tradition exported to America, has that reputation.

The Catholic politician knows this; he may decide in Boston or Providence to play along. But nationally or even in statewide politics, a politician knows that, even if 'smut when smitten is front page stuff', you can smite too often, particularly if you are a Catholic. For more will be forgiven to a representative of the indigenous tradition of using the secular arm to enforce morality than to a representative of what is still thought of as a largely foreign body.

*

This alienation of the Church, and of the groups which it represents, alters the role of the American Catholic politician. He is not thought of merely as the representative of Bloody Mary or the Inquisition or of the Syllabus of Pius IX or of the harassers of Protestants in South America or Spain. He is, or at any rate was, thought of as being no doubt an American citizen, but a second-class citizen. Possibly, before the great immigrant waves of the nineteenth century, the few Catholics who lived in the United States were treated according to their positions in life; if they were servants, they were treated as servants; if they were great landed magnates like Charles Carroll, they were treated as great landed magnates; if they were great lawyers like Roger Taney, they were accepted as Chief Justice, as Edward Douglass White from the semi-Catholic state of Louisiana was later accepted in that great office. He was, after all, not a 'Mick'; he was that much more respectable thing, a former Confederate officer. Something of the same acceptance of the old Catholic families could and can be seen in New Mexico. Senator Dennis Chavez of Los Chavez is not just a Catholic politician; he is 'Chavez of that ilk', as they say in Scotland.

Now, there was some justification for the snooty attitude of old American stocks to the political ambitions of the newcomers. Ireland and, still more, Sicily did not provide a good training in political ethics. Their governments, British or Bourbon, were too bad for that. Few of the Irish Catholic bourgeoisie and few of the small body of Irish Catholic aristocrats emigrated to America. (The Emmets and the Mitchels, prominent in New York social life and politics at a high level, were not Catholic by origin.) What the Irish were expected to do was to provide top sergeants in the political army, at most. The result of this political role was not always edifying. Catholic Boss Croker was not much more honest, though much more intelligent, than Protestant Boss Tweed. Since municipal politics was often corrupt and since Catholics were so numerous in the lower echelons, understandably a great many Catholic politicians were grafters or tolerators of graft. But one would have to know very little about the inner history of city and state politics to believe that only Catholics were grafters or that their religion bred their corruption. William Allen White made the proper distinction between the 'governing class', the politicians, many of them Catholics, and the 'ruling class', few of whom were Catholics. Both classes encouraged and profited by corruption. The ruling class profited more.

It was, of course, natural and right for Mugwumps to be angry with the Catholic local grafters, but if Henry Cabot Lodge and Theodore Roosevelt held their noses and voted for Blaine and bitterly resented the superior sensitiveness of the Mugwumps, why should a local Catholic politician, with no benefit of Harvard, be totally condemned for supporting a local and Catholic equivalent of Blaine? How many proper Bostonians remember Patrick Collins, a good mayor of Boston (as the late Edward Channing used to tell his Harvard classes)? It is easier to remember that much more entertaining and probably more significant figure, James Michael Curley. With the name of Curley, we come to the crux of the Catholic question as it affects contemporary American politics. It is not only that there is a Catholic President (and Attorney-General), but that there are nearly twenty Catholic governors, and that the leaders of both houses of Congress are Catholics. In some states, both senators are Catholics. Catholics are numerous in city halls, including the city halls of some of the greatest cities. The naïve anticlerical in France would see the hand of the Jesuits in this. I am not quite convinced that there are not a great many American Protestants who think the same. And, of course, since Catholics are just about a fourth of the population, they are over-represented. But it should be noted that they were elected, and, in nearly every state, necessarily by Protestant majorities.

What the sudden flood of Catholic politicians into office, culminating in the entry of a Catholic into the White House, represents is not a Jesuit conspiracy, but America's coming of age, in a new sense. The great immigrant blocs of the nineteenth and twentieth centuries are being assimilated, and this is reflected in the sphere where immigrant blocs have already made their claims to assimilation most effectively, in politics. It is not only the Catholics, it is also the Jews who benefit—and alarm. The last great immigrant group whose assimilation is far from complete is overwhelmingly Protestant, the Negroes.

Some of the old suspicions have been diminished by the Kennedy Administration. Some are silly. Moreover, it is something in a country like the United States (less so than in England) that the Catholic President went to a good Protestant school and not to a good Catholic school and college—to Choate and Harvard, and not, for example, to Canterbury and Georgetown. President Kennedy is not a product of the Fulton Street Fish Market, like Al Smith, nor is Mrs. Kennedy as shocking a chatelaine of the White House as the nervous clubwomen of 1928 thought Mrs. Al Smith would be. The Catholic Church in America has come out of the catacombs. It is in every way more respectable intellectually, socially, and economically than it was even when Al Smith ran. The decline in immigration has relieved the Church of what was its most important task, keeping and training the immigrants. This was a kind of training that only the Catholic Church could have given. That role is over: the immigrants are now Americans; they are much more at ease than they were in Al Smith's time.

It would be idle to pretend that American Catholics are totally mature, politically speaking. They are very American in their willingness to believe in conspiracies. Thus, the late Joseph McCarthy was not much admired in his ancestral country, but he found supporters among American Catholics. Many American Catholics believed, like many French Catholics at the time of the Dreyfus case, that the enemy of my enemy is necessarily a friend. But from the beginning the two chief organs of the Catholic intellectuals, *America*, run by the Jesuits, and the *Commonweal*, run by laymen, were vigorous, courageous, and acute critics of the Wisconsin demagogue. That Catholics have no monopoly on this kind of folly, Mr. Welch has shown us. And it could be argued that since it was inevitable that some demagogue would capture the lunatic fringe of frustrated Americans, it was just as well it should be the disreputable Catholic ex-Democrat rather than a sound teetotal Baptist.

In other ways the Catholic community is now at home. Its most important groups, the Germans and the Irish, are not in any reasonable sense of the term recent immigrants. Probably more than half of the genes of the present American population come from nineteenth-century immigrants. And Joseph P. Kennedy has reasonably complained about being constantly described as an Irishman, and has asked why he isn't occasionally called an American. The reason is that he is a Catholic. The Kennedys are no more of new immigrant stock than were the families of Woodrow Wilson and Charles Evans Hughes in 1916. But they were Protestants: there's the rub.

*

Should there be a rub? There will, I am convinced, be many rubs, and there should be some. No American Catholic can give that unlimited adherence to Caesar that hundred-per-cent American patriotism too often asks for; too often, because I do not believe *any* Christian can worship *Divus Caesar* as some of the more noisy, flag-waving, oath-imposing Americans would seem to think is right. The United States, for a Christian, is really *under* God; that means that God need not approve of all, or even of most, of what the United States does. A deeply conscientious Catholic converted, say, by the English Dominican Gerald Vann to the belief that an atomic war would be a sinful war would be in an ambiguous position as President (and Commander-in-Chief). Christians have always thought that holding civil office had its special moral dangers. The Catholic politician is no worse off than the deeply believing Protestant Christian.

But in the American context he is worse off than a Protestant. It is not that I really expect that the medieval controversies over the two swords are going to be revived. No Pope in his right mind will stress all the doctrines of the more extreme canonists. But there are possible dangers of rifts between Catholic politicians, especially in the federal government, and the hierarchy. There are minor grounds of friction. The freedom of American foreign policy might be limited by uncritical and unrealistic anti-Communism. There is nothing surprising and wrong in violent anti-Communism among American Catholics, especially among Catholics of Irish origin. Jews were not asked to think kindly of Hitler (they are not asked to think critically of Israel). But an innocent black-and-white view of the external world might be a nuisance. I do not think it more than that.

There are two topics, however, which, on the local level in one instance and on the national level in the other, will perplex any Catholic office-holder who has—and knows he has—to steer between what would please the more vociferous bishops and the mass of Protestants. One, the attempted ban on contraception, is much more a source of irritation than of permanent grievance, but it irritates non-Catholic Americans even more than the imposition of Protestant Manichaean views on liquor did. But contraception is not so serious a question as the schools are. No one knows how effective the ban on contraception is, except in the most devout Catholic households, and there are some Protestants who share Catholic dislike of contraception. A Catholic politician can dodge the problem of contraception. He cannot dodge the schools question, specifically the question of federal aid to parochial schools.

For here the Church is not demanding something negative; it is demanding positive action from Catholic politicians, including the President of the United States. And it is running into two very formidable forces. The first is the belief that a non-denominational system of public eduaction is part of the American way of life, one of the most sacred parts of that way of life. Whether this tradition is as old as the Supreme Court seems to think is doubtful, but, as the Dred Scott case shows, the Court has never been very sound on history. But that is neither here nor there; the wall of separation has been erected. What does a Catholic President do, what does a Catholic senator do, when an attempt is made to breach the wall? I may say, as a foreigner, that the case is not so open and shut on either side as controversialists think. How seldom in these debates or quarrels is any foreign experience called on, say the experience of the Netherlands or Scotland. Politicians with a big Catholic vote will be under great pressure to act one way; politicians with a big Baptist vote will be under great pressure to vote another. I do not see how some, and possibly bitter, conflict is to be avoided. And I do not mean only or mainly controversy between Catholics and Protestants. It will be a different quarrel. It will be a quarrel between bishops and politicians who think that a battle in which the Catholic Church stands as an obstacle to what, more and more, the great industrial states will want and need, federal aid to education, will be disastrous. The politician will want to avoid quarrelling with the bishops, and he will want to avoid quarrelling with the voters. And the contemporary Catholic office-holder will differ from the old-time ward leader (who was the representative Catholic politician even a generation ago) in two important ways. First of all, he will often not be a product of the Irish tradition at all. He may have only a modified respect for the political judgment of bishops; he may have no respect at all. Governor DiSalle (and Senator Lausche) of Ohio have a different background from Al Smith's or David I. Walsh's. So has Senator Pastore of Rhode Island; so has Governor Rosellini of Washington.

Then, probably more important, American Catholics have now a large, growing, wealthy middle class. Even if the male members have gone to Catholic schools from kindergarten to college, they have had a less restricted access to the Protestant world than have priests brought up in parochial schools and in seminaries sheltered from the heretical world, brought up in what a leading Catholic friend of mine calls 'the Catholic ghetto'. In many things in the future, the spokesmen of the Catholic community (as apart from the Catholic Church) will be laymen who may or may not be politicians. If they are politicians, they will have more worldly wisdom and probably more independence than their predecessors had. They will not denounce Harvard as that 'Kremlin on the Charles'. They have doubts about Catholic education at all levels and may not want to commit the Church to a losing battle. There will be no Al Smith or Commissioner Murphy again. And Mayor Daley of Chicago and Governor Lawrence of Pennsylvania compare favourably with some not very remote Protestant predecessors.

The growth of the Catholic middle class and the slower but visible growth of a Catholic intelligentsia will alter the picture of the Catholic in politics, of the Catholic office-holder. What have the late Frank Murphy of the Supreme Court and Justice Brennan of the Supreme Court in common? What has either in common with the late Judge Martin J. Manton, who tried in vain to save America from *Ulysses* before going to jail for corruption? The Catholic office-holder, the Catholic active in politics, will be seen more and more as a representative American of an accepted minority group. With the rise of the intellectual quality and prestige of American Catholicism, a Catholic will no longer be regarded as *ipso facto* the victim of a dying superstition. Perhaps the bishops will take the advice given by Judge John M. Murtagh not to expect the state to be a force for sanctity or even a force for punishing sin. Perhaps even Southern Baptists will learn that they and the papists have a common enemy and that, in America, the enemy is not so much atheistic Communism as a great deal of the American way of life which insists that gaining the whole world *is* saving one's soul. Nothing will make the role of the Catholic politician, especially the office-holder, easy in a Protestant country. It is not easy in a Catholic country, not even in Ireland.

1962

14

UNCLE TOM'S MESSAGE: THE BOOK OF WAR AND FREEDOM

'SO THIS IS the little lady who made this big war?' So, in the famous anecdote, the gigantic President Lincoln greeted the tiny Mrs. Harriet Beecher Stowe in the White House at one of the darkest moments of the Civil War. Mrs. Stowe had come to Washington to reassure herself that the President, of whose lack of anti-slavery zeal all the Beechers were suspicious, would stick to his word and issue the final Emancipation Proclamation. Lincoln *had* made up his mind. He had made it up long before he issued even the first proclamation, as Professor John Hope Franklin has recently reminded us, but Mrs. Stowe, like most of the New England Abolitionists, old or new, did not wholly trust the enigmatic man of the White House. And Lincoln, who had his hands full of problems of all kinds—problems for which, in many instances, he did not see any good solution—was not exaggerating very much when he attributed the outbreak of the Civil War to Mrs. Stowe, or, to be more accurate, to *Uncle Tom's Cabin*.[1]

Uncle Tom's Cabin has many claims to be regarded as the most remarkable propaganda novel ever published. It is unjust to think of Mrs. Stowe as simply the author of *Uncle Tom's Cabin*, but had she not written that, she would be a minor author dug up, like so many other even more minor authors, in courses in American studies. She wrote some good and humane books, but for once in her life the

[1] Harriet Beecher Stowe, *Uncle Tom's Cabin*. Edited by Kenneth S. Lynn. 460 pp. Harvard University Press. London: Oxford University Press. £2.

Daemon took over. When she used to say, as she often did, that God had written her book she was, in a sense, speaking the truth. Before the publication of *Uncle Tom's Cabin* controversy over American slavery was not only muffled by leaders both North and South, but by a kind of conspiracy of silence about the contrast between the American dream and the reality of the slavery system. After the publication of *Uncle Tom* it could never be 'bright confident morning again' for the South. The South was at last on the defensive. And as far as *Uncle Tom* helped to convince them that they were isolated, surrounded, endangered by a hostile climate of opinion, the book did in fact make 'this big war'.

*

It is, of course, true that other novels have had a great effect on the climate of opinion. There are half a dozen English social novels, half a dozen American novels on social topics, which have had an impact on public opinion greater than that produced by solemn treatises or by parliamentary debates. Thomas Hood, Charles Reade, Charles Dickens, Upton Sinclair, John Steinbeck—all, to some degree, changed public opinion. Turgenev's *Sportsman's Sketches* is said to have helped to induce the Tsar Alexander II to abolish serfdom. But we do not read Turgenev because of his impact on the system of serfdom and we do read Harriet Beecher Stowe because of *Uncle Tom's Cabin*.

It is impossible to estimate how many million copies of this most successful of all propaganda tracts (with the possible exception of the Communist Manifesto) have been printed in all the major languages of the world. It was not very fanciful for the author of the libretto of *The King and I* to revive the memory of the impact of this moral tale a hundred years ago even in remote Siam.

*

The immense propaganda success of *Uncle Tom's Cabin* resulted in an almost total neglect of its literary qualities. When Mrs. Stowe, by then a very old woman, died most obituary notices, although they admitted the historical importance of her most famous book, were extremely patronizing about its literary merits. Then, as various people have pointed out, a great many people not only in the United States but in Great Britain got their impression of *Uncle Tom's Cabin* not from reading the text but from what were called in

America 'Tom Shows'. Many grew up actually believing that Eliza was pursued over the ice by bloodhounds, and bloodhounds were provided in the 'Tom Shows'. It is, in fact, more against the Uncle Tom of the 'Tom Shows' that American Negro opinion has protested than against the Uncle Tom of the book. In his remarkable essay on Harriet Beecher Stowe the greatest living American critic, Mr. Edmund Wilson, has pointed out how far the 'Tom Shows' diverged from the text of the novel. Indeed, Mrs. Stowe, when taken to see one of the dramatic versions of her book, had to have the plot explained to her! The lesson of her book, which was written as a moral tract, had been almost completely lost. Probably Mr. Wilson exaggerates the degree to which the book was ignored and forgotten. It was certainly never forgotten in Great Britain or on the Continent; but since it was regarded as a propaganda book or, more oddly still, as a children's book, it was not studied seriously by professional literary critics and was used by historians merely as a *document pour servir*. As Mr. Wilson wrote: 'To expose oneself in maturity to *Uncle Tom* may therefore prove a startling experience. It is a much more impressive work than one has ever been allowed to suspect.'

This admirable new edition of the most famous, if not the best, of American novels makes it possible for us to read *Uncle Tom* not as if it were quite a new book, but as if it were a book and not a tract. And yet one must constantly bear in mind that it was designed as a tract. The ailing, overworked, impoverished wife of an unsuccessful biblical scholar had no intention of writing a novel or of writing a book of the length which she was inspired to make it. Up to the time of her sudden ascent into the firmament of literary fame Mrs. Stowe was a minor writer of a type common enough in the mid-nineteenth century and later. She was an inferior Mrs. Gaskell and perhaps the nearest British (or Scottish) equivalent to Mrs. Stowe before *Uncle Tom* is Annie S. Swan. The book was written under great difficulties, because on no account in those male-dominated years could her husband's laborious biblical researches or her formidable father's theological investigations be interfered with. So she wrote hurriedly, week by week, on the corner of the kitchen table, looking after the children, arranging the cooking, looking after unsatisfactory servants, worrying about the bills. It would be idle to expect in these circumstances the austere devotion to literary discipline that one expects from a Flaubert or a Henry James.

And it must be remembered that not only was *Uncle Tom* treated as a tract, it was designed as a tract. It was begun as a serial in a religious paper. A great deal that a reader today finds most off-putting was part of the lesson that Mrs. Stowe wanted to teach, and that lesson was the lesson not only of the wickedness of slavery but the goodness of Tom.

Harriet Beecher was the daughter of one of the most formidable neo-Calvinist preachers of the early nineteenth century. Lyman Beecher was a man of immense mental and physical activity, a man who knew few doubts and no hesitations. Suspected by the extreme right of American Calvinism, he was yet a determined and convinced Calvinist. He detested the latitudinarian theology of Harvard almost as much as he detested and feared Rome. He had immense belief in his own powers of convincing others. He thought he could have saved Lord Byron, and perhaps he could have, for Byron never got over or, if you like, recovered from his Scottish Calvinist education. All Harriet Beecher's brothers became ministers—in one or two instances with hesitation. But none of them became Calvinists of their father's school. A lesson, perhaps *the* lesson, of *Uncle Tom's Cabin* is that God is really love, that he is not the God of Jonathan Edwards who loves to be loved. A great deal of the religiosity of *Uncle Tom* which irritates present-day critics, white and Negro alike, is simply a projection of the religiosity of the Beecher household. They were a very remarkable family, provoking an emendation of the famous jest about the Herveys: 'The human race consists of Saints, Sinners and Beechers.' But the question of whether God was really love or whether he was the God of Calvin was one of intense interest to the Beecher family. They did not face their abandonment of their father's views as clearly as did Theodore Parker when he said to an orthodox minister, 'I see: your God is my Devil.' Like the rest of her family, Harriet was 'converted'; but her conversion was not taken seriously because it came so easily. Her aggressive elder sister Catherine had been very much in love with a brilliant young professor at Yale who had not been converted and who was drowned at sea, leaving his fiancée in anguish and despair about his fate in the next world. This side of Harriet Beecher's education comes out in many more of her writings than *Uncle Tom*.

*

A great deal of what seems to us irrelevant and nauseating in *Uncle Tom* comes from the religious preoccupations of its author. The sanctity, the humility, the resignation of the hero were, for Harriet Beecher Stowe, not only proofs of the Christian character of the Negro and the proven reality of his religion but they were also exemplary in the strict sense of the term. Whether it was conscious or not, Harriet Beecher Stowe meant Uncle Tom to be a Black Christ. In her other anti-slavery novel, *Dred*, the hero is a rebel who is *not* resigned. He is obviously a leader of Negro Jacobins like Denmark Vesey or Nat Turner and his apocalyptic rhetoric is very unlike the Christian resignation shown by Uncle Tom.

Other things in the novel irritate a reader today. Little Eva's death, so successful on the stage, where she was often hoisted to heaven in a kind of tackle to the strains of an angelic orchestra, was very popular in an age in which stage shows, except edifying shows of this type, were forbidden to the evangelical population for which, basically, Mrs. Stowe was writing. But the relationship between Uncle Tom and Little Eva, their common Bible reading, the references to the Book of Revelation, the spectre of a dying little white girl helping the threatened Negro to acquire a better knowledge of his faith accounted in great part for the immense success of the book. Mrs. Stowe was delighted to learn that *Uncle Tom* had created an increased demand for texts of the Bible even in sinful Paris.

But what was the main theme of the book, slavery or, as the South preferred to call it, the 'peculiar institution'? When Mrs. Stowe wrote *Uncle Tom's Cabin* she knew very little of slavery at first hand. She had made one visit across the Ohio river to a plantation in Kentucky, which she paints in very glowing terms in the first chapter of *Uncle Tom*. She had read a certain amount of Abolitionist literature, presumably reading Theodore Weld's famous book of atrocities committed under the shadow of the peculiar institution. And although she finally settled in Florida 'after the War', she had very little first-hand knowledge of the slavery system. She had some knowledge of Negroes because she both employed them and taught them in Cincinnati. She knew of the existence of the 'Underground Railroad', and her family had helped to organize the escape of a fugitive slave, an incident of which she made great and good use in her book. But the Southerners who attacked her for not knowing anything about the slavery system at first hand were not wrong. But, as she showed in her reply to her critics, *A Key to Uncle Tom's Cabin*, she had very seldom to use fiction in her descriptions of the possibilities of the system. It *did* make possible the destruction of family life, indulgence of sadistic tastes, indulgence of sexual irregularity and at times very horrible crimes very insufficiently punished by the law. As has been recalled more than once, one of the most horrible crimes of the old régime in the South was committed in Kentucky by members of Jefferson's family. More than that, the doom hanging over Uncle Tom of being 'sold down the river', sold into the very deep South, into the Mississippi delta, was a matter of terror for the slaves in the comparatively civilized states of Virginia and Kentucky. Professor Allan Nevins has recently told us of the reaction of Union soldiers as they moved from the border states, where slavery was in many instances a genuinely patriarchal system, to the plantations of the deep South. The propaganda of the Abolitionists was often extreme and described abuses as normal. Sometimes, as a recent publication by Professor Dumond has shown, mere rumours were taken as truth. But it appears to be a fact that by the time *Uncle Tom's Cabin* was written slavery was a great deal worse than merely odious, it was a great abuse and, in the biblical sense of the term, a source of scandal for thousands.

In any event, the book scrawled on the corner of the kitchen table and published in instalments in a not very important religious magazine made Mrs. Stowe famous overnight. Only Byron and Kipling have known such sudden fame. It was not only fame in the United States: there was what was very important for a mid-nineteenth-century American, fame in England. It was fame in Europe, where *Uncle Tom* was almost at once translated into French by Hilaire Belloc's grandmother. From being very poor, Mrs. Stowe suddenly became decidedly rich. From being simply the daughter of Lyman Beecher, the sister of Henry Ward Beecher and the wife of Professor Stowe, she became the most famous American woman in the world, whom all western Europe wanted to see.

It is not for nothing that fame of this kind is acquired, and *Uncle Tom* is a book of very remarkable qualities. It suffers from its composition as a serial and, possibly, from the bringing in of George and Eliza. But they were a necessary foil to the tragedy which was about to fall on Uncle Tom; and in Cousin Ophelia and her wayward ward, Topsy, Mrs. Stowe showed some of that talent for social observation she was to display in her New England novels. The faults of construction are very obvious. The death of Uncle Tom is made too unavoidable and the happy ending for the other characters wrenches the long arm of coincidence right out of its socket.

Mrs. Stowe was astonished at the violence of Southern reaction. For she thought she had tried to show the bright side as well as the dark side of slavery, and in a sense she did. She was also, probably much more than she realized, as her most recent biographer, Mrs. Johnston, has pointed out, much more concerned with the problems of sexual relationships than was considered decorous in the mid-nineteenth century. Even here she pulled her punches. As the intelligent Mrs. Chesnut remarked bitterly in her celebrated *Diary from Dixie*, Mrs. Stowe evaded one of the greatest problems of plantation life, the planter's habit of visiting 'the Quarters', that is to say using his female slaves for his pleasure. She also noted that Mrs. Stowe made a great mistake in making Simon Legree a bachelor: in *her* experience the men who had the Negro women in the Quarters were married.

*

Almost everything after the success of *Uncle Tom's Cabin* was destined to be anti-climax or worse. It is true that both Queen Victoria and Harriet Martineau thought *Dred* a better book than *Uncle Tom*, but although *Dred* remained in print a very long time and sold hundreds of thousands of copies, it was not the block-buster *Uncle Tom* was, and, to some extent, still is. If we laugh at the sentimentality of Little Eva, we must remember that, like so many other mothers of that day, Mrs. Stowe had lost a baby. Her brilliant eldest son was drowned while bathing in the Connecticut River at Hanover, her second son, badly wounded at Gettysburg, became an alcoholic and finally simply vanished, leaving no trace. Her very learned husband was a hypochondriac of the most advanced type; and Mrs. Stowe, though writing very successfully and, in some instances, with more than merely financial success, novels and *chroniques*, showed her family talent for indiscretion by publishing in the *Atlantic Monthly* the confidences made to her by Lady Byron about the relationship between Byron and his half-sister. Like most literate young women of her age, she had been in love with Byron, whom her father had hoped to convert, so to discover that he was a monster was a blow like the discovery of the realities of slavery. The *Atlantic Monthly* was nearly ruined and Mrs. Stowe's reputation suffered very badly.

At this time the great Henry Ward Beecher scandal broke. Her beloved brother, the great preacher (who does not seem to have estimated his sister's writings highly enough), was charged with adultery, a charge which led to the longest and most avidly discussed trial of its kind in nineteenth-century American history. It was noted that Mrs. Stowe, perfectly willing to believe every word she heard from Lady Byron about the wickedness of Lord Byron, firmly refused to admit any shadow of doubt on the assertion that her brother was totally innocent. Another brother had committed suicide, and there can be no doubt that the Beecher family, including its most famous member, was passionate, unstable, indiscreet and uncritical.

Thus Mrs. Stowe believed the most preposterous atrocity stories that she heard during the Civil War and was indignant that her English friends were not as moved as she was. It did not seem to dawn on her that one reason was that they did not believe in the horrid crimes alleged to be committed by Southern soldiers and Southern women.

*

In minor matters indiscretion did her harm. Macaulay (who greatly admired *Uncle Tom's Cabin*) was infuriated by her report of his conversation which Mrs. Stowe cheerfully printed without consultation or permission. She greatly enjoyed being taken up by London society, especially by the Duchess of Sutherland, who was a leader in the anti-slavery movement. Stafford House was certainly a great change from the ministerial manses and poor professorial houses that she had known. But unkind critics were quick to point out that the Sutherland clearances, still odious in Highland memory, might excite almost as much moral indignation as the horrors of the internal slave trade. Innocently ordering a dress in London, she found herself attacked for buying from sweat shops, a kind of institution that she did not know existed and was certainly unknown at Bowdoin, Maine, or Andover, Mass.

She was not a woman of great reflective power and certainly not a great artist, but that does not diminish the importance or the potency, even today, of *Uncle Tom's Cabin*. Many in the North wondered whether Lincoln would, in fact, issue the final Proclamation of Emancipation due on January 1, 1863. Mrs. Stowe had been among them, although her visit to the President had given her trust in his good faith, but she went to the great meeting held in the Boston Music Hall to wait for the news that the proclamation had finally been issued. The telegram came and the hall burst into cheers. Then news came that Harriet Beecher Stowe was in the hall, and the whole audience rose, crying out, 'Mrs. Stowe! Mrs. Stowe!' She went to the front of the balcony and looked down on a sea of faces cheering the woman who, as she thought, had by the direct inspiration of God helped to remove the great national sin and helped her to justify the justice as well as the goodness of God. For her they were the same thing.

1963

15

ANOTHER PRESIDENT

THE ASSASSINATION of President Kennedy has lent a graver interest to his predecessor's memoirs. The merits and defects of General Eisenhower's first volume are discussed below. But at a time when the whole world is shocked, in the strictest sense of the term, at the murder of President Kennedy, it is perhaps worth noting how, possibly unconsciously, General Eisenhower reveals to us not only the august character but also the immense burden of the presidential office. For quite a long time now the President of the United States has shared with the Chairman of the Soviet Council of Ministers the power of destroying the whole human race—a power that doubtless will sober even the most light-hearted and light-headed candidates for the White House or for the Kremlin. And it must be noted that President Eisenhower, like President Kennedy, steadily refused to be panicked into using or even threatening to use the power that science had, possibly unfortunately, given them.

*

The most famous of American political correspondents, Mr. James 'Scotty' Reston of the *New York Times*, is reported to have remarked of General Eisenhower's memoirs that General Eisenhower is too nice a man to be a good historian. One can see what Mr. Reston means. General Eisenhower is no Tacitus. There is no Swiftian *saeva indignatio*. The most that one can say is that there is a drop in the temperature when certain people are mentioned; but he never gets down to zero and hardly ever gets below 50° F.

Mandate for Change[1] is a book of great charity and generosity. And

[1] Dwight D. Eisenhower, *Mandate for Change, 1953–1956*. The White House Years. 650 pp. Heinemann. £3 3s.

if it must be wished that General Eisenhower had not pulled his
punches so much, it must be admitted also that his astonishing
popularity, as great in 1963, as the polls show, as it was when he left
office, is in part based on the public belief that General Eisenhower
is a nice man, full of concern for the public weal and at the most
inclined for brief moments to 'blow his top' and to display in no
offensive fashion a harmless and often quite justified vanity.

There are, however, drawbacks to General Eisenhower's temperament when it comes to writing memoirs which are *documents pour
servir*, and these drawbacks are no doubt what Mr. Reston had in
mind. For, like a sundial, General Eisenhower tends to register only
the serene hours. He makes it plain that he had great responsibilities
and, as is sometimes forgotten, he again and again showed that
sagacity which made him an admirable commander-in-chief of a
coalition army. But there is a lack of edge to these memoirs which
was not so visible in *Crusade in Europe*. It is hard indeed to think of
any of the military memorialists of the last war who are less open to
the charge of scoring off enemies or what is even more tempting,
allies, than is General Eisenhower. And although he glides over
faults and failures in his administration and perhaps claims a little
too much for it, there is none of that assumption of infallibility which
has marked so many accounts of the late war from its leaders.

*

This amiability of temper in his writings, of course, detracts from the
dramatic value of his memoirs. We know in fact a great deal more
about the Eisenhower administration from the now quite numerous
confidants of the President who have 'told all' than we learn from
General Eisenhower himself. The General, in discussing the reasons
which led him to campaign for the Republican nomination in 1952,
puts very high indeed the desirability of rescuing the Republican
Party from the self-destructive frustration to which it had been condemned by five terms of exclusion from the White House, an exclusion made all the more bitter as victory had seemed inevitable in
1948. Above all, General Eisenhower, head of Nato, had been
alarmed at the signs of the resurgence of the 'fortress America' idea,
a natural nostalgia for a day when it did not matter what happened
outside the territory of the United States. General Eisenhower
knew that this nostalgia was an illusion and a dangerous illusion,
but he feared that it was an illusion very popular with a great

section of the Republican Party (and not only of the Republican Party).

Revulsion from involvement in the affairs of the outer and wicked world had been reinforced by the unsatisfactory character of the postwar world. That hot war became the cold war was an immense deception for the mass of the American people. The Korean War, the fourth most bloody war ever fought by the United States, whose sacrifices in men and money it is fashionable to underestimate or ignore in Europe, was the last bitter ingredient in the cup. That after the most complete victory in history, with the Germans surrendering to General Eisenhower at Rheims and the Japanese to General MacArthur in Tokyo Bay, there should not have resulted *at once* an America free from any concern for the outer world and free from the pressures of war and preparation for war, was a wounding insult to American pride. And for many Americans the situation existing in 1952, with an uneasy truce in Korea, with a Europe which was very far from stable and very far from total commitment to the American side, could only be the result of treason. For they suffered from 'the illusion of American omnipotence'. General Eisenhower knew better, and there can be no reasonable doubt that his decision to enter politics, which he had refused to do earlier, was based, above all, on his desire to save the United States from the stultification of its victory, and, indeed, its possible ruin if some of the Republican politicians whom he mentions too kindly came into command.

*

That General Eisenhower is sincere in this description of his motives cannot be doubted. Just as Robert E. Lee is probably the only general in history who has taken command of one army after refusing the command of the opposing army, General Eisenhower is probably the only man in American history who could have run, and won, as the Democratic or the Republican candidate. Had he accepted President Truman's offer of support, he could have been nominated in 1952 and no doubt would have been triumphantly elected. He accepted the Republican nomination and was triumphantly elected as all competent observers of the American scene in 1952 realized was certain to happen.

General Eisenhower tells us candidly that the Republicans were in some doubt whether he was a Republican, and they had reasons for their doubts. The only other West Pointer ever to enter the

White House, Ulysses S. Grant, voted only once before he entered the White House and he voted against the Republican candidate not because he was a Democrat but because he knew the Republican candidate, John C. Frémont. General Eisenhower was, in the Greek sense, almost as 'idiotic' as General Grant. From this political innocence came many of his troubles. With a generosity which is charming, but also regrettable, General Eisenhower pulls his punches when he comes to discuss his dealings with the Republican high command. He does, it is true, report his disgust when he discovered how narrow were the views of the Republicans whom he was carrying to victory, and how much their motives were local, personal, and even base: but he names no names, again a sign of amiability but of an amiability which makes his book less valuable than it might have been. One is led to hope that General Eisenhower has left, for the benefit of posterity, an unexpurgated version of his years in the White House.

*

It was widely reported in 1952 that General Eisenhower, when he consented to run, assumed that opposition to his nomination would cease. He soon discovered his mistake. He was opposed on two different grounds—the first the narrow and professional ground that he was a 'Johnny-come-lately' not only to politics but also to the Republican Party. The labourers in the vineyard who had borne the burden of the day and the heat were not at all amused at the spectacle of the amateur going in and taking the prize without any contest. As it was, General Eisenhower and his party managers, like Senator Henry Cabot Lodge, had to fight hard to put the nomination over. There was a paradox in how this was done which General Eisenhower either failed to notice or has failed to comment on. In 1912 Senator Lodge's grandfather had organized the Republican Convention to secure the renomination of President Taft by the use of the Southern votes always given to the dispenser of patronage. In 1952 it was necessary to overthrow in the South, above all in Texas, the existing Republican machine in favour of the Eisenhower supporters, many of whom were very recent Democrats, and this was done in great part by Senator Henry Cabot Lodge, reversing the role of his grandfather in 1912.

One of the few really interesting human notes of this worthy book is not only the account of the distress of the Taft supporters when

'Mr. Republican' was again, as they thought, cheated of the nomination he had earned, but the account of the relationship which grew up between General Eisenhower and Senator Taft. Obviously, General Eisenhower resents the suggestion made at the time, and repeated often since, that he surrendered his principles to Senator Taft in order to get his support and there is no evidence that he did. Indeed, General Eisenhower reports his astonishment to learn how 'liberal' in the American sense Senator Taft was—much more liberal than General Eisenhower was in domestic matters. And, indeed, Senator Taft, the head of a great, wealthy, and patrician family with a long tradition of public service, was far more willing to use the power of the states and of the Union to heal social wounds than was the very self-made man from the wrong side of the tracks who was about to enter the White House. But Senator Taft was only slightly converted, if converted at all, to the Republican nominee's views on international affairs and was as devoted to budget balancing as most Republican and Democratic members of the Senate are in theory today.

General Eisenhower suggests, and it is not a baseless suggestion, that had Senator Taft lived he would have been an effective ally of the new President in his dealings with Congress. This is highly plausible because Senator Taft had very great weight in the Senate and was a man of very great ability and of great public spirit. He was succeeded by a senator whose political career had been largely accidental and who is now, as a result of vaulting ambition, editing a worthy provincial paper in California.

*

The Republicans had been out of office for more than twenty years; only one Senator had ever served under a Republican President. Those Representatives who had known a Republican President in the White House were old, and, in some instances, very old men. The new President required a kind of leadership in each House which he did not get from the top brass of the Republican Party. In part, of course, President Eisenhower was to blame for his illusions. Used to the army chain of command system, he could not understand the very delicate relationship between the White House at one end of Pennsylvania Avenue and 'The Hill' at the other. He was at the beginning of his term at as great a loss in dealing with politicians as were the great businessmen he brought into his cabinet.

Although he had been a kind of army lobbyist when serving on the staff under General MacArthur before the Second World War, he seems to have learnt no more about the handling of politicians than did General Grant, who had more excuse for his innocence.

The frustrations General Eisenhower faced in dealing with his Party are reported, but not stressed. We have only an allusion to the project of leaving the Republican Party, of starting what would have been in effect a new party, cutting out those barnacle types who encrusted the ship of state. We have, in fact, learnt far more of this interesting if impractical project from Mr. Donovan's *Eisenhower : The Inside Story* which was published before President Eisenhower ran for his second term.

Without vanity, President Eisenhower knew that he was far stronger than the Republican Party. This lesson was reinforced by the Republican loss of control of Congress, very narrow even at the beginning of the first term, in 1954. Indeed, President Eisenhower was to have the odd distinction of being the only President serving two terms with Congress in the hands of the opposition party for three-quarters of the time.

President Eisenhower knew that the American people had not turned against either the New Deal or the Fair Deal and that they had no desire to go back to 1932 or even to 1929. (It is worth noting that one of the people who supported President Eisenhower in this belief was ex-President Hoover.) President Eisenhower reasonably complains that his administration was given no credit for continuing and expanding the social service legislation of the Roosevelt and Truman administrations. This is true, and public ignorance of this fact was unjust, but President Eisenhower does not notice one cause of the injustice. Although most Americans voted in 1952 (and again in 1956) for 'Ike', a great many Republicans and a great many highly conservative Democrats came to interpret these personal tributes as a repudiation of the welfare state.

This was the attitude of many of President Eisenhower's most vociferous supporters and helped to spread the belief that the Eisenhower administration wanted to repudiate the New Deal and the Fair Deal.

President Eisenhower does not mention the odd effect produced by his nomination of a man who professed to want to abolish the income tax to head the Bureau of Internal Revenue, and he alludes only once to the curious career of Dr. Clarence Manion, quondam

Dean of Notre Dame University Law School. He does not notice the nomination of a man who was an enemy of public housing to head public housing (actually, this nominee rapidly became a friend of public housing, but the public perhaps did not know this). Much more than President Eisenhower realizes, he has not appreciated what his appointees said and did.

*

For example, General Eisenhower reports his defence of the Civil Service system and in a sense his defence of his administration is valid. But no one who knew Washington in 1953 and 1954 can quite accept the defence, for there were plenty of enemies of the Civil Service in Washington, and some very odd things were attempted. The Republican appetite for office after twenty years' exclusion was ravenous, as the Democratic appetite had been in 1933, but it ran against the law and against an obstacle curiously neglected, 'Veterans Preference'; but not until a good deal of damage had been done to the morale of the Civil Service. This damage was especially notice-able in the State Department where Mr. Dulles displayed a con-temptible disloyalty to his subordinates. It is perhaps worth noting that the name of Mr. Scott McLeod occurs only once. Yet he did nearly as much damage to the morale of the State Department and the Foreign Service as Senator McCarthy. When the damage had been done, he was sent off to the unfortunate Republic of Ireland where *teste* Mr. Claud Cockburn, he was known as 'the copper's nark'.

In the same way, General Eisenhower's speech at Dartmouth College against book burning had little resonance when the public reflected on his silence in face of the antics of Messrs. Cohn and Shine and of what were worse than antics on the part of their great patron, Senator Joseph McCarthy. General Eisenhower does discuss briefly why, when he spoke in Wisconsin, he was induced to drop his tribute to General George Marshall, his great patron, lest it should offend the junior Senator from that state; but he does not seem to realize the shock it gave to his admirers, a shock which has not totally disappeared even today.

President Eisenhower deserved better support than he got from the Congressional leaders, but he is probably wrong in thinking that his difficulties with Congress arose from the fact that for six years out of his eight in the White House he had a Democratic majority against him. President Kennedy did not do much better with a nominally very large Democratic majority in both Houses. With great charity, President Eisenhower passes over some of the actions of his appointees, like Secretary Weeks, who began his administration of the Commerce Department by an ignominious and doomed battle with the Bureau of Standards, an institution much more serious than Secretary Weeks appreciated. The very amiability and innocence which Mr. Reston commented on, if they have made President Eisenhower the most popular figure that America has known in the twentieth century, limited his efficacy as a President. His predecessor Mr. Truman is reported to have noted his successor's reluctance to engage in close infighting. 'If he doesn't like the heat, why didn't he stay out of the kitchen?' It is understood that ex-President Eisenhower and ex-President Truman are not on the best of terms; but Mr. Truman's comment had some validity.

On foreign affairs there are few or no revelations in this book. There are not many on domestic affairs either. And we know a good deal more about the external and internal history of the administration from insiders and semi-insiders than we are likely to learn from this amiable book. Professor Oscar Handlin, of Harvard, has rightly raised the question of whether people like Mr. Emmet Hughes should be encouraged to quote from confidential documents and give an 'inside' view. Probably they should not, but they have done it and it is impossible to read this book without thinking that but for the work of Mr. Donovan, Mr. Hughes, and others we should be still very much in the dark about what went on in the White House and at Camp David. It is gratifying to note the obvious sincerity with which General Eisenhower recalls his wartime and post-wartime partnership with Sir Winston Churchill and the Earl of Avon. But it is odd to be told how anxious the American administration was over the political fate of that most sterile of Fourth Republic politicians, Joseph Laniel.

Mandate for Change, then, will be a valuable source for future historians and it will interest and inform *aficionados* of American politics and policy. In writing, it is clear but flat: it cannot for a moment compare with that masterpiece of American narrative, *The Personal Memoirs of U.S. Grant*. President Eisenhower mildly and delicately protests against the insinuation that he reads nothing but Westerns and that his grammar is peculiarly defective. As he points out, 'off the cuff' speeches often make very odd reading when taken down and shown to their author; and with what is an obvious allusion to his brother, Dr. Milton Eisenhower, the President of the Johns Hopkins University, he reports that a very experienced and highly erudite public speaker has often been horrified at the sight of his verbatim remarks. And even President Kennedy, who graduated *cum laude* at Harvard, sometimes produced very tangled paragraphs at his press conferences.

We should not forget that again and again President Eisenhower, like many distinguished soldiers profoundly pacific in temper, refused to pursue policies that might well have ended in an atomic war. He kept the peace and reinforced the general American position in Europe and to some extent in Asia at a time of great difficulty. This should be enough to give him respectable rank among the occupants of the White House, a much more respectable rank than that of a much better writer, President Grant. His greatest weakness was his inability to understand and either manage or intimidate the professional politicians. His reluctance to run for the Presidency perhaps came from an apprehension that he would be out of his depth. Of him it could be said in contemplating such figures as ex-Senator Bricker:

> He only in a general honest thought
> And common good to all made one of them.

1963

DATE DUE

~~JAN 0 1999~~			
			Printed in USA

HIGHSMITH #45230